D1369682

The
Jew
and
Civilization

The Jew and Civilization

By

ADA STERLING

Author of
"A Belle of the Fifties," "Mary, Queen of Scots,"
Etc., Etc.

Published by
AETCO PUBLISHING CO.
16 East 41st Street
NEW YORK CITY
1924

DEDICATED

to

the work of promoting a better
understanding amongst the
members of the human family

Table of Contents

CHAPTER I

Introductory

"I am glad to be able to say that while the Jews of the United States have remained loyal to their faith, and their race traditions, they have become indissolubly incorporated in the great army of American citizenship prepared to make all sacrifice for the country, either in peace or war, and striving for the perpetuation of good government and for the maintenance of the principles embodied in our Constitution. They are honorably distinguished by their industry, their obedience to law, and their devotion to the national welfare."

THEODORE ROOSEVELT.

(In letter dated "Washington, November 16th, 1905")

THE purpose of this book which it seems best to declare in the beginning, is to re-state, on the *pro* side, the "Jewish Problem"— the *con* side having been so widely stated by others—to a people more or less disturbed, according as they are conscientious or careless thinkers; or, according as they have become infected with the idea that "humanity is an illusion," an idea which the over-intellectualized have been disseminating for years and to which the name *Kultur,* or *Efficiency* has been affixed. This new theory of human relations, this *kultur* is a curious fungus which grows upon the surface of today's civilization, but its roots do not reach down to the heart. Its manifestations have all the allure of the spectacular. Its flaming flowers wave in the wind of popular speech and in that still more evanescent quantity, "public opinion" like little inciting banners of anarchy. "Humanity is an empty word" writes one of these; and living sympathy, or sympathy with the living, is "a folly of the past." But it seems quite clear— and history repeatedly confirms this—that extremes of this sort sooner or later set humanity upon a renewed search,

9

as Dr. Petre has said, for a restoration of its rhythm and a re-establishment of harmonic balance.

In this way the present author has re-acted from the many-volumed attacks upon the Jews for which Mr. Henry Ford is responsible; from the nightmare of exaggerated spleen exhibited by Houston Stuart Chamberlain, and which, more than once becomes incoherent and even comical in its paroxysms of frenzied antipathy; from the artificial, narrow, and even shallow arguments of Mr. Hilaire Belloc, who does not hesitate to define his belief that the Jews must be got rid of by hook or by crook, and to state openly as we shall presently see, that both of these implements will be used if the Jews themselves do not voluntarily withdraw from participation in today's normal activities.

The records of the past show that sectarian bigotry and racial animosities have come invariably as the aftermath of bitter wars. In the case of the recent world unrest in connection with anti-Semitism the fact should be faced squarely that the late war merely lulled racial ill-feeling to sleep, nothing more; for it had been openly indulged in and cruelly displayed all over Europe, for the better part of the last half of last century. In the recent conflict, in the great hour of humanity's need, the fires were merely banked for the time being. Almost co-incidentally with the firing of the last shot they burst again into visible flame. The armies of Eastern European countries had scarcely been mustered out after the armistice had been declared, armies which in each instance had included brave Jewish soldiers, and whose lot had been eased by Jewish philanthropy, whose ill and wounded had been soothed by Jewish nurses, before exciting newspaper articles and pamphlets began to appear, warning the world of a coming racial conflict. One such, entitled *"A Knife for the Jews"* was circulated openly in an Eastern European coun-

try. Immediately thereafter the most unprovoked persecutions of the Jews were reported from many quarters of
that bloodsoaked continent. They were but the first clashes
arising from calumnies suddenly sprung, but whose trail
leads back to the middle of the nineteenth century.

Within a year anti-Jewish feeling began to appear in
England where the Jews have had their greatest opportunity, and in return for which they have rendered loyal
and patriotic service. Antagonists of the late Lord North-
cliffe threw out adroitly-framed hints that he was of Jewish extraction; and inimical factions and countries immediately took this up using it as a text by which to hurl
anathema upon him and the race. The "Times" of London
came out with an extended notice of one of the most pernicious of the many printed attacks upon the Jews, which
book included the matter which, since, has been separately
printed as a pamphlet, and is now known to history as
"The Protocols".

This matter, which but for its vicious character and
the lives it has already cost and endangered, might well be
called the greatest of literary hoaxes. The book was
caught up and printed in several languages and circulated
all over Europe. Copies found their way to the Western
hemisphere. To their credit it must be said that many
heads of European Governments recognized the peril of a
free distribution of a work of this character, and forbade
the printing and circulation of it. This, however, continued, and the contents of the strange documents soon
became the popular topic of the notable drawingrooms in
the great cities of the world. They began to figure as the
theme of all others in private correspondence. Gossip soon
carried the word from capital to capital, through the
medium of persons honest enough, no doubt, in their intentions, but who were horrified by the perfidy of the Jews as

accused by these *"Protocols"*. Now these proved to be the yeast that has since set the world in a ferment.

From that moment on the Jews have been put under the microscope. The motives of the every act of their most representative men have been impugned, and every short-coming of the less worthy members of the race has been magnified into a concerted movement of the whole Jewish people that menaces the community and the safety of the world. Copies of these *"Protocols"* crossed the ocean. Soon credulous publishers of the United States were issuing reprints of the vicious sheets, and the poison began to work down into popular thought. In an astonishingly short time bookshop windows were featuring in bright-covered volumes *"The Jewish Peril"; "The International Jew"; "The Jewish Problem"*, etc.; and, as this sort of thing was sure to do what it was intended to do, the masses hurrying by were caught by this exciting matter. They were all at once suspicious of their neighbor, the Jew. A feeling of great indignation swept over the country against the presence here of a so-called treacherous enemy; one who, certain malevolent sheets would have us believe, was like to nothing that has been since the days of belching dragons and the workers in magic. Though the Jews, as Mr. Roosevelt had said, "have become indissolubly incorpo-rated in the great army of American citizenship", though they had given innumerable proofs that they were pre-pared to make all sacrifice for the country, yet at the first outcry against them, the first raising of Europe's tarred stick, there were those who were ready to use that stick upon the entire race.

The most regrettable part of it all is, that while the London "Times" which may be said to have started the ball rolling, i. e., in English-speaking countries, was discov-ering the fraudulent character of the whole cruel *canard,* frankly admitting it and so correcting, as far as might be, the evil it had been first to do, the American Jew-baiters, who had found their great opportunity, continued to arraign the race, and even to the present, have nowhere admitted their error, if charity may so name proceedings so scandalous.

As to large numbers the import and history of the *"Protocols"* is still an intriguing mystery, it may be well to outline this here. Their supposed character was that of an official programme devised by leading Jewish Elders for world conquest, not by arms, but by moral pollution; by the reduction of spiritual stamina, if this term may be used, among non-Jews, who by education in debauchery of mind and body were to be led on to such self-indulgence, the Jews, meanwhile to keep themselves morally clean while performing this diabolical work, until, themselves rising in spiritual values, the non-Jewish world, of its own pollutions, would ultimately fall into subjection to the Jews.

The *"Protocols"* read like the frothings of a madman; but as mania often causes "sympathetic mania", they affected the minds of many. The London "Times" was among them. It thought, about 1918, that it perceived proofs in events which then were taking place that "certain passages in these *"Protocols"*, had been prophetic; that the great world-pollution had already begun. What! exclaimed its editor, "Have we escaped a 'Pax Germanica' only to fall into a Pax Judaica"! and it called for an open investigation of the documents which purported to be addressed to Jews, by some learned "Elders of Zion."

An investigation was begun that extended through the highest channels in Europe and even to the Congressional Library at Washington. The fantastic propositions contained in these mad documents were traced by devious paths to a literary lawyer of France, one, Maurice Joly, who, in 1865 published some imaginary *"Dialogues in Hell between Machiavelli and Montesquieu"*. It was a satire on Napoleonic practices, and the author put some of his most malicious speeches into the mouth of an imaginary Jewish Elder. The book was confiscated; but it is known that one copy found its way to Russia even as many copies of the forbidden *"Protocols"* have found their way into other lands, and that a writer there, imbued with a traditional prejudice against the Jews, copied and embellished passages from that work and in turn set these on their devastating way.

The London "Times" having inaugurated the work, published on August 16th, 1921, an account of the fraudulent character of the *"Protocols"* and stated that, after all, these were only clumsy forgeries. There was ample time for the cable-united continents to bring the news of this exposé to the Western hemisphere and so invite as prompt a recantation and as frank on the part of those who, for a year, had been engaged in the most virulent attacks upon the Jew. It was not forthcoming. For a year or more thereafter the Ford periodical continued to trust to the ignorance of its readers and to detail the ways in which, it said, the Jews were attempting to pollute the world through book and bulletin, through magazines; through moving pictures; through the theatre and even through music. These defamatory volumes may still be purchased, and are even displayed in book-shop windows.

Zola was not more dramatic than were the thundering "J'accuse's" which issued from the West; but Zola's purpose was honest; with righteous resentment, he was espousing the cause of the much-wronged Dreyfus. That of the Ford periodical could have no other aim than to rouse the varying groups of the land to a pitch of alarm and prejudice which held in it the possibility of bloodshed. Ancient as well as current history was searched by this group to find and to fix crime and obloquy on the Jewish race. The most ordinary act of a Jew, the most kindly, even the noblest, through these agents have been made to take on the air of plotting against the peace of society. A rich Jew dies and leaves his fortune to be devoted to the redemption of his race through education. He defines his beneficiaries. They are not all in one spot; but, "Never mind," he says: "Go seek them out and help them;" that is the message he leaves behind to the world. But such phenomenal nobility in a Jew strikes these anti-Semites as a suspicious circumstance. They instantly raise a cry. "The rich Jews are educating their less fortunate brothers; for what purpose?" and promoters of hatreds answer: "In order that they may become masters of the world. Haven't you read the *Protocols?*"

We have been warned by these same factions that the Jewish press is sowing industriously "The Jewish Idea": that it is encouraging Jews to cling still more closely to their faith; that they are inaugurating a "revival" spirit in Judaism; that this is inciting Jewish people to a higher self-esteem; that they are being spurred industrially, and to educate themselves. Through these means, reacting upon them, the race will rise mentally, morally, physically. "But," these agitators protest, "These Jews are getting on too fast as it is. They no longer cringe before us. It must be stopped!" What the Jewish press is doing is to hold up to the Jewish people, to those who but a generation ago went bowed under the yoke of Eastern despotism, modern democratic ideals of the rehabilitation of the race by education; by self-effort, by faith in their own ideals. This is exactly what the presses of all other religious bodies, all other racial and social groups are doing, the majority of them having at their command far vaster machinery for the carrying on of their work in the uplift of their people. The Jewish press is doing its work in open and legitimate channels, and in the most praiseworthy manner; yet from the attacks made upon them, the public can scarcely avoid regarding their editorial rooms as hotbeds of sedition.

Because an especially conspicuous example of the daring of the prejudiced, an instance may be cited here of a Jewish weekly paper, the publisher of which, as a great war-correspondent, has looked on human suffering from very serious view-points both in the Jewish quarters of the old and new worlds and on the battle-fields. He has watched the clashings of prejudice and from the evidence offered by various random issues of his publication would seem to have brought into his publishing enterprise an especially inspiring and high purpose. Like a declaration of faith, he puts on the title-page of every issue of his paper, the question put by Malachi: "Have we not one father? Has not God created us all?" But this publisher has been made the object of a vicious onslaught, all the more surprising in that he had previously been a guest of the western publisher on the Peace Ship which by this time has been forgotten by the majority.

Something happened on that voyage, however, which may explain the disfavor into which the editor and his race subsequently fell. When in mid-ocean, one of the party predicted that their efforts would meet with no success abroad where President Wilson was unpopular because he had restrained the United States from entering the war. Thereupon, a protest was drawn up, which in its nature was a censure of and to the President, and the voyagers were asked to sign it. All did so with two or three exceptions. One of these was the Jewish editor referred to, who declined to sign on the ground that such a proceeding was not only an unprecedented impertinence to the nation's head, but a disloyal and unpatriotic act. He furthermore disembarked at the first port the ship made, and, declining to accept further courtesies at the hands of his host, paid his own fare home. A similar instance: a native-born and educated American—graduated from Columbia University, and a distinguished humanitarian as well as international jurist, was similarly pilloried for daring, in the face of these rancorous attacks upon his race, to ask the question: "Is ours a Christian Government?"

The Right Honorable David Lloyd George, who, as one has said, "sees with amazing clearness what must happen if this course is persisted in, has written in his recent book *"Where Are We Going"?* a sweeping protest against the wide-spread revival of the Jew-baiting spirit. "Of all the bigotries" he says, "that savage the human temper there is none so stupid as the anti-Semitic. It has no basis in reason; it is not rooted in faith; it aspires to no ideal; it is just one of those dank and unwholesome weeds that grow in the morass of racial hatreds. How utterly devoid of reason it is may be gathered from the fact that it is almost entirely confined to nations who worship the Jewish prophets, revere the national literature of the Hebrews as the only inspired message by the deity to mankind, and whose only hope of salvation rests on the precepts and promises of the great teachers of Judah. Yet, in the sight of these fanatics the Jews of today can do nothing right. If they are rich they are birds of prey. If they are poor they are vermin. If they are in favor of a war it is because they want to exploit the bloody feuds of the Gentiles for their own profit. If they are anxious for peace they are instinctive cowards or traitors. If they give generously— and there are no more liberal givers than the Jews—they are doing it for some selfish purpose of their own. If they do not give, then what can one expect of a Jew but avarice? If labor is oppressed by great capital, the greed of the Jew is held responsible. If labor revolts against capital as it did in Russia—the Jew is blamed for that, also. If he lives in a strange land he must be persecuted and pogrommed out of it. If he wants to go back to his own he must be prevented. Through the centuries, in every land, whatever he does or intends or fails to do, he has been pursued by the echo of the brutal cry of the rabble of Jerusalem against the greatest of all Jews—"Crucify him"! No good has ever come of nations that crucified Jews. It is a poor and pusillanimous sport, lacking all the true qualities of manliness, and those who indulge in it would be the first to run away were there any element of danger in it."

This is an admirable protest against the most unjust and most unwarrantable prejudice which the late history of the world has shown; which appears, moreover, to be increasing in particularly significant quarters; but can a few paragraphs of generalities, however, strong and red-blooded, overtake and dislodge from the human mind the multipled and widely distributed vilifications which the book press of the world has been issuing for now six years and the insidious reasoning of which may well blind the unthinking into an acceptance of them?

Let us consider for a moment the arguments set forth by Mr. Hilaire Belloc. This author views the efforts of the Jews in high places to uplift the less fortunate of their race as so menacing that, if it is allowed to go on gathering momentum "Civilization presently will not be able to cope with it." Nor is this all. In finished language he proceeds to press the need for "segregating the Jews, either by persuading them to go peacefully into a separation from non-Jews; *or, if they will not, civilization will oblige them to it by compulsion!*" This, if you please, in the year of our Lord, 1922!

This author, who, indeed, has uttered other works as feverish against other human groups, and for which he has been roundly chided by the conservative and reasoning forces of England, looks upon the Jew as being entirely "different from ourselves"—not as a Frenchman is different; not as a Greek, an Italian, a Spaniard may be said to be different, but "as a Chinaman, or a negro, or an Esquimaux". He specifically refuses to consider the fact which is the common possession of the informed, that every spiritual concept which western civilization lives by today, has come to it through the Jew. He is as definite in stating that he has no interest in Jewish literature, a rather damaging admission, it would seem; for, as innumerable authorities in this field have testified, Mr. Wells and ex-President Eliot among many others, as will hereinafter be shown, in the Hebraic literature is contained the wisdom of the world; the kernel of all education.

Throughout his volume Mr. Belloc's determination, expressed with all the dogmatism of a bigot of the Middle Ages, is to warn the world against the Jew, and to menace the Jew with what will happen if he does not slink away of his own accord. Rising to a paroxysm, he presently goes so far as to say: *"We have already a formidable minority prepared to act against the interests of the Jews, which, in all probability, will become and that shortly, a majority; for if the quarrel* [which the non-Jew is thus seeking with the Jew] *is allowed to rise unchecked and, to proceed unappeased* [this word is noteworthy] *we shall come unexpectedly and soon upon one of those tragedies which have marked for centuries this peculiar people and ourselves."* . . . It should be said, parenthetically that the Jews' peculiarities bear a remarkable resemblance to those of the rest of the human species, even when exhibited under such false glasses as these strange authors employ.

It is unnecessary to point out what Mr. Belloc emphasizes so plainly, namely that his is not the raving of one who is self-deluded and who speaks for himself alone; but of one who speaks for others who are possibly under the impression that the soil is already prepared for such seditious matter, and who make through him an open threat that if a quarrel, which such unblushing attacks so

easily might provoke breaks out, the Jews will pay for such
human indignation as they may be unable to restrain, by
slaughter. It should be equally unnecessary to point out
the need for rousing the fundamental good sense of the
fair-minded, who, when the test comes, are usually in the
vast majority, to see the injustice of allowing these pernicious appeals to continue. It is not enough, for it has no
appreciable effect upon the great public who have read and
listened to these modern preachers of persecution, to dismiss their utterances as the merest triumph of irrational
impulses over intelligence. It is not enough that the injury
is admitted in the quiet of the friendly circle; too many, as
Addison is said to have done, speak justly but faintly. The
evil thing has gone abroad. The barbaric instinct, as a
recent publicist has said, is coming West; it has pressed
forward from behind the Russian boundaries and lingers
to gather force at the borders of the Rhine. A counteract-
ing common sense should be brought into the situation
before these unrecoverable diatribes of lawless and malicious minds have worked a mischief that is beyond repair;
before they are transmuted into deeds that may set a shame
upon the forehead of today's civilization. It boots us
nothing to reiterate the Biblical wisdom as to the danger
that a house runs which is "divided against itself." Grotius has put that proposition in more modern legal form in
his statement that society cannot subsist unless all parts of
it are defended by mutual forbearance and goodwill; but,
whatever the form, it is a commonly accepted truism;
nevertheless the world is imperilled today for lack of the
application of its own proven axioms. If the present acrimony were displayed against bad Jews only, who deserve
to be reprobated equally with bad non-Jews, and that not
because they are bad Jews but because they are bad men,
none could take exception to it; but, as Mr. George has
pointed out, this is not the case. A kind of vitriolic rancor

is being sprayed over the whole Jewish people. We are asked today to accept the statement that all Jews, the world over, are committing, or planning to commit frightful and treacherous crimes against organized governments. We are told that these crimes, alleged to have been committed or which are in process of being committed are so crafty, so subtle as to demand, not merely eternal vigilance, but a craft superior to the Jews' own in order that this guilty people may be circumvented. What is really required is a willingness and zeal to investigate the charges, and those who make them, and who, in so doing reveal themselves as possessing a craft at least equal to that which they ascribe to the Jews; for, while dealing in the scurrilous and making their basic accusations to appear as a peril sudden to today, they have been merely manipulating very old matter indeed; charges which, in fact, were ancient history two thousand years ago.

In the chapters that follow some of these specific charges will be taken up which have re-appeared in recent years against the Jewish people, and will be offset by facts which all the right-minded should become possessed of at this time. Meanwhile, it will not be amiss to direct their attention to the venerable age of the charges which, in the hands of the unscrupulous, have become again living themes, and have been made to appear as matter of current importance and interest.

One of the most interesting of the documents that have come down to us from the ancients is the fiery rebuke of Flavius Josephus (written about 90, A. D.) to the derisive Apion, who had made then a vicious attack upon the whole Jewish race. The methods Apion employed were identical with those re-employed by the authors already mentioned as the spokesmen for the anti-Semitism of today. Apion was an Egyptian who frequented the courts and upper society of Athens and Rome, where the patrician and scholarly Jew, Josephus, notwithstanding the unpopularity of his race, enjoyed an esteem and favor which lesser men envied.

Apion, who, but for this attack would long ago have perished from the memory of man, appears to have gathered from Apollonius, who lived about 300 B. C.; also from Posidonius, Cicero, and Manetho the Chaldean, who lived about 150 B. C.; consequently from an array of witnesses who began some two hundred and forty years before Apion's own time, every disadvantageous accusation that had accumulated against the Jews of earlier as well as of his own time. These he caused to be published in all directions. We can measure the effect of this upon the old Athenian and Roman worlds, by fancying what would happen if some scribe of today were to gather all the objectionable things that have been said about the Americans up to the present—or, for that matter about any other modern people,—mass them and set them before a public ever keen for the dramatic, ever avid to scent catastrophe, or to spring to strife against a fancied enemy!

Thanks to this rejoinder by Josephus to the malice of Apion, a useful parallel may be offered between those ancient and the basic modern charges against the Jews.

Retailed by Apion, 93 A. D.	*By 19th and 20th century accusers.*
(1) That Jews hate all Gentiles. (Gentiles means foreigners, or strangers.)	(1) That Jews hate all Christians.
(2) That they are and always have been cowards, lack courage, and are headstrong.	(2) That they are cowards and will not fight.
(3) That they are ignorant and uncultivated; barbarous.	(3) That they are ignorant traditionalists.
(4) That they cannot lay claim to having invented anything of value to mankind.	(4) That they have never invented anything worth while.
(5) That they have not participated in the work of civilization.	(5) That they have had no share in the building up of civilization.
(6) That they have no public spirit.	(6) That they are not public spirited.
(7) That they lack patriotism.	(7) That they have no patriotism.
(8) That they are irreligious.	(8) That they have no moral law.
(9) That for ritual purposes they kill Greeks.	(9) That for ritual purposes they kill Christian children.

etc., etc.

The parallel might be lengthened, but is this not sufficient? Does it not show the lengths to which the modern addict to prejudice will go to attain his unholy end? Does it not show the imposture by which the credulous public is being misled into a dangerously false state of mind, and the need for acquainting ourselves with the Jew's real place among the builders of Civilization?

CHAPTER II

The Jew as Soldier, Citizen and Patriot

*"When with true American enthusiasm we recall
the story of our War for Independence and rejoice
in the indomitable courage and fortitude of our Revolutionary heroes, we should not fail to remember how
well the Jews of America performed their part in the
struggle, and how, in every way, they usefully and
patriotically supported the interests of their new-found
home. Nor can we overlook, if we are decently just,
the invaluable aid cheerfully contributed by our Jewish fellow-countrymen in every national emergency
which has since overtaken us."*

GROVER CLEVELAND.

(In address delivered at Carnegie Hall, November 30th, 1905)

WITH a vast heap of anti-Semitic tomes before one,
a thought sharpens in the mind, of surprise at
the unwisdom of which the embittered and mendacious
are guilty when they publish in a volume or set of volumes,
their varied and voluble venom which first had appeared
in the more transient form of newspaper or magazine articles; for now what appeared startling, even terrifying
when administered in small doses, under "feature" head-
ings, when seen *en masse* assumes the appearance of a
mere exhibition of bile.   The matter in a book may be
matched, statement for statement and its discrepancies
compared, though few readers would take the trouble to
preserve and compare the utterances from week to week,
or from month to month that appear in what is spoken of
collectively as "the press".

This is what happens with Messrs. Ford and others
in their wholesale criticism of the Jews. Not that Jews
more than others should be immune from criticism. Criticism, as President Coolidge has recently said, is good; but

it attains its best worth when it makes for construction. Your professional critics in this day of free speech, however, when given an opportunity to dissect a group or a race, are like nothing so much as mad mariners with cutlasses in hand, who, running amuck slash indiscriminately right and left. Invariably they lose their judgment and sense of justice in the enjoyment of an orgy of destruction. While often ingenious in their thrusts, they are even more often contradictory to the point of defeating their own ends. Mr. Belloc, for example, speaks of the great world war, with which, he says, "the Jews had nothing to do, and which their more important financial representatives did all they could to prevent"; and a few steps farther on he denounces as dangerous these same representatives, who, he declares, are liable to foment wars because they control the metals of the world. He offers questionable "proof" of this last statement; but makes it plain that though it was cutting off a profit to themselves these Jews did all they could to preserve peace, and to prevent war, which, necessarily would bring them large returns.

It should be said, in passing, that this author, who has been previously referred to, has elsewhere denounced another and larger group than the Jews with even more vehement fanaticism; and, in this instance having worked himself into an ectasy of sectarian zeal, he has cried out that "the sword fits the hand of the Church" which institution, he says, "is never more alive than when it is in arms". He regrets that Spain did not come to "handgrips with the Reformation at home, did not test it, come to know it, to dominate it; to bend the muscles upon it, and to re-emerge triumphant from the struggle, revivified as was France" after enjoying her religious wars.

But the thought that follows the reading of such utterances by a twentieth century author, necessarily is sober; it may well hold in it somewhat of despair that forces still exist, that men pretending to uprightness of purpose may still lend themselves to the propagation of hatred and malice and all unkindness; may still find pleasure and personal profit in disintegrating all hope of a mutual understanding among the peoples of the world; in the opening up, as a Ford author puts it, of "new angles of the *Jewish Problem*' in order "that people may know the true character of the Jews' influence in America."

One such "angle" which has not merely been "opened" but hopelessly split, has to do with Jews in war. By various means, including a certain sledge-hammer way of pounding out his charges, the author leads you to believe that he is about to give you a study of the race and its part in the late war. But he does nothing of the sort. What he does is to make statements in which you find an occasional atom of truth which in each case, is imbedded in a solid block of mis-statement. This is deplorable, for, as the axiom says: The lie that is part truth is the worst lie of all to combat.

Beginning with the statement that *"Wars are Jews' Harvests"* this apostle of prejudice goes on to deny the race personal courage, though his competitor in the dissemination of the same sort of calumny, Mr. Belloc, gives them credit for having a disproportionate allowance of it. The Ford author, following the Apion charge of two thousand years ago, denies them patriotism, civic worth, and military bravery, and ascribes to them an avidity for war arising from a pitiless willingness to trade upon other peoples' tragic experiences and needs. In supporting this ancient charge this author, and others no better informed who have followed his lead, disparages the Jewish race so unsparingly that one wonders that governments, which know better, should allow the circulation of such unjust, unfounded, one-sided and disrupting matter through the mails. One bag of it contains more of the potentials for mischief in a commonwealth than a carload of sermons might hope to counteract.

Such wilful assaults upon a class, or race, or creed in the United States, for instance, which bases its well-being on the complete freedom of such classes, races, or creeds, tends to brand the whole people as pretenders and self-deceivers, if not hypocrites. In allowing such vilifications to go unchallenged and unreproved, we negate every precept which natural laws, religion or philosophy have taught us. Were the Jews all they are accused of being, what end would be attained by the spiritual torture which fanatics would impose upon them? Mr. Burbank has demonstrated that the cactus and other prickly plants merely borrow their thorns for self-protection. When cultivated and protected from the rough interference of passersby, they shed them. The need for protection has taught even what we call inanimate nature to find its own means for keeping marauders off.

History clearly demonstrates that the world has forced the growth of the thorn which, it is now complained, exists in civilization, in the shape of the Jew. He has known nothing but the need for eternal vigilance for his own preservation since the time of the Babylon captivity. The last hundred years have liberated him as no century in his previous history has done, and yet though while in this freedom he has contributed unmeasured benefits to the world—as he has from the beginning of known history as we shall show from time to time as we proceed—we come face to face with the fact that persecution, petty, it may seem, while limited to calumnious screeds, is taking breath for a fresh attack upon him; with the fact that in many parts of Europe it has already gone much farther, and that unless the conscientious enter upon an enquiry into the charges made so boldly and sowed so assiduously against the Jews, we may see conditions in our own land which will at least tarnish its often boasted-of glory.

It is time for the American people to come out intelligently in the work of helping to rid the Jew of his thorns, and in aiding him, rather, in the putting forth of blossoms. A first step, as the reasonable will agree, which should be taken toward this end, is for the just-minded to range themselves outspokenly on the side of truth, at least to the extent of examining into the nasty charges (no other word can fitly describe them) which fanatics, counting upon the ignorance which so generally prevails concerning the real Jew, so boldly brings against him.

Let us look, for example, into those of that especially strenuous Jew-baiter, the author of *"The International Jew"*. To prove his point, which is to make the Jew appear as a menace to the nation, and as a coward, he causes it to be understood that the arguments and "facts" he is about to project, relate to the late war, and especially to the Jews of the United States of America as identified with that war. He begins his dramatic arraignment with a copious excerpt from the *annals of the sixteenth and seventeenth centuries,* as presented by a German author nearly two decades ago, and which relate to events which, he says, took place in Germany.

These state that *four hundred years ago, and in Europe* "Jews were Army Contractors," and made profits by it. The statement is so put as to cause the reader to infer that they evaded military service, and sought by trickery of some kind, the commissary department because of the profits that were to be gained in it. By not so much as a hint does this quoted author, in so far as he is quoted, suggest that four hundred years ago, and in Europe, Jews were barred from all European armies; that not only was this so, but, also, they were forbidden the bearing of arms, even for their own self-defense at a time when any bully might carry his sword or rapier openly.

In Spain, so early as 408 A. D. this exclusion of the Jews from all things military was in force. Under Omar, in the eighth century, they were forbidden to serve in the army in all of the several countries over which the rule of that potentate extended. In England, in 1181, when all freemen were compelled to take up arms in defense of the realm, Jews were forbidden to own, handle, sell, or transfer arms, hauberks, suits of mail. These are instances caught up at random; but similar conditions existed in every European country and continued there to exist to the middle of the nineteenth century, and in Russia practically to the present time.

Nowhere in this quotation from the German is it hinted that the occasional Jew who served as army contractor in the sixteenth century did so at the command—as often at the plea—of governments which needed him, particularly in the commissary departments, where politically free and consequent stay-at-home citizens were less well equipped to serve. "Who travels much," says the old adage, "has much to tell." So the Jews, enforced travellers, denied the joy of calling their native lands their "home", without civic standing or political affiliation, and wandering, not for centuries but for thousands of years, could tell much of many lands. They were especially qualified to serve in that branch of the military service which called for an acquaintance with markets in which supplies in large quantities might be purchased. Moreover, there were always near by such markets, Jewish kinsmen as detached, politically, as themselves, who, in various ways, might cooperate with them and smooth the difficult processes of providing for the war-needs of the belligerents.

Though dishonest Jews, like dishonest Christians, rise at every public crisis, seizing it as their "opportunity", yet the majority, the honest ones—and fortunately the honest in this race, as in other races, are in the great majority—of these it may not be said truthfully, that theirs was a shameful association with European wars. In most of the wars of the past, and in even more recent times, the Jews were, and have been helpless victims. Austria, England, France, Germany, Italy, Russia, *et al,* until recently all refused the Jews citizenship, though they *permitted them the privilege* of sojourning in any and all of these lands, if, and when the governments needed them, and even then only upon the payment of heavy taxes.

What was more, the grantors of these privileges might call upon these sojourners to perform services which non-Jews could not, or would not undertake. It is unnecessary to recall that to be in trade in those old aristocracies, was to be socially demeaned. (If we may place any reliance upon the modern novelist's acquaintance with the standards of the present day, the same strange idea still prevails in some countries and circles). Not because the Jews were cowards, but because they made the best of conditions that were forced upon them, are they to be found "in the commissary departments" of the armies of four and more centuries ago.

But another point that here should be made, is this: Jews have been mercilessly conscripted for the fighting forces by every government under which they lived, century after century, when free subjects failed them or their regular Army ranks grew thin. In rare instances a commander was sufficiently decent to commend them for their valor as was the case in Venice, after a war with Turkey.

In the light of these facts, of which abundant proof exists, (and very interesting reading it makes, too) it should not be possible for anyone to arraign the Jew of this century upon charges based on events occurring four and more centuries ago, or to judge him by any but this century's standards and records, without adducing all the facts.

Leaving the German narrator of long-ago events, the author who would "open up angles" on the part of the Jews in war, proceeds to strengthen his argument against today's Jews by telling of two Jewish army contractors who aided in provisioning the Revolutionary and Civil wars. Here, omitting all reference to the many of the race who fought and fell in the ranks, dying, as did non-Jews, to secure the freedom of the Colonies, the author describes, in scathing detail, the acquaintance and commerce the two (related) Jews had with Benedict Arnold. Several Christians were equally involved but these are put aside as negligible. As a climax to much contempt the author in question adds that his two Jews "also traded with Indians." It is hardly necessary to call attention to the fact that trading with the redmen was a common occupation of practically all of the Colonists, and that the foundation of many American "first families'" fortunes were the outgrowth of it.

A highly theatrical tale is now told of the "treasonable dealings" of one, in particular, of these two Jews, with Benedict Arnold. Though, after the traitor's successful flight, his "accomplice" if he may be called such, "was acquitted in court of all suspicion; nevertheless," continues our author, "he was suspected ever afterwards . . . What his end was, no one appears to know."

It will be seen that the statement is so worded as to cause the reader to infer that this Jew's end may have been disgraceful or mysterious. What are the facts? That after his trial, which he personally demanded, he served the Government in diplomatic missions abroad, once being intrusted with despatches to Franklin, then at the Court of France, and again as vice-consul at Marseilles; and that the United States Government conferred a grant of several hundred acres of Pennsylvania land upon him in recognition of his services to the country. As there is not a scintilla of evidence to the contrary, it is at least as reasonable to suppose that he died under his own vine and figtree, as to conclude that his end was, in any way, one of obloquy.

Whether this recital be viewed as a sin of omission, or of commission it provides pretty clear proof that the ranks of the non-Jews are not wanting in unscrupulous members, and that when the passion-blinded set out upon a fanatical course, they will stop at no form of libel. It seems opportune, in view of this incident, to cite here a paragraph from a biographical list of the *"Wealthy Citizens of New York City"*, prepared "for Bankers and Others" by Moses Y. Beach in 1845, and published by *"The Sun"*. It relates to Haym Salomon, son of Haym Salomon, of whom Madison, when Congressman wrote, "I am a pensioner on his bounty".

"If this man" wrote Mr. Beach, "had received his just due from the National Government, he would now be worth more than a million dollars. There is now in the archives of the Government, documentary evidence that his father, a wealthy Jew of Philadelphia, loaned without security to the United States a sum not less than $355,000. Mr. Madison, in his posthumous papers, says that during the Revolutionary War, at a time when the Government could not borrow on its own credit, and could not raise a dollar on its best Virginia Drafts, Mr. Salomon came forward and freely lent his aid in support of the Government". In a continuation of this case, Mr. Beach refers handsomely to the patriotism of the entire family of Salomon; and to Colonel Franks, one of the Salomon kinsmen, whom he calls a patriot. Colonel Franks, however, is the officer who has been held up as a proof that Jews, whether in the eighteenth or twentieth centuries, encourage wars, in order to cull profits; who, because he had dealings, as had other honest citizens, no doubt, with Benedict Arnold, he was a traitor whose end was a dubious one.

Let us turn to the Jews' status as citizen and patriot as patriots and citizens of another rank have rated it:

Ex-President Cleveland, in addition to the tribute which is to be found at the head of this chapter, has said: "I know that human prejudice, especially that growing out of race and religion, is cruelly inveterate and lasting; but, wherever else in the world prejudice against the Jew exists, there can be no place for it among the peoples of the United States, unless they are heedless of good faith and recreant to every pledge involved in our boasted equality of citizenship . . . The Jews have become our fellow-citizens, and, like us, have at heart the prosperity and safety of our common country."

If any was capable of understanding and impartially approximating the value of citizenship, it was the distinguished John Hay. Endowed with a live conscience and just mind, as Secretary to President Lincoln he had unusual opportunities for estimating the many-sided values of the Jew in the Civil War period. He is quoted as saying that of all immigrants to this nation, none has proven himself worthier of citizenship than the Jew. Mr. Hay knew the Jew when he fought in both armies, North or South, according as his patriotism drew him. Nearly eight thousand Jewish soldiers are recorded in the two armies, exclusive of some six hundred and sixty staff officers, chaplains, surgeons, etc. *Nine generals of the Jewish race commanded during that internecine strife.* Lincoln bestowed medals on a number of Jewish soldiers for their bravery during it. Many German-Jewish names figured in those Civil War lists, as many in the Northern Army as in the Southern ranks, where were inscribed, too, the names of native Jews of the fourth and fifth generation born in America.   These fought side by side with new-comers of the race, and with their non-Jewish compatriots.

On more than one occasion ex-President Roosevelt expressed his opinion as to the fine qualities of citizenship that have been displayed by men of Jewish faith and race. "Even in our Colonial period," he has written, "the Jews participated in the up-building of this country, acquired citizenship, and took an active part in the development of its foreign and domestic commerce.   During the Revolutionary period, they aided the cause of liberty by serving in the Continental army and by substantial contributions to the empty treasury of the infant republic.   During the Civil War thousands served in the armies and mingled their blood with the soil for which they fought."

He might have added that at the outbreak of the Spanish War, a regiment of Russian Jews from New York, and a second from Philadelphia, though this order possibly should be reversed, were among the first to offer their services to President McKinley, and that it was generally believed that the first American blood spilled in that war was that of a young Jew.   The *Washington Star,* reviewing the Jews' history in America, observed that here they had always been soldiers when the call came.   This was overwhelmingly true during the great world war.   An estimate which made a vivid impression upon the writer stated that from the Jewish people, representing four per cent of the population of the United States, six per cent of the enlisted men of a given district in a given time had come. The number of "honorable mentions" among the Jews for gallant conduct on the battlefield during the World War is enormous.   There was no branch of the service in which they did not have part.

Because of the accusation brought against them of having a leaning towards the Quartermaster's corps, the present author has carefully looked into the question to see if facts would bear out such an assertion. It is found that Jewish names figure in every branch of the army and navy. They served in the ordnance and medical corps; in infantry and artillery; in cavalry and aviation corps; in the engineering, dental and ambulance corps. Less than ten per cent of the whole enlistments from this citizen group were in the Quartermaster's corps, and these, generally, represented the more delicate men who were of much greater assistance in that department than they would have been in the actual fighting ranks.

The Jew as a soldier is what might be termed a neglected source of pride to the nation; of joy to the historian and to those who delight in stories of martial adventure and prowess. It has been so long unfashionable to praise him that to hear that he can be and often is a physical as well as a moral hero, strikes those who have accepted their opinions of him in the usual second-hand way, with amazement. From the very beginning of his association with American history, he revealed himself as a stout fighter.

Asser Levy was the name of this first comer, and he arrived in New Amsterdam about 1654, some thirty-odd years after the *Mayflower* made her historic landing at Plymouth Rock. He was alive with the true citizen's spirit which Spain's persecutions and Portugal's in driving the Jews from Brazil had in no way stifled or subdued. He was ready to do his part as a citizen when, upon a memorable occasion, the call came to the settlers to arm and defend the tiny hamlet at the end of the Island of Manhattan. But, no! says the redoubtable Peter Stuyvesant, full of old world habits of mind and prejudices; "Jews may not fight with us. But you may pay a fine for not doing so!"

Did Levy submit to this? No! He was not an ignorant man, and he refused to forego his man's right

and to pay a fine for the privilege of doing so.   He argued
the matter, but Stuyvesant was obdurate.   Then Levy
appealed to the Dutch Company in Amsterdam which was
financing the new settlement, and among whose directorate
were several of his race, and, eventually, he won his right
to be a man as others were in this new land of the free
and home of the brave!

It should be said, too, that when it became necessary
to build the "wall" from which Wall Street took its name,
Levy was one of the few who would and could and did
subscribe the sum of one hundred florins toward it.   That
determination to fight his way, rather than to sink into
inferiority by the payment of tribute, to claim his full citizen's rights, and not buy "privileges" is the base on which
the political freedom of the Jews in America rests today.
An excerpt from *"Jewish History in the United States"*
which forms part of *"The International Jew"* by Mr. Ford
may prove illuminating here as an example of the strange
history writing, which serves as foundation for much of
the vituperation which has been spilled upon the race.   It
reads: "Unwillingly, old Peter Stuyvesant compelled the
Jew [in 1660] to make New York the principal port of
America, and though a majority of New York Jews had
fled to Philadelphia [this occurred 110 years later] most
of them returned to New York [some 25 years later]
instinct seeming to make them aware that in New York
was to be their principal paradise" etc., etc.

Each war that has arisen in the United States, since
Levy insisted upon bearing arms, has had its Jewish as
well as its non-Jewish contingent of fighters.   Back in
the Seminole wars; out on the frontiers, at a time when
their numbers were few, there were military heroes of this
race.   One of them, David de Leon, won his *soubriquet,*
"the Fighting Doctor," at Chepultepec, and twice received
the thanks of Congress for his bravery.   He was a native-

born American, graduate of the Pennsylvania University. Twice when his commanding officer met with disaster, he led a charge of cavalry "into the cannon's mouth," and on to victory. There is the case, too, of "Little Frauenthal!" whose non-Jewish comrades of the Civil War, up to a very old age thrilled as they told of how "that little Jew" stood, never flinching nor blanching, as he filled and refilled his gun amid a hail of bullets, and went on shooting.

Nor is this bravery a something characteristic of the American Jew only. It may be the reawakening of primitive traits in him, but if it is it is an awakening that runs through the veins of his people the world over; a something rising as political liberty has become more and more extended to him. From every army in the recent war you may gather news of his bravery if you look for it. An enormous number of Jewish soldiers were honored by the Italian King for their military services. France had a great multitude of Jews in her armies, among them Alfred Dreyfus, victim years ago of such malicious persecuting plots as have no counterpart in recent times. He fought eagerly, and came out of the war with promotion and honor while the disgraced miscreant Esterhazy, who was the author of his sufferings, lay hiding and starving in a London garret, whence he has since gone before the Great Judge of all.

So early in the World War as 1917, in Austria, four hundred and seventy Jewish soldiers were decorated for gallant services, a fact which was brought to light in order to silence the charge of an Austrian Jew-baiter who accused the Jews of "lack of enthusiasm for field service." As an interesting accompaniment to this (and a side-light which is valuable), at the time when this charge was brought the knowledge was current among these said-to-be reluctant Jews that while they were serving their country, the Government was transporting their wives—mothers, torn from their little children—to distant cities where labor was needed to keep up with the demand for war supplies. This was hardly the sort of knowledge which would incite the normal man to zeal.

When all is said and done it will be found that, no matter what their race, in the human family when the martial spirit is invoked, there are "family resemblances among the heirs of enthusiasm." From the very beginning Jews have produced martial heroes. 'Abram leads the list. Even the people of Heth hailed him as a mighty Prince. Whether you read of it in the Scriptures, or in the account given of it by Josephus, Abram is shown to be in every way a red-blooded and determined man. Upon learning that his brother was taken captive, he led forth his trained men, "born in his house," and pursued the captors. He overtook them, "and brought back his brother, and his brother's goods, and the women also, and the people."

We find him once more at the head of an army not so unlike those raised among the early settlers of America; and again his army is made up of his family and household. This time he is rushing to Lot's aid against the Assyrians. We are told that he routed them valiantly, and that few escaped slaughter, "thereby demonstrating," says Flavius Josephus, "that victory does not depend upon multitudes, and the number of hands; for the alacrity and courage of soldiers overcome the most numerous bodies of men. Abram conquered the Assyrian hosts with no more than three hundred and eighteen servants, and three of his friends."

The Laws of Moses have obscured from the general view that patriarch's record as a warrior-General directing the military forces of Pharaoh; but non-scriptural historians describe his leadership as wonderful. They tell in a spirited manner of his strategem in leading his troops upon one occasion through a land infested with deadly serpents.   In the story of this feat there is no admixture of the unreal, or of the superstitions.   It is a fascinating account of early war experiences.   It seems that Moses desired to lead his troops across a land which lay between the Egyptian and the opposing Ethiopian troops, a sort of no-man's land, which was regarded as impassable because of the swarms of serpents that infested it.   Moses, however, brooding over the problem of how to cross this territory and get at the enemy, devised a plan by which to solve it.

He caused his troops to catch a number of the ibes, a native bird which was the one enemy that could engage and conquer the serpents.   They collected, too, a number of rush baskets.   Into each basket he placed and secured one of the birds.   When a sufficient number had been caged, and all was ready, his troops stole up to the borderline and let loose the birds, before which the serpents scattered, many of them prey to their enemies.   In this way Moses secured his passage to the encampment of the Ethiopians, whom he quickly annihilated.   It was long after this triumphant campaign that jealousy began to flame about him, and to sow such scandalous suspicions concerning him and his people, that the King presently viewed him with doubt and even as a possible rival.   The history is marvellously modern and thrilling.   There is no grander moment in the career of the great Lawgiver than that in which, leaving his military glory behind him, and fleeing to the desert, he is presently seen tending his sheep upon the slopes of Mt. Sinai, which, through his stay upon it, was to become immortal.

Coming directly down the Ishmaelitish line we see military hero after military hero in a blaze of glory.   We may not linger here to consider them, not even General

Joshua, and his successors; not even David, who rises, a
true prototype of Napoleon.   When he comes into view
Israel is but a small country, comprised entirely between
Dan and Beersheba.   A few years of war, and he commands the land between the Nile and the Euphrates, practically all of old Chaldea.   We know it today as Syria,
where the Jewish race is again to be found in numbers.

Long after their kingdom was divided, and then lost,
the Jews retained their reputation for being dauntless and
loyal soldiers even to those who had conquered them.
Ptolemy I of Egypt, who took Judea from the weak hands
of a successor to Alexander the Great, showed full appreciation not only of the Judean valor, but of their loyalty
as citizens.   He entrusted to them the fortresses of Egypt
which he manned with thirty thousand Jews.   He believed, and this because of their deeply religious sense, that
they would keep their charges faithfully against all comers.
It is said, too, that when he desired to secure the Government of Cyrene and other Lybian cities to himself, he sent
a party of Jews to hold them for him.

It would seem as if the traditional accusation against
the Jew of cowardice arose among the coarse about this
time, when occurred an incident which was highly ideal
on the Jews' part, highly admirable as religionists of the
most austere piety but deplorable to them in its after
results.   Under what has been called the "pacifist" preaching of Ezra, Nehemiah and others, a religious awakening
had occurred among them, which made them place a new
value upon their traditional rites and laws.   Among these
was one which forbade them to fight, even in self-defense,
upon the Sabbath.   This the generals of Ptolemy I knew.
They decided upon the clever stratagem of attacking Jerusalem upon the Sabbath day, when the Jews, too pious to
fight, would be easily overcome.   Their ruse proved effective.   Because of their idealism, which today would be

called quixotism, the Jews' military glory was lost. In its place came derision and scorn from the practical outside world. For the ribald, and especially for the ignorant, their "cowardice" has since been a byword, carried down from age to age, even to the twentieth century A. D.

Yet, despite this stigma, one of their greatest military men was yet to come in the heroic figure of Judas Maccabeus. Here again, lovers of martial adventure find a field that is nothing short of thrilling in its recital of splendid and fearless deeds, not alone by the great Judas of the Maccabees, but by those of his father. In some respects he appears as the greater man, as we trace him as instigator and inciter of his sons to all that they later accomplished. For a hundred years they gave a period of glory to Judea, over which they ruled until shortly before the present era.

The story of the old father inciting his stalwart sons to the re-habilitation of Judea, the drama of it, is marvellously stirring viewed quite aside from its historic values. From the moment the scene is disclosed, you follow it with strained attention. You leave it with the recognition that despite the sadness and suffering which is accented in all histories of the Jews, theirs is no mean past; rather it is a mighty one, and unquestionably a mighty military one! The whole story of the Jews until the period immediately before the present era may be said to lie between the soldier's tent and the priest's temple. From the time of the dispersion as a nation, records are lost of them except as individual heroes rise against the backgrounds of other nations. Of these, however, there are many notable ones. Sometimes they appear under the banners of a Hindu prince; sometimes fighting in Turkey; some identified as "soldiers of fortune" who fared forth to many lands in search of adventure, but especially for the opportunity of being free like other men.

One of the most spectacular of these was Emin Pasha, born Schnitzer, who was, by turns, explorer, physician, warrior, and scientist. Scarcely arrived at manhood, he set out for Turkey, pausing awhile at Constantinople. Next we find him in Egypt, physician and aide to Gordon, who was then Governor of the Equatorial Provinces. It was Gordon who gave Schnitzer his new name of Emin Pasha. Through all Gordon's long and dangerous conflict with the Mahdi, Emin Pasha was with him, even to his death at Khartoum. Thereafter he becomes a figure of world importance, commanding the Gordon forces with unlimited freedom of action conferred upon him by the British Government. Throughout his continued strife with the indomitable Mahdi the cables rang with such accounts as they were able to get of him. His gallantry was the wonder of the world which shortly sent expeditions to relieve him—Stanley from England and a group of men of Germany—but so resolute was he to carry out alone the campaign with the Mahdi, that, in spite of the desperateness of the situation, he almost resented the aid that came to him. A strange and colorful career, his was, that ended, no one knows how, somewhere in the Congo State. All that was known of that end was the tale brought in by an Arab, who told of the assassination of Emin Pasha somewhere in the back country.

There were Jews in the armies of Marshal Saxe; in the Napoleonic wars, many in all the contending armies. Of those who fought in 1815 with the German forces, Prince von Hardenberg wrote to Count de Grothe: "Young men of the Jewish faith have been companions-in-arms of their Christian fellow-citizens, and we can point to examples among them of true courage and complete disregard of the perils of war no less than among the rest of the inhabitants. Their women, also, have mingled with the Christians in sacrifices of every kind."

Similar appraisals fell to the Jews' share for their participation in war under Wellington. It was estimated that in times of peace and prior to the breaking out of the last war, some ninety thousand Jews were in the military service of the different European Governments. Nothing better demonstrates the patriotism of which the Jews are capable than the loyal spirit shown by the immigrants who have settled here, to their native lands. It takes nothing from their love for their adopted country that their hearts retain tender remembrances of their earlier homes. Rather it holds the assurance of a stability of sentiment as strong for America when they shall have taken root here. German Jews in the United States, notwithstanding centuries of very harsh treatment received at the hands of Germany, like Caesar, who forgot all injuries and remembered only the kindnesses he received, have forgotten their injuries and remembered that country with tenderness as the nest from which they have flown. Surely a natural sentiment in a well-constructed human being! Russian Jews who for generations have starved and cowered under the tyranny of Russian misrule, refer with moist eyes to that country as their motherland. The Jews who came first to America felt the same traditional love for Spain and Portugal; but by the time of the Revolutionary war, all of them were rooted in America. So loyal were those in New York, that, when the British took possession of that city, rather than to enjoy the protection of those enemies of the country's independence, almost to a man they emigrated to Philadelphia, to Newport, where notable memorials of those early patriots are still to be found.

Forty soldiers of the race were decorated by the Sultan of Turkey, early in this century. Italian Jews fought with Garibaldi. They were part of the Royal Italian Army that marched into Rome in 1870. Many

Italian Jews have risen from the ranks to places of distinction in other lines.   General Giuseppe Ottolenghi, who died in the early part of this century, was a gallant soldier, who became first Senator, and then Minister of War. French Jews fought in the Franco-Prussian war, and German-born Jews were with the German Army which entered Paris in 1872.

Wherever they have had the semblance of a reason to call a land their home, they have given that country their love, their devotion, their lives in her times of need. Patriotism with them is a creed.   All their religious teachings impress this upon them as a necessity.   They have before them constantly in their Rabbinical teachings, God's admonition, as sent to them while captives in Babylon, by Jeremiah, then in Jerusalem: *"Seek the peace of the city whither I have caused you to be carried away captive, and pray unto the Lord for it; for in the peace thereof shall ye have peace."*

There is no reason to doubt, even though from time to time a speckled sheep appears among such a flock, the purity of heart, of motive, and of life of the great majority of Jewish people; no reason to look for disloyalty or lack of patriotism among them, nor any ground upon which a doubt may be cast as to their courage; rather, reason after reason presents itself for believing that the Jews, as a whole, represent a real spiritual asset to any country which makes living reasonably comfortable for them.   From the utterances of the first Jew to arrive in this land, they have proven and pledged their loyalty to it.   To George Washington the Newport colony declared themselves as follows: "This Federal Union, whose base is philanthropy, mutual confidence and public virtue, we cannot but acknowledge to be the work of the great God. * * * Deprived as we hitherto have been of what should be the inalienable rights of free citizens, we now, with a deep sense of gratitude to the

Almightly Dispenser of all events, behold a Government erected by the majesty of the people, a Government which to bigotry gives no sanction, to persecution no assistance, but generously affords to all, liberty of conscience and the immunities of citizenship, deeming every one, of whatever nation, or tongue, to be an equal part of the great government machine."

During the world war the Jews of the United States came together, as all other religious groups did, and formed a Welfare Board. Its first announcement reads: "Primarily the purpose of the Jewish Welfare Board is to help America win the war." An American Rabbi at that time was asked to give his definition of America. He replied: "To me America is all that the submerged races of the world wish to be and cannot be; the concrete realization of what the ages have hoped and labored for. That is my definition. It is a creed. It is a challenge. God built a continent of glory and filled it with untold treasures. He carpeted it with soft-rolling prairies, and pillared it with thundering mountains. He studded it with sparkling springs and traced it with winding streams, graced it with deep shadowed forests and filled these with song. Then He called unto a thousand peoples * * * and they came from the ends of the earth each bringing a gift and a hope. The glow of adventure was in their eyes and the glory of hope within their souls. Out of the labor of men and the bounty of earth, out of the prayers of men and the hopes of the world, in love God fashioned a nation, blessed it with a purpose sublime and called it 'America'."

The reaction of such preachments and such dogma upon the Jews' daily life cannot fail to produce impregnable patriotism. We have dwelt upon the military side of their citizenship for reasons which will have been seen. In their purely civic relationship they are the most active of all citizens. They are in every movement that has to do with the public good. They fill offices which others may crave but will not contest for. Above all men do the Jews regard political service honorable. They appreciate political freedom, so new to them, as a class. They go to the polls while only too many non-Jews go fishing. As we shall presently indicate, they are in the vanguard of all civic improvements. They create industries, demands for them, and markets for the fruits of them. But this aspect of the Jew and civilization we shall consider in our next chapter.

CHAPTER III

The Jew in Industry

*"The recurrence of the Jewish New Year is always
a reminder of the debt which the modern world owes
to the Jewish people and their wonderful national
culture. The occasion is one of significance, not
merely to the people of the Jewish faith and race, but
to all who have been the inheritors of some part in the
splendid estate of leadership, spiritually, and the service which they have given to the world for the common advantage."*

CALVIN COOLIDGE,
President of the United States of America.

TURNING to the Jew in industry, we come upon him
in a field in which he has been misrepresented with
especial acrimony. None has done this in a more petty
and unworthy spirit than has a writer in the *"World's
Work."* This author's aversion to "the exotic mass of
Jews which the steamships," as he puts it, "began dumping
on the Atlantic seaboard forty years ago" causes him to
go to great lengths in making disparaging comparisons between those victims of Russian tyranny in the nineteenth
century and the first immigrants to arrive in America in
the seventeenth and eighteenth centuries. The reasonable
will at once recognize the impossibility of making any comparison whatsoever between the two groups; but this author, none the less, has attempted it. He says that the
first immigrants had "the pioneering spirit" which the
more recent comers lack.

"Take the original settlers," he says, "those colonists
from the British Isles, who at the time of the Revolution,
formed 80 per cent of the young country's population,"
"and whose descendants form not far from 60 per cent of
its population today. We first see these hardy frontiers-

men in the seventeenth century, making accessible to civilization the Atlantic seaboard." (He has forgotten that the first pioneer to step upon that coast was a Jew, and this in the late fifteenth century.) These hardy frontiersmen, says this author, pressed westward, founding cities and great industries, which, he adds, was "real immigration" as was the coming of later Scandinavians and Germans, and, presently the Irish and the Italians. But the Jews, he goes on (whose communings with their God appear to be particularly offensive to him) stayed in cities, when "three thousand miles of continent beckoned to them," and where, "like Jacob of old, they could have practiced sheep herding and all the arts of husbandry; but, apparently, only the teeming cities had any attraction for them."

This is loose reasoning, but worse still, it is distortion of facts. In the first place there may have been three thousand miles of unused territory in the west in 1880-1-2 but we need no over-sharp imagination to fancy what would have happened to the Jewish newcomers of that period had they attempted to take possession of it as the pioneers took possession of the primeval land two centuries earlier. Most of these late arrivals, moreover, were refugees, whose passage was paid for them by the pitying; who in addition, had planned for them opportunities for living nearer to groups of their own race who could understand and help them. But here, again, with a view to alarming the public, other bitter accusations have been made of the "organized movement into America of masses of Jews" and an unworthy significance has been given to the fact that rich Jews and aid societies had furnished means to these Jews (forty-three years ago), to fly the terrors of Russia and seek asylum in the United States.

The fact is entirely overlooked, in these bitter attacks

upon the Jews, that the progeny of this same "exotic mass" that then was "dumped upon the Atlantic seaboard, have, in many instances risen as scientists, and in various professional avenues today are to be found all over the land.

It is worth a moment's turning aside from these perverted views of the Jew, these oversights, if so they may be termed, of the actual value to the country of those immigrants of the '80's, to look at the subject through the dispassionate eyes of a thoughtful economist. Speaking of immigration in general, Professor Commons, in his *Races and Immigrants in America,*" says: "We have seen the conditions in their foreign homes which spurred the emigrants to seek America . . . religious persecution, race oppression, political revolution; taxation, famine poverty conspiring to press upon the unprivileged masses and to drive the more adventurous across the water. But it would be a mistake should we stop at that point and look upon the migration . . . as only a voluntary movement to better their condition." He then traces the immigration that has peopled America.

"While various motives and inducements have always worked together," he continues, "and it would be rash to assert dogmatically the relative weight of each, yet to one who has noted the circumstances, it is scarcely an exaggeration to say that even more important than the initiative of immigrants, have been the efforts of shipowners and Americans to bring and to attract them. Throughout our history these efforts have been inspired by one grand, effective motive—that of making a profit upon the immigrants. The desire to get cheap labor, to take in passenger fares, and to sell land have probably brought more immigrants than the hard conditions of Europe, Asia and Africa have sent. It is to this mercenary motive that we owe our manifold variety of races.

. . . Working people of the colonial period were hood-winked and kidnapped by shippers and speculators who reimbursed themselves by indenturing them to planters and farmers. . . ."

Professor Commons cites the means employed by William Penn and his lessees, John Law and the Dutch East India Company, to people his new estate in America. Pity for the persecuted mingled with his project, without doubt; but a need for the development of real estate lay side by side with it and led to the prepaying of the passage of the emigrants who were to act as pioneers for civilization. Professor Commons adds: "In the nineteenth century new forms of induced migration appeared. Victims of the Irish famine were assisted to emigrate by local and general governments and by philanthropic societies, and both Irish and Germans whose migrations began in the middle of the century, were, in this measure, exceptions to the general rule of immigration for profit."

It should here be recalled that the refugees who were "dumped on the Atlantic seacoast" in the '80's were, likewise, exceptions, and that their predecessors met with a scarcely kinder treatment than the Jews have since received. They, too, were reviled in the press of the day, and racial ill-feeling here and religious strife there will be come upon by those who are sufficiently interested to look into the history of last century.

The fact is, as Professor Commons makes plain, that the industrious emigrant arriving in a strange land in the modern world is always resented and rebuffed, and the more vigorously as he at once sets out to repair his fortunes and to "dig in" for a permanent home. This attained, his own next step is to keep others out. History repeats itself in these economic facts in every land and in every age. It also shows that in the course of time no means have been considered beneath the dignity of the first arrivals which would enable them to besmirch and hinder the progress of those who came after. It is a wise precaution, then, before accepting the statements of the passionately prejudiced, to look into the economic facts of the case. What appears to be religious and racial antagonism (Professor Commons makes plain), and what the blindly fanatical regard as social and political animosities, are actually, at bottom, economic problems. An examination into the charges brought against the Jews today by each and every writer will reveal this economic factor at the root of every slander, of every accusation.

It is in the field of economics that the interests of all men meet, that all conflicts arise. All sorts and conditions of men operate in it from the humblest artisan to the richest manufacturer; from the simplest handicraftsman to the distributor of the finished product. The Jews, entering this field have prospered signally. A very high percentage of them have shown themselves skilled workmen, notable for their sobriety, frugality and willingness to work hard, and these qualities have brought their own reward. But, as a result, we find the modern Jew-baiter rising up to impugn their motives and methods at every point. There are those, on the one hand, who declare that the Jews are crowding into, and, by inference, crowding others out of many trades; and, on the other, those who declare that the Jews will not work at all if they can help it, but will, if they can make the opportunity, live by the sweat of non-Jews. This, in the very beginning, is belied by both Jewish practice and Jewish preaching. Let us look at this from the records of the race:

From the first chapters of their Scriptures work has been commended by the Jewish teachers, and idleness condemned. "The sleep of a laboring man is sweet;" "He

that gathereth by labor shall increase;" are among the
Biblical proverbs of this people. In post-Biblical writings
labor is be-praised by the Rabbinical teachers. "Who fails
to teach his son a trade," says a Talmudic verse, "teaches
him to become a thief." The urge to industry again
appears in the parable of the "ten talents." Contrary to
the opinion so insistently projected by those inimical to
the race, the Jews who labor with their hands are many
times more numerous than are those who enter commercial lines, into which they are constantly forced, however, by discriminations that shut them out, even in these
"enlightened" days, from the trade and professions open
to the non-Jewish applicant. Forced into "individualistic"
enterprise they are next attacked because of this "tendency" to individualism and to petty mercantile pursuits;
or, as the *World's Work* author has put it, because of
their preference for becoming "shoe-string capitalists"
rather than to be numbered among the idle and dependent.

Look where you will, as Mr. David Lloyd George has
said, the disposition is evident to mis-state the Jew; to
misrepresent him, and to make him again the victim of
prejudice deliberately roused. The ways of the public
are barred by hysterical criers, announcing that the Jews
are seizing upon—for the anti-Semites are frantic users of
the superlative,—the economics of the western hemisphere
so boldly as to threaten its future; that the rising tide
of Jewry—one of the smallest peoples, numerically, in
the world, will shortly overwhelm the vast human family
unless "something be done." That "something" has been
pointed out by Mr. Belloc. The sane, getting this whole
commotion in a proper perspective will scarcely fail to
see the resemblance it bears to Kingsley's "children of
Prometheus who go telling folk what will happen, instead

of looking to see what has already happened"; or, that author's Pantheon, wherein all the philosophers and scribblers are busy contradicting each other.

On one side the maddest alarmists trumpet the warning of the *"Jewish Peril,"* and on the other the superficial and preoccupied deride both the complainants and the complained of. In the meantime, the voices of the first drown those of the second, and, even more effectively, those of still another class who estimate the Jews at a higher value. A Ford periodical scents economic disaster in the Jews' appearance of prospering, and sows fears over the whole land; while the utterance of the Chicago Mayor, who sees blessings in that prosperity, and states it openly in the press, is negligibly given to the public, and passes unread by those whose views might well have been modified into a kinder appreciation of this people. The present mayor of that western municipality, which has a large Jewish population, has said: "Their notable accomplishments in industry and all branches of human endeavor which constitute the basis of every civilization, have secured them an honorable position in this city . . . They are, in addition, a God-fearing people and have contributed greatly to the growth and development of this city." Governors of states and the heads of nations have again and again told in unstinted praise of the value of the Jew to the nation and community. Preachers have added their testimony of the same sort; nevertheless the honest seeker after the truth is confronted on every side by the most contradictory proclamations of prejudiced sowers of sedition, who attribute to the Jews a super-craftiness which would make them, if true, the most dangerous mortals imaginable. They are accused, even the humblest of the race, of possessing the most incomparable cunning and selfishness; of acting in stealth in all things; of seeking to subvert governments; of destroying industry; of being a race which now menaces the world's well-being; and, again, as through the pen of Houston Stewart Chamberlain and his follower, the editor of the *"World's Work,"* they are held up as inferior, mentally, to other races, and stupid even to delinquency.

Surely it should be apparent that bigotry and not reason or honest purpose is at the bottom of these laboriously worked out attacks upon this race. They present a very confusion of accusations. At times it would seem as if, in their determination to prove the Jews models of stupidity and its opposite, cupidity, these modern fanatics tumble pell-mell into each others' ways, reveal what they take pains to conceal, under ingenious and even momentarily blinding arguments. For example, H. S. Chamberlain, son-in-law of Richard Wagner, himself a notable Jew-baiter as well as musical genius, in one breath accuses the Jews of 800 and 900 A. D. of having been too stupid to perceive the mercantile value of paper, and in the next of having perceived it, but, out of mercantile greed, of having held back the knowledge of it from the rest of Europe.

There is a common characteristic displayed by all anti-Semites, a propensity to run back into ancient and indistinct history, into that, usually, of thousands of years ago, for proofs of the low worth of the Jew of today. This we shall have occasion to recall as we go on, in order to show the lengths to which Mr. Chamberlain has frequently gone to dispraise the Jew in the various avenues of effort in which the human race has operated. For the moment we may examine into his treatment of this people in their relation to paper and to printing, lines of industry in which the race has been conspicuously active and important in late centuries.

In the ninth and tenth centuries there were numerous lusty races in Europe each one of which was in far better position to examine into the value of and undertake the development of this industry than were the Jews, who had neither political nor domiciliary rights, nor even an unrestricted choice of trade or occupation in which they might engage. But, in a manner entirely his own—a dazzling manner, too, as we are assured in the introduction to the Chamberlain book written by Lord Redesdale, G. C. V. O., K. C. B., etc.—this author is able to twist facts in such way as to inculpate the Jews as hoarders upon whom rests the responsibility for the belated appearance of paper in Europe, and, in consequence, for the still further delay in the invention of printing. The Jew, Mr. Chamberlain asserts, kept back "the flow of intelligence" in the west, in order to preserve paper for his own and sole use in the the form of bills of exchange and promissory notes. This invites a looking into.

It appears that the Indo-Aryans invented paper made of rags which improved upon an earlier and simpler product of China, manufactured from papyrus. By the natural migrations of peoples, but chiefly by utilizing the knowledge of war captives and refugees, Samarcand, in time became the paper-making centre of the East. Haroun-al-Raschid, contemporary of Charlemagne, and a Semite, or half-Semite, as Mr. Chamberlain might say, though he was a Mossulman and not a Jew—in the course of time became interested in the Indo-Aryan product and built a factory in Bagdad for its manufacture. But he guarded carefully the formula for making it. Now, Mr. Chamberlain says, "wherever the Arabs went, paper accompanied them, particularly to Moorish Spain where Jews, for a long time, were predominant, and where paper can be proved to have been in use from the tenth century. Hardly any came to Teutonic Europe, and, if it did, it was only as a material of unknown origin."

This is both singular and contradictory; for the Teutons, who in Mr. Chamberlain's opinion were from the beginning, the superiors of all other races in Europe, were sprung from the Eastern Indo-Germanic stock and should have been in possession of very early knowledge of paper manufacture, especially in its primitive form. But Mr. Chamberlain very adroitly directs his readers from a possible enquiry into this, and points them towards Spain, and the Arab who, he says, carried paper to that country. The chances are as ten to one that the Jews and not the Arabs brought the first paper to Spain. Though some among the Spanish Jews had lived there, legends say, since the days of Nebuchadnezzar, yet Jews were not then the dominant figures in Spain which later they became. A few of them were rich and powerful; but, until well into the tenth century, Babylonian teachers of the Jewish race were centered at Sora, to which the eyes of the Jews of the world were turned. The Jew in general had no national home, and he became the great link between the east and the west in that period, not withholding, but spreading knowledge, intellectual and spiritual as well as commercial, between the lands he had commerce with.

Saadiah, the great builder-up of the Jewish religion of that period, presided at Sora. It was the Mecca for Jews of that century, and for Arabian and other philosophers who would take issue with Saadiah, and disciples who would profit by his learning. It is certain that the most intelligent Jews of those times from all lands made pilgrimages to this school, and continued to do so until the disturbances in the surrounding world began to affect them unpleasantly. Then the Talmudic school and all its interests were transported to Spain. Meanwhile, defined routes of travel had been trodden between the East and the West, over which, thereafter, Jewish merchants on foot, or camel or on courser, travelled regularly.

When Christianity and Islam arrived at scimitar and javelin points, the Jews were called upon to play an important role. A Christian was not permitted to enter Islamic territory, nor a Mossulman to enter that of Christians. The Jews being of neither faith, were, in consequence, in demand as messengers and interpreters between the two; as mediums in trading between the opposing groups, as well. So early as the ninth century Jewish merchants are known to have brought from the east various products, such as spices, drugs and slaves, and to have returned to eastern countries with the products of Europe.

Even then Jews settled, where they were permitted to settle, and took up trades. There were glass-workers, goldsmiths, silversmiths, locksmiths in many of the Mediterranean cities, and even scattered members of the race in Northern Europe. But those familiar with that eastern travel are known to have served as ambassadors between Haroun-al-Raschid and European kings; Charlemagne, among others, who then ruled over the Germans. Paper must have passed in those embassies, but it does not appear to have stirred curiosity among the Teutons more than among the Jews, of whom, though Mr. Chamberlain makes no mention of it, there were numbers in Germany, some of them having lived there so early as 315 A. D.

Many of them were scholars from whom distinguished lines have sprung. The Fratelli Treves, whose Italian books lie on the tables of the cultured of today the world over, are descended from one of the most remarkable Jewish families of whom there are records, and they are first found in Germany in those early times. The Jews there lived comfortably, prosperously, serving the king as faithfully as did non-Jews. Some of them unquestionably travelled East to Saadiah's school. In all probability there were merchants among them. But when, about Charlemagne's time the agitations began in Christian countries which were to culminate in the Crusades against the Moors, the Jews in Germany, because they, too, were "infidels" and looked not unlike the Moors, came in for much hatred. False accusations, persecutions and wholesale massacres thinned their ranks. Their homes destroyed, their goods seized, and life become so very uncertain with them, many of them fled to such sanctuary as they might find, in other lands.

As the first and second Crusades cover a century's history, and their aftermath a still longer period, and as the Crusaders were to be met with on every highroad in Europe, the Jews must have had a pretty hard time of it in the keeping of body and soul together. It is small wonder that the minds of non-Jewish inventors of that period ran to the needs of war rather than to the evolving of the mysterious fabric we call paper. It is no wonder at all that the minds of Jews, pursued by the persecuting zeal of the Crusaders; obliged to exercise their wits night and day to secure their own and their families' safety, were content to leave matters as they were, for the time being, at any rate. Bigotry augmented with the war; and the zealous devised some very strange ways of inciting the people against those who did not believe in the prevailing religion. It was during the Crusades that the story of *"The Wandering Jew"* was invented to fill the superstitious with the belief that the Jew was accursed—reprehensible in God's sight, and should be, therefore, in the sight of good churchmen.

"However," continues Mr. Chamberlain, avoiding the truth—"avoiding" because it is impossible to believe him unaware of it—"for nearly five hundred years the Semites and half-Semites held the monopoly of paper; time enough, if they had possessed a spark of invention or experienced the slightest longing for intellectual study, [Oh, oh! And this at a time when all Christendom was warring and the Jews were practically the only unattached people who might and did concern themselves with things intellectual!] to have developed this glorious *weapon* of the intellect into a power; and what did they do with it? Nothing, absolutely nothing. All they could do was to make promissory notes of it, and, in addition, a few hundred soul-destroying books."

Among those books were Maimonides' philosophic work, the *"Guide for the Perplexed,"* which Grotius drew from and which has affected human thought for centuries; the laboriously copied Scriptures, and numerous early geographical, astronomical and mathematical works, original and translated from the Arabian. These were made by Jewish scribes, often by flickering torch-light, who copied over and over again these works for the scholars and clerics of those centuries. But, continues Mr. Chamberlain, "in the course of the Crusades, the secret of the manufacture of paper, guarded with such intellectual poverty, was revealed. What the poor Iranian, wedged in between the Semites, Tartars and Chinese had invented, *was taken over by the free Teuton."* (The italics are the present author's.)

It took the free Teutons quite a century thereafter to come to the building of a paper mill, and two hundred more years before they made the discovery of block printing. Again fifty more passed ere movable type was perfected, and Gutenberg printed his Bible, or Jewish Scriptures. But during all this time Europe continued to be

torn with wars. In the chaos Jeanne d'Arc had run her
career and had perished at Rouen, and kingly lines had
risen and fallen. During these troubled times the European Jews sustained themselves as best they could. Most
of the occupations in which they engaged must have been
followed by stealth, since the laws of many lands prohibited them from practicing the majority of trades and
callings then known. There is evidence that Jewish goldsmiths, silversmiths, locksmiths existed. Some of these
must have been searching for a means of printing, for laws
were enacted to prohibit them from practicing the cutting
of seals, a trade which was the direct predecessor of type-
cutting, and one in which the Jews must have operated,
else why the laws to prohibit them?

When, in 1450, steel movable type was an assured fact
—Coster had worked with wooden type some thirty years
earlier—the Jews were among the first to invest their
money, time and intelligence in perfecting it. Within
twenty-five years after Gutenberg's discovery, the Soncini,
descendants of German Jews who had fled to Italy from the
persecutions of earlier times, were making Italy famous for
its fine printing, and their race joyful with new hope. "Out
of Zion shall go forth the law, and the word of the Lord
from Soncino," became a famous saying. The Soncini
printed the Hebrew Bible as well as Italian works, using
a fine type cut by the expert type-cutter whose letterings
distinguish the choice volumes issued by Aldus from his
Aldine press.

In England, France, Holland and Spain the clicking of
type was heard simultaneously. It was the advance guard
of the great work-multiplying machinery which has since
changed the economy of the world. The facts of that epoch
suggest that the Jew, as a stupid, was in rather good company; but it cannot be said that this was on equal terms;

for, as has been stated in several countries, and notably in Germany and Austria, he was specifically prohibited by law from engaging in seal-cutting.

By 1500, Gerson Soncino, who came to be dubbed "The Wandering Jew of Italy," had planted Italy with printing shops and his race permanently before the world in modern industry. Mantua, Naples, Brescia, Rome all had their Soncino printing establishments. Twenty years later Gerson Cohen, a member of the same family, returned to Germany and set up a press at Prague. From him a great family of printers derived who, for generations, were known as the Gersonides.

It should be said here that type-making, type-setting and printing for which, from the first, the Jews showed a marked aptitude, was hailed by them as "the art of writing with many pens." The early printers looked upon theirs as "holy work." "Certainly," wrote Jansen, "printing gave wings to intellectual life." "Gave wings to our intellect!" exclaims the irascible Mr. Chamberlain, quoting inexactly, as he so often thinks, "On the contrary, it was winged intellect that forced the invention of printing!" Mr. Wells in his *Outline of History* says of that wonderful discovery that it not only set ideas trickling, but running in floods. Probably nothing greater has ever happened to humanity, than this invention of printing. It has set undreamed-of forces in motion in the world.

It is not short of romance to trace the upward rise of the Jewish printer from those early beginnings to the present day, when the various occupations opened up through this invention give employment to multitudes of Jewish craftsmen the world over. Today the Type-setters' Union, said to be the strongest in the Federation of Labor, is composed largely of Jews. The same might be said of the unions of tailors and clothing makers and many other numerically strong labor groups, which in themselves should be sufficient to disprove the statement so often heard, that Jews are not willing workers with their hands. Available statistics prove that as artisan in many crafts the Jew occupies an important position in the industrial world, though he has had to battle for the respect he now enjoys.

In the last forty years he has risen steadily as a factor in United States industry, and in it has proven to be a living denial of the charge that the Jews are, primarily, a money-seeking and ease-loving race. The industry the poor among them display is passing into a proverb; and the poor and industrial classes among the Jews represent seventy-five per cent of all Jews, go where you will, but these, due to their self-respect, are less discernible among the general population than are the poor of any other of the numerous races that make up the population of the New World.

Some reasons for this will develop as we proceed in our story; but the basic reason of all is the Jew's determination to be independent, at no matter what cost in self-denial or labor. He is intelligently seeking a way out of poverty. He labors long and hard, and often in despised trades; but, meaning to better himself by and by, he studies as he works. And, as many have observed, he puts ideals into his work. He may not express his ideals in our terms. He may even express them in a way to us unlovely. He will be sure to do this if he belongs to the ill-fed class. The ill-fed of all races fight strenuously because they are and know themselves to be at a disadvantage. Mr. Belloc, observing certain forms of struggle in the Jewish race, says, fastidiously, as another reason why the Jew should be got rid of: He is not like us. He does not reason like us. His manners are not like ours.

But the battle with want, with hardship of any sort, inevitably leaves its scars, and in nothing more than in manners. Dr. Johnson, whose boyhood was spent in penury, could never shed a certain unpleasant awareness of the need for economy. If a philosopher of his stern type was custombound by a mere lifetime habit, how shall we demand of the Jews the immediate shaking off of the race habit of self-defense, of distrust of the world which has been forced upon them for millenia? Yet the industrial Jew, in particular, goes courageously on, perhaps even a bit desperately, since he knows that if he does not care for himself, none else will care for him. One of the first things he does is to educate his children so that their future may be an improvement over the life he has known. What is altogether amazing in the Jews of the working-classes, is that after long days at work-benches, fathers and mothers themselves seek mental improvement through evening public school classes, and by attendance at the public lectures which in New York, at least, are now part of the educational system of the city. They sacrifice leisure, and, it may be needed rest, to hear of science, literature, music, travels. The corridors and reading rooms of public libraries show the Jews to be omnivorous readers and students.

A confirmed anti-Semite will, of course, discount all this as an indication of Jewish worth. He will probably tell you it is mere sentiment to recall it; that the Jew "pushes" out of mere dogged will; that it is part of the Jewish scheme to conquer the world. The prejudiced today do not hesitate, in discussing the Jew, to transmute what are virtues in others, into vices when displayed by him. A most unpleasant example of this has been furnished by an editor of the *"World's Work"* within the year.

"The Jew," he writes, "scrapes together a few hundred dollars at his sewing machine or pressing board;

with this he purchases an equity in a tenement house, giving first, second, third, fourth, and fifth mortgages for the remainder. He then moves his family into the least desirable apartment; he himself becomes the janitor; his wife does not disdain the job of scrub-woman; his sons do service as painters, paper hangers, and general repairmen. In this way his "overhead" is very light; everything is very light; everything is kept within the family, which labors eighteen hours a day with one consuming determination—to get together enough money to pay off the series of mortgages as they fall due. The family can subsist on the modicum of food and can wear the cheapest clothes; it spends no money on amusement or general frivolity; it has but one purpose in view—to meet those payments!"

Could a picture be painted that represented better citizenship than this of a family, coming to the land of the free, hoping to become more than grovellers, and willing, meantime, to endure incomparable hardships to attain it; avoiding the foolish, dishonest running into debt, and winning by sheer labor, by long personal self-sacrifice? This is the moral stuff of which a fine nation is made. It is the stuff of the Pilgrim Fathers, of the true pioneers; but their path was easier, since there were none to cry "shame" upon their heroism. Far from sneering at them, we, in free America, should encourage people who have such fortitude, and rectitude to contribute to the national character. These are the true qualities that may stay the decay of over rich countries. Out of many of the Russian homes thus established in the eighties and nineties have come scientists and professional men; teachers and preachers, who today hold notable positions.

This same writer describes some of these strangers who come to America seeking asylum. It was rather "disconcerting," he says, "to see their half-starved appearance, their furtive movements, their hollow chests, their undeveloped bodies, the outward physical signs of the centuries of city dwelling that had been their portion." He perceives nothing of the wonderful in the miracle of these men courageously going to work and starting life anew in a foreign land, among not friendly glances, supported only by their marvellous faith. On the contrary, through the insistently prejudiced mind the virtues of these people are transformed into vices; every timid glance of enquiry is interpreted as a sign of cupidity; every necessary frugality as an indication of mercenary traits.

These immigrants take up dress and clothing and boot-making, and are accused of seeking only the "softer berths" in industry. They have been especially attacked for "taking possession" of the clothing manufactory of the country. One would think they had ousted some other group who wished to retain control over it. This is not true. They have taken what no one else particularly wanted. The Jews of Eastern Europe, especially from Russia, which group, as has been seen, has been picked out for some especially harsh treatment, have come into the country like so many confiding sheep into the American fold, not to beg or to borrow, or to steal, but to work and emancipate themselves from want. They come, as a rule, skilled in some branch of industry. Seventy-five per cent of Jewish handworkers have been listed as "skilled workers." They look for an opening in the avocation they have followed abroad. That is frequently the making of clothing.

Much might be said of this trade, and the manner by which the Jews have been inducted into it. In the first place, it is one of the avocations into which, centuries ago, they were forced; in the second, it is associated with much in the past which has caused the majority of non-Jewish men, at least, to turn from it. Part of the tyranny of the past practiced toward the Jews has consisted in making them ridiculous. Rulers are recorded who have passed laws prohibiting Jews from riding on horseback and obliging them to ride upon donkeys. One king, as all know, chose what he regarded as an amusing way of forcing more money than was his due from a Jewish subject by drawing his teeth, one by one, until he consented to "pay up."

It may be noted in passing that this sportiveness later took the form of forcing absurd and insulting names upon the Jews, which jest continued to be indulged in until a comparatively recent period. It originated, no doubt, in the discovery that the old Jewish name forms began to be obstructive, since they carried with them what was practically a geneological tracing of ancestry, as: Benjamin-ha-Levi-ben Moses, and so on, meaning Benjamin son of Levi, son of Moses, etc. The Jews were ordered to change their names and to choose new ones from a list prepared and selected for them. The numerous 'heims and 'steins, 'bergs and 'wassers which figure among present Jewish names are but the brands put upon them by sportive non-Jewish rulers of scarcely one hundred and fifty years ago.

Where Jews resisted this parting from their names so long identified with their race and history, choice was denied them, and such names as pleased the jocular in authority over them, were forced upon them. Some of the race who have since tried to rid themselves of such unbeautiful names have been heaped with abuse. Though as shopkeepers and workmen these names have been most serious drawbacks to them, they are branded at once as would-be imposters when they seek even legal authority for changing them. Nor will it be amiss to give here a few of the least offensive names imposed upon the Jews by the royal wits of Austria in the eighteenth century. The German name is given and its kindest equivalent in English, as an illustration of why, even in translations, many old world names are unbearable to Jews, and why those who wear them so unwillingly should be relieved from the burden and indignity of them:

Drachenblut, dragon or serpent blood; *Nachtkafer,* blackbeetle; *Rindskopf,* wooden or blockhead; *Veilchenduft* (the mildest interpretation), odoriferous; *Bettelarm,* old pauper; *Eselkopf,* ass's head; *Singmirwas,* sing-me-some thing; *Katzzenellenbogan,* cat's joints or elbow; *Wohlge-ruch,* stinker; *Wanzenknicker,* bedbug-squeezer; *Sauma-gen,* hog or pig-belly; *Nashorn,* hooknose; *Gottlos,* God-less; etc., etc. Anti-Semites have made much of the Jewish tendency to change names, and where mere vanity, shame of race or desire to perpetrate a fraud animates, no possible excuse can be made for the practice; but a little examination into this topic on several sides would go far to lessen the suspicion which is expressed often against a people who, in America are eager, less to deceive, than to throw far from them, all remembrance of past humiliations.

Returning to the charge that the Jews have "taken over" the industry of clothing making: were any others by, who wanted to take it over and develop it? We have no evidence that there were. People manu-factured clothing here, we are told, in 1850, before the Eastern Jews came, but it was not of a kind to raise the general standard of dressing here, or to increase our industrial standing or output. It in no way approached the standard of product offered by Vienna, Paris, or Lon-don. Hence great fortunes were spent in those centres by fashionable Americans. American men were not interested in making women's clothing as Jewish men today are doing. In fact, the facetious aphorism "it takes nine tailors to make a man," though many centuries old, never lost its power over the imagination of the average man of Anglo-Saxon race. The tailor was in the beginning and ever has been a source of ridicule among the comic writers notwithstanding his usefulness. In an often quoted line of Percy's *"Reliques,"* the "tailor lown" is referred to with good natured contempt. This ridicule had no reference to the Jews, who at that time were not in England; nor was such reproach as was attached to the calling brought upon the trade by reason of the Jews' association with it. Quite contrariwise, it was because of its supposed absurdity that it was one of the avenues left open that the Jews might enter, when other trades and occupations were closed to them.

Nearly fifty per cent of the Jews in the Pale of the Settlement in Russia earned their living in the manufacture of clothing. Cap-making, shoe-making, paper-making, box-making, certain departments of chemistry and agriculture, and other scattered trades engaged the remainder. It was and is the most natural thing in the world for them upon arriving in America, since the majority have brought their trade knowledge with them (this notwithstanding much that has been written to prove the contrary) to seek work in the lines with which they were familiar. The transference of these clothing-makers from European clothing centres is responsible, without question, for the fact that today New York has taken its place with Paris as a fashion centre, and that the standard of American dressing has risen immeasurably beyond what it was even thirty years ago.

The influx of these workers has had a most diversified economic value for the country. It has diminished our dependence upon foreign countries, shorn us of some

of our provinciality and broadened our world acquaintance and real interests. It has stimulated American silk
and cotton industries, to name two of the most familiar
articles, such as the manufacture of dress and hat trim-
mings now largely produced here, and opened up new industries which previous to the Jews' coming were never
thought of. The circle of remunerative employment
whether for men or for women, has widened to take in
thousands where once it engaged ten, and this expanding
process is still going on.

The air has never been so full of the spirit of progress. It is the comment of travellers that shopping streets,
even in small towns, are smarter than they used to be;
their shop windows better dressed. Finally, in the case of
the clothing makers, their coming has raised what was
a fourth or fifth class industry and certainly a despised
avenue of livelihood-earning into a great national industry
of the first consideration and the calling itself into one
that excites envy; else why this loud outcry against the
Jew in it?

And in this, too, we see a notable characteristic of the
Jew. Forced in the past to take the world's leavings and
make what he could of them, he has at once set about
the creation of a virtue out of his hard necessity. In addition to being accused of having "taken over" the clothing
trade—though today Italian, Rumanian and Serbian workers in this trade are almost as numerous as the Jews—he
is further accused of having taken similar control of the
tobacco trade, which has been a traditional occupation of
the Levantine people for centuries.

One of the few worthwhile things which Ernest Renan
has said of the Jews is this: "Examine at close range the
enemies of Judaism, and, in general, you will find that they
are enemies of the modern spirit." The modern spirit: that

is what is conspicuous in the Jews of today. The old Jewish tree is sprouting new leaves of hope and unparalleled energy. The young Jews, those in industry, are progressive. Some one said of them a decade or more ago: "The immigrant of yesterday is tomorrow's millionaire; the poor sweater of ten years ago is today a manufacturer —and the tremendous energy of this people is becoming a factor in the industrial life of the United States. If so much can be accomplished in twenty years what must be the result in a century? What will the national spirit of which they have become a part, achieve? Trained in the schools of the country, their souls freed from the anguish of centuries of persecution, moving with perfect political freedom is it not a natural thought that as the years go on the Jews will render illustrious service as Americans?"

Though reference is here made to such chief occupations as printing, clothing-making, tobacco-working, Jewish industry is by no means confined to these. It extends into every other field of human activity in which effective work can be done under conditions that yield considerate treatment free from suspicion and distrust, and a moderate living. Given a chance that calls for his best qualities, the Jew exemplifies every ideal that has been evolved concerning thrift, economy, perseverance toward a goal.

Again it may be necessary to interject that the Jew as understood here is the Jew who represents at least ninety per cent of his race, and not the "awful examples" which the hostile seize upon in order to point their immoral tales. The type of citizen which this ninety per cent of the Jewish race represents, has, even at the very bottom of the ladder of life, that combination which President Coolidge so recently has described as "deep faith in spiritual things, tempered by a hard common sense adapted to the needs of the world."

Nor should the topic of the Jew in industry be closed without pointing attention to the fact that some of the loudest voices that cry to us warnings against the "Jewish Peril," are not natives of the United States, but of other lands. They have gained their own American followers who have rushed into hatred by the impulse of their falsely excited emotions. They have sought violently to *create a Jewish peril idea,* which must vanish before an honest examination into it. A Jew here and there, of whom none is more ashamed than his own people, has been the brand with which to scar a whole race. But this is as unjust as was Balzac's attacks upon the French peasants, the lowly of his own people whom he charged (in *Les Paysans*) with being, with scarcely an exception, liars, petty thieves, sly, models of cupidity and dishonesty, and, withal, religious hypocrites.

The facts in the case disprove the statement so often made that the better Jews connive at hiding and upholding the misdeeds of the frail ones of their people. As one of the most notable writers of their race, the late Joseph Jacobs, has written: "Mr. Abramsky, or Mr. Isaacstein, 'or let us even say Mr. Jacobs, has no diploma entitling him to do inefficient work or a piece of underhand trickery because he may be a descendant of Samuel or Hosea. In fact . . . the possession of so illustrious a pedigree only creates the greater disappointment if its possessors fall short of the standards of manners or morals in the ordinary citizen."

But there will be other occasions to touch upon this side of the Jewish citizen as we follow him through the developing field of economics, into commerce, domestic and foreign, and, necessarily, trace his career as barterer, merchant, and organizer.

CHAPTER IV

The Jew in Commerce

"Wherever we read human history, the answer is always the same; where commerce has flourished, there civilization has increased. It is only when the exchange of products begins that development follows. This was the case in ancient Babylon, whose records of trade we are just beginning to read. Today it is not the battle-fleet, but the mercantile-marine, which, in the end, will determine the destiny of nations."

CALVIN COOLIDGE.

(Before the Brockton Chamber of Commerce)

WHEN the Jews began to affect commerce, giving it, ultimately, its present international character; when the clearer-minded of them began to figure it out, as Jews have a way of doing, and of systematizing it, it was a mean, if useful career, and spelled with a small c. It was a work which rich men engaged in, but behind the screen of an agent. Today, as all know, it has ceased to be a lowly interest and has become the great one of every government in the world. Chambers to direct Commerce rise in every community and in every land, and those who once scorned an active participation in it, now crowd to enter it. Economics has become a science.

Mr. Wells has deduced from numerous sources that the Semites, to whom, Mr. Chamberlain says, the Jews are half-brothers, early displayed the peculiar "gifts of the Semitic peoples to mankind" of trade and of exchange; and he points out, further, that "the moral teachings of the Hebrews was saturated with the ideas of equivalents and reparation". "With what measure ye mete, the same shall be meted unto you," he quotes, and adds: "Other races and peoples have imagined diverse and fitful gods, but it was the trading Semites who first began to think of

72

God as a Righteous Dealer, whose promises were kept,
who failed not the humblest creditor, and called to account
every spurious act." Apropos of which, according to
Jewish laws, a discrepancy of one-sixth in weight or
measure enabled the wronged party to secure the cancella-
tion of the sale or purchase. Overcharging by the merchant selling to the customer was the most frequent
instance in which the law was invoked; but the deceived
customer could recover from the merchant, the condition
being that the claim must be made as soon as the person
defrauded had had an opportunity to show his purchase
to a witness.

However, notwithstanding these laws, the Jew, of all
Semitic peoples, appears to have been the last to enter into
monetary transactions. He appears to have had nothing
to do, directly, at any rate, with money until a century or
so before the present era, and little to do with barter save
the simplest. The Romans, Greeks, and Phoenicians were
all centuries ahead of him in this field though there seems
to be no dispute of the often declared fact that the Semites
were the first people to arrive at a form of civilization.
Archaeologists today generally agree that they precede the
Aryans.

Mr. Chamberlain, whose attacks upon the Jew are the
most remarkable and violent that have been made in centuries, naturally denies them this rank and every quality
which even the unfriendly, heretofore, have conceded to
them. And he goes still farther; for he denounces their
"selfishness" as that of a "one-God people", who, though,
"beggarly poor in religion" have yet been able to dethrone
the many gods of Greece and of the Indo-Aryans. He
proclaims his passionate longing for the return to those
ancient "artistic" beliefs. With outlived paganism, of
course, we have nothing to do; but this author has undertaken, and stuck to his task with a pertinacity a Jew might

envy, to prove that in everything appertaining to acquisition, barter, or sale, the Jew is inherently crafty, and by inference, dishonest; and that, indeed, in every phase of past and present life, he has exhibited only the mercenary motive.

Of course the man who believes that because a few artists existed in early Greece, all the race must have been artistic, and still are so—Edmond About has written some very amusing descriptions of the modern Greek, which might prove beneficial reading for this author—of course the man who believes that all Romans were great, because a few were so, and that because a few Jews, or, as he intermittently calls them, Semites, have been cunning, and have grasped at great possessions, that selfish calculation and mercenary motives are bred in the bone of every member of the Jewish race, can hardly be taken seriously.

Unfortunately, his arguments have been caught up deliriously by a pack which appears to have scattered over the world to terrify it with their own cries of transmitted hate and warning especially against the Jew "in business". This means a very large percentage of Jews, since, for thousands of years, circumstances have forced them into trade, and even today, by a kind of race habit, by the fact that prejudice bars their way, too, in many professions; and, particularly, because they realize that all other careers are assisted by the possession of a competence, many more Jews, according to their numbers, enter commercial life than non-Jews. It would seem to be time well spent, before surveying the Jew and his connection with commerce, to look over specific attacks made by Mr. Chamberlain, and to examine the nature of the warrant he offers for making them. By this means we shall the sooner arrive at a fairer valuation of them, and of his reasoning generally.

His first proposition is that the Jewish race is a mongrel and not a pure stock, *which preserves its purity by inbreeding!* He says it has held its strain unadulterated and its primitive shortcomings intact for thousands of years through a course of elimination of foreign blood. Prior to the beginning of this elimination process, however, that is, some eight or ten or fifty thousand years ago, Jews intermingled freely with other races of the ancient world, from which Mr. Chamberlain deduces, and therefrom has been able further to deduce an amazing number of mean, cowardly, and unlovely qualities with which to invest the Jew of the present day.

He has gone at this work with a vim. He explains throughout his book that he has "vigorously attacked whatever is un-Teutonic". The Jews are so, he says; but if his elaborately argued pages be read cautiously by one fairly disposed to arrive at a better understanding, the objectionable traits which he identifies as "Jewish" will be found to be characteristics quite common to the human family; very natural ones, whether the family be new English, old English, South American, Italian, French, yes, even Teutonic. Nevertheless, this author proceeds to prove them to be exclusively Jewish race inheritances, by instances drawn ostensibly from the Scriptures and beginning with the charmingly human anecdote of Rebekah. The story will scarcely be recognized in the form in which Mr. Chamberlain presents it. It would be interesting to know whether he has drawn it from any known version of the Writings, or from his own Teutonic deductions. These, as Matthew Arnold pointed out fifty years ago often go "splay."

By the Oxford authorities Rebekah is placed at about 1857 B. C. or, about 3780 years ago. The Biblical story paints her in a masterly bit of character delineation, as a mother. It shows that in that matriarch were all the proverbial "mother-in-law" likes and dislikes, and also the partial fondness a modern mother may possess for her

youngest-born.   You will find it paralleled today among
any nation you may select.   A very amusing illustration of
a similar situation was portrayed a few years since in
Robinson's *"Whiteheaded Boy"*, the Irish name for the
youngest son who is also the spoiled child of the family.

The account of Rebekah's partiality for Jacob will be
found in Genesis, chapter 27.   There you will come upon a
picture of Rebekah "fussing", critical, and resentful of her
elder son's wives.   They were not like the girls she used to
know when she was young.   They were Hittites, and
strange to her.   As a natural consequence, she resented
Esau, who had brought them into the family, and doted
on Jacob, who was still left to her.   Presently you find her
conniving to secure for him the blessing of Isaac, which
should have gone to Esau.   She accomplishes her purpose
and deceives her nearly blind husband.   Of course, as soon
as Esau finds out the injustice, he is angry over it.   His
wrath, very naturally, is to be feared.   But Rebekah's
mother-heart knows his nature.   She gives him credit for
being very tractable and forgiving, once he has cooled off.
So she urges Jacob to keep out of his way; to go away for
awhile until this has taken place.   She wishes he would get
a wife and settle down; but, and here the mother-in-law
spirit shows again:

"I am weary of my life of the daughters of Heth," she
tells her husband, as they talk the matter over.   "If Jacob
marries one of them, what's the good of my living"!
Thereupon Isaac, quite like a husband of today, and to
put a stop to her worrying, sets about comforting her.
He advises Jacob to pay a visit to the land of his forefathers and get a wife from there.

It is a homely story, but human, and wholly without
the mercenary motive which, for example, we may find in
Tennyson's *"Northern Farmer"*, who assuredly was not
Jewish.   It will be remembered how *he* impressed upon his

son continually the value of "Proputty! proputty, proputty! Now, don't 'ee marry for money," said he, "but go w'ere money is." A dozen similar pictures may be found, commonly at hand in the literature of all lands, to prove the universality of parental ambition and cupidity. This, however, neither Rebekah nor Isaac displayed in so far as any proof remains. Their chief concern was to see their son escape his brother's wrath, and have him married to a nice old-fashioned girl, the opposite of those forward daughters of Heth.

But what does Mr. Chamberlain, who has set out to prove a point, say of this simple tale? He writes:

". . . the younger son, Jacob, is sent to Mesopotamia, that he may take a Hebrew woman for wife, and from this we must conclude that there was none in Palestine, no Hebrew girl, at least who would, *as regards wealth* have been a suitable match for him"! Nor do Mr. Chamberlain's "instances" and liberties with the Scriptures stop here. A few pages farther on he comes to Judah, one of Jacob's twelve sons, who, in his day was an out-and-out scalawag; but, it is from just this one of the twelve-branched house of Jacob—one who, by the way, is another human type of which so many perfectly drawn ones are to be found in Genesis—that our Jew-baiter has been able to trace in the Jew of today, every possible undesirable characteristic. Indeed, as he skips from century to century, he catches up every example he can find of obliquity in the story of Israel, and weaves it into the race structure to add to the undesirable qualities which he says all Jews now possess. He dwells much upon the "rich elders of the race", and "the heartless matchmaker, Jacob."

His meaning is far from clear to most of us, who are accustomed to think of Jacob, despite his early cunning, as a patient and faithful lover with sufficient heart to labor for fourteen years for the woman he loved.

However, Mr. Chamberlain is not to be deterred by any mere generally accepted fact. He is a discoverer; a modern writer with modern ideas in his head; and these indulge, as Mr. Wells has said, in his *"Outline of History"*, in lapses "into picturesque romances which are at once the joy and the snare of historical writers." But I am forgetting; Mr. Chamberlain is more than historian; he is an ethnologist, in search of racial traits. Having, in his devastating journey, arrived at David, from whom so many proud lines of Jews are said to have descended, he proves that all traditions we have held heretofore concerning David are absolutely erroneous, and does so in this wise:

David's grandmother was Ruth, the Moabitess. In the country in which he lived there were many races, among them Hittites and Amorites, and "probably", since there is nothing to guide the historian in this respect, David's mother may have been a Hittite or an Amorite. She also may have been and probably was, an Israelite. But Mr. Chamberlain bases his "probability" on questions, which, it seems have engaged the attention of European ethnologists, and which rest upon suppositions and probabilities as to the color of David's hair.

Accounts of this disagree apparently. Someone, Herder, it appears, has said that it was fair. It has even been described as auburn. Hence, there is a "probability" that David's mother may have been an Amorite.

Now, the Amorites, Mr. Chamberlain identifies as "our own kinsfolk"; for they were all tall and strong and so terrible in their appearance of might as to strike fear into the hearts of the Israelites who beheld them. To this splendid people, "our kinsfolk", says our author, "belonged the brave Goliath killed by the treacherously slung stone" from the hands of little David! And David being full of the despicable characteristics of the Jews made this cowardly attack, notwithstanding that many of the Amorites carried "gigantic spears and heavy mail of iron!"

Nor is it enough to show how "Jewish" cowardice and treachery inherited through his Moabite grandmother, and "possible" Amorite mother, is marked in David; but our historian goes on to show that Solomon, being the son of Bathsheba, who was "probably" a Hittite, was of a still more composite race and really not as much of a Jew as David was. Yet it is through these two ancestors that many modern Jews (quite a nation being possible from Solomon, as we all remember) have drawn their many "evil" qualities.

But we must come back to the subject of commerce:

It cannot be ascertained that the Jews had anything to do with trading until long after David's time, not, indeed, until after their stay in Babylon. Undoubtedly, while in that opulent country, they saw much of bartering and of commercial transactions generally.

It is not unlikely that the Babylonians, holding the Jews in captivity, taught them somewhat of their own method of buying and selling; a sort of give-and-take of opinion and custom must naturally have obtained between them and their captives. It is not unlikely that a kind of highroad commerce may have been carried on later between Babylon and Palestine. Not all the freed Jews returned to Jerusalem, and those who did so may well have trafficked later with their kindred whom they had left behind.

We know that at that period there was great maritime activity among both Romans and Greeks, and that vessels were plying about the Mediterranean and the Bosphorous, with cargoes to and from the sea-ports of those days. But there is nothing to indicate that the Jews were interested in or desirous of taking part in these activities. Their neighbors, the Phoenicians, on the other hand, a vigorous

sea-faring people, are described as having had a natural
genius for commerce; but their overland transactions by
no means began to reach the importance of their maritime
interests. Phoenicia has been called a sort of "clearing-
house" for the products of the Mediterranean and Syria;
but the Jews, an inland race, seem to have known little and
cared less for ships or ports in those early days, though
they took to both very naturally some centuries later.

Such insignificant external trade as they knew, which
is first to be noted as occurring under Solomon, was the
exporting of wheat and oil, and the importing of peacocks
and apes, designed, no doubt, as contributions to the "glory
of Solomon's court." Palestine, which was the assured
home of the Jews, was notable for its olive-groves, oranges,
and grapes. Its wines were famous in the early world and
today as elsewhere noted the Rothschilds have set up
presses to encourage the Zionist emigrants to attempt the
revival of its ancient wine industry.

Such trading as the early Palestinians knew was carried on chiefly through the "wanderer" or Soher, an itin-
erant merchant, to whom the housewives sold their wools
and perhaps their eggs and milk, getting in return the
wares he carried; the transaction being almost identical
with that carried on sixty years ago or less in our own
New England, Southern and Middle West provincial
towns. Camels, instead of covered wagons, may have
borne the pedlar's wares, or even oxen or donkeys; but
a very pleasing and colorful picture may be conjured of
those primitive peoples and their modest tradings, while
chattering and questioning the pedlar concerning the happenings in other lands.

The merchants who thus supplied the Jews in Palestine were often Philistines or came from the land of
Canaan. In the course of time we hear of dress fabrics
and even jewels reaching the Jews through these traders.

Presently there is note of a street being set aside in Damascus for the holding of Jewish bazaars; but of what was brought to it and offered for sale we have no record. When the contiguity of those little countries of the primitive world is considered, the various nations noted among the early peoples would seem to lie as near together as the counties in the States of our country. Many of these counties are of larger area than the greatest nations of the early world could claim.

In considering these very practical points we find it easier to realize the interchange of even weighty commodities between those early people. After their return from Babylon, the Jews in Palestine are said to have remained very poor, but changes were beginning by that time, which ultimately were to prove very momentous to them. Travel was increasing. By 400 B. C. or thereabouts, Herodotus was going about and writing his impressions of strange people, that were to become immortal. By the 5th century, too, Sophocles comes into view. Persia, Greece and Rome were enjoying a remarkable commercial prosperity. The Jews, as "The People of the Book," seem to have been occupied chiefly with their Scriptures, which were now being brought together and compiled. They were content to live away from commercial turmoil. They had been stirred by the preaching of Ezra and Nehemiah, and appear to have been concentrating their entire attention upon things religious. "The less business, the more Torah", was the answer made to those who criticised their indifference to commerce.

Nevertheless traders passed to and fro through their country, Tyrian silk traders, notably, and those who carried luxuries from other countries to pique the Jewish curiosity and desire. Undoubtedly they carried tales as well as silk with them, and it is not long before we find Jews here and there venturing out of Palestine to seek

acquaintance with the outer world with its foreign learning and luxury. But notwithstanding these exceptions,
their progress, as a race, toward commercial life was slow.
Josephus, who was writing in Athens about the year 93,
said of his people: "we do not dwell in a land by the sea
and therefore do not indulge in commerce by sea or otherwise." Perhaps Josephus was not aware of it, but so
early as the year 43 of the present era and nearly thirty
years before the Destruction of the Temple, some of his
people had already made their way into Mauretania, then
a province of Rome. It is said that Rome welcomed the
Jews enthusiastically, desiring their aid in civilizing the
Mauretanians.

From the time of the Dispersion, 70 A. D., which
scattered the Jews over the known world, their experiences
make very colorful reading; if often sad and sometimes
tragic, yet generally it is courageous and inspiring. In
the 4th century we find them branching out as sailors,
some owning their own vessels and trading along the Bos-
phorus. Colonies of Palestinian Jews were shortly settled
in Greece, where scholars of the race had thronged for a
century or two. This is the point in this era where they
definitely "enter Western civilization." It seems as if in
those early days the expatriates were generally recognized
as an interesting people which had something to bring into
European civilization. Hence, Rome in particular, invited
them.

A picturesque colony was soon engaged in raising
mulberry trees and silk worms in Greece, in which country
the Jews prospered until the 12th century, becoming
famous manufacturers of silk and of other fine fabrics.
It is said that the rich of Corinth and of Athens paid great
prices for the beautiful product of the Jewish looms. A
traveller of the early Middle Ages, observing a Jewish
community in Stamboul, or as we know it today, Constan-

tinople, has described the residences of the Jewish silk manufacturers of the twelfth century as the richest in the city, outdoing in splendor the palaces of the Viziers; and they were notable for their beautiful gardens.

Jews had dwelt in Turkey from the time of Alexander the Great, and to this country, and to Persia, too, the persecuted Jews from Jerusalem fled and prospered greatly. We now find them returning to Babylon in numbers; and to the better-known Persian cities, which were like a second home to them. There Jewish learning had first begun to express itself in written form. There, now, great Rabinnical schools were established. Quite in the beginning of our present era they began to sustain themselves in such leading centers as Ispahan, Hamadan, Kermanshaw, Shiraz, Teheran, Iran. Today all of these cities are rug centers. Their products which beautify many American homes, were early made known to the western world through the enterprise of Jewish merchants and traders. In all probability Jewish workmen engaged in their manufacture. All through the Levant little communities of Jews were to be found, energetically seeking a way to maintain themselves against decidedly bitter odds. Many of them, being Hebrew and Aramaic scholars, sustained life by teaching; but all, even the Rabbis, occupied themselves necessarily, with some trade or commerce.

More numerously, however, the Jews turned to the newer world of Europe.

They were silk manufacturers and traders in Spain, and those of Cordova were famous. There are legends which connect them with Venice, during the war with Hannibal; legends that describe the Jews as befriending the Venetians by bringing supplies by small boats from Egypt. These legends say that the Jews were able to steal in under cover of night to the beleaguered people and that Venetians thereafter always held them in affection. However, there is a long interim in which history makes no mention of them in connection with that land.

Late in the 10th century, long after the Islamic troubles had come up, there is mention of another sort of the Jews in Venice; or, rather, of a protective measure which the Senate passed, to prohibit "Jews and other merchants" from coming into the town. By this time it would seem that "Jew" and "merchant" were synonymous terms, and this metamorphosis from bookmen to trades-men appears to have been brought about coevally with the rise of Islam, about the sixth century. From this time on, the Jews, being linguists, were able to serve as interpreters and even as ambassadors between the antagonistic forces of Christianity in Europe and of Islam in the East. Jews have been traced as travelling in this capacity between Byzantium and Prague so early as the seventh century.

Shortly thereafter they are mentioned as having pushed up to the Baltic, with little stocks of wines and condiments, which the Northern nations are said to have bought in quantities, as relishes to go with their salt fish diet. These trips, threading primeval forests, crossing mountains, subject to highway attacks and those even of wild animals, equalled in their demand for courage, those taken by our pioneers in the early settlement of our own country.

In Venice, by 1100-1200, the Jews had a special island, among the many that form the city. They were again highly valued by the Venetians, who credited them with having been instrumental in establishing the com-merce between themselves and the Levant. This commerce did so much to enrich that government, that the Senate advised the minister to encourage the merchant Jews, and to build store-houses for them, "for the sake of the im-portant advantages which will accrue to our Customs' Duties."

It is vastly interesting to trace the history of the Jews' truly heroic commercial courage. So often they were rebuffed in their bread-winning efforts; so often they were lean and underfed; yet to each rebuff of fate, they have begun again, with indomitable courage and amazing hope. They have shown a special gift for taking waste and converting it into wealth; for taking up despised callings and making the envious desire them. They had money-lending and money-changing thrust upon them, yet when they made both profitable these, too, were taken out of their hands.

With the influx of precious metals the Jews performed prodigious commercial feats, making, as did all in Spain and in Portugal in those days, great fortunes, only to suffer in turn the losses of most of their gains. The law of compensation has ever acted with them, however; and, scattered as they are, with kinsmen all over the world, they have been able to speed the commerce of every modern land which has given them asylum. It is noteworthy that within the present century Spain has taken steps to invite the race back to the land in which it once flourished and the glory of which the Jews, very largely, helped to bring about. It was President Castelar of the short-lived Republic of Spain who pleaded: "Let there be no more accursed races on earth . . . Let us be so just as to be enabled to see even to what degree each race has contributed to the universal education of humanity."

The Venetian Jews experienced frequent and hard vicissitudes. Having raised the commerce of the country to so high a point; the itinerent merchants of the race having succeeded in getting control of the trade from upper and lower Rumania; having fearlessly ventured in every direction whence Venice might draw valuable trade, you come upon local laws being enacted to keep them out, "in order that the native merchants may be protected."

A century or two later Venice prohibited the Jews from dealing in new things; in anything but money-lending. Practically they were ordered to take this up. They, therefore, became lenders of money as best they could, on any collateral they could get; wearing apparel, jewelry, carriages, etc., which articles they had permission to sell when unredeemed. This is the origin of money-lending, which presently became known as pawn-broking, and of the Jew's dealing in second hand things. In the matter of money lending, the state fixed the tax or interest, which was allowable, at first, at 4 per cent. with a rise to 12 per cent., according to whether the loans were made on substantial security or on written obligations. All the *roués* of Europe, turned to the Jews to get them money. They would borrow on any terms. Usually they had no collateral whatever to offer, and were therefore willing to pay any "usury". Great tragedies lie along this path which we may not risk recalling.

After the Inquisition, many of the Jews, who, in the early centuries of our era resided in Spain and who were identified there with manufacturers, together with non-commercial groups of their race in Spain, went over to Venice, which, with the other Italian States, was in the full excitement of the new invention, printing. Here it was that the ghetto was first established as a device which would give the Jews an exclusive section in which they might be free from the interference of non-Jews in the following as they desired of their racial customs. While in after years many other cities imitated the example of Venice, with very unpleasant results for the Jews, yet that first ghetto, that secured them quarters in which they might be free to perform their religious rites and ceremonies, was, as one writer of the race has put it, "a potent factor in the spiritual life of the race."

The Jews of Europe were among the first to open commerce with the western hemisphere, and upon arriving here themselves, in the middle of the sixteenth century, immediately began to suggest outlets for available goods. We find among shipments arriving in the new land, sent through their efforts, cargoes of knives, bells, scissors, and pearls for the good wives of New Amsterdam. The Jews met with hostility here, but less, it will be conceded, than had been their share abroad; and there is a curious demonstration of their loyalty (previously referred to) to the country of their adoption in the fact that when the British took New York, the Jewish well-to-do group there moved on to Newport and other cities.

There, in 1753 we find one of the many early builders of American commerce, Aaron Lopez, of a Portuguese Jewish family, with thirty ships engaged in trade with the West Indies. A hundred others might be cited, even from among these early Jewish citizens, who were forces in the colony's development. Quoting from the *"Journal of Commerce and Commercial Bulletin"* and speaking of the plastic character of the Jew and his indomitable energy which asserts itself under the least favorable conditions, we find: "While New York was still New Amsterdam the Jews were among the chief exporters and importers of this city. When Newport was a mart of trade, they ranked among its foremost merchants; they were trading on the Delaware in 1655, and in the eighteenth century, their names stood high in the community of Philadelphia. With connections extending throughout the whole civilized world, and able to command the facilities of credit and exchange in Europe, the American Jew's breadth of view, his foresight and his enterprise were powerful factors in securing for the young Republic the place it early took in international commerce."

It has been said that the Jew excels in the "commerce of intangibles"; in other words, in just money; and this leads us naturally into consideration of the Jew in banking; in what may be called "broad finance", which we will next proceed to take up.

CHAPTER V

The Jew in Finance and Banking

"The character of a people, like the character of a person, should not be measured by its worst, but rather by its best; not by the depths into which it has at times sunken and declined; and, reckoned by that rule and by that standard, Israel's rank is high. For what department is there of social or civil economy that has not been and is not now illustrated and adorned by the unimpaired vigor, the unslackened energy, the immortal youth of this so ancient nation!"

Right Reverend DAVID H. GREER.

(In address at Carnegie Hall, November, 1905)

WHEN we come to the Jew as banker and financier we find ourselves crossing the boundaries of the real and entering the field of the magical; a field all the more astonishing because it offers such contrasts in facts, personalities and motives to those of whom we have heard such strange accounts through the writings of Messrs. Belloc, Chamberlain and others, not omitting, of course, those of Mr. Henry Ford. These all declare, and wave a red flag of warning, that the Jews have designs upon the wealth of the world. Mr. Ford, who is rated as being worth personally, $500,000,000 has launched a four-volume attack against the Jews of America, whose richest member, Mr. Otto Kahn, and he is alone in his class, is rated at $100,000,000. The late Mr. Jacob H. Schiff, also alone in his class, which, however, includes a dozen or more non-Jews, was rated at $75,000,000.

On the other hand fabulous fortunes have been earned or inherited and are owned by the non-Jewish of America, Mr. John D. Rockefeller being listed as worth $2,500,000,000; while several others are rated at $500,-000,000, $200,000,000, and $100,000,000. Most of these fortunes have been made through enterprises with which Jews are not connected. Is it strange that a thought springs up, in facing these facts, that this anti-Semitic outcry against Jewish financiers may have for its purpose the directing of the public attention less to the Jewish rich than away from the super-rich among the non-Jewish? In the meantime we may with interest trace the path of the Jew from his earlier thraldom to lesser things to latterday finance.

There is nothing more picturesque in fiction; nothing more stimulating; nothing more inspiring to the humble than the story of the Jew in today's finance. From itinerent pedlar to manufacturer; from manufacturer to international commerce; and thence to banking, railroad building, international finance—this would seem to be the regular progression in which the race has travelled ever since the inquisitorial happenings in Spain and Portugal sent it scattering through the world. The stone which those builders discarded in that dark period has become of the first importance in the building of the world's present prosperity. Could we sweep with a telescope the travels of the Jews in their nomadic wanderings of the centuries and scan the wide earth as they pass on, to the east, to the west, to the north, to the south, seeking peace and sometimes finding it for a while, our eyes would rest upon a panorama of great wonders unfolding in the wake of that expulsion of a people.

Prior to that period of catastrophe, for persecutors as well as for persecuted, banking, as we know it, was nonexistent. A bank, it is true, had been established at Barcelona, early in the fifteenth century, which secured monies and loaned them in a simple way for foreigners as well as for the citizens of that locality. There are mentioned, as well, banks at Florence, and at one or two other Italian cities; but Jews do not appear to have had any connection with them. There had been deals in high finance of amazing scope as we see them today against the background of modern progress, and some of these had been affected by Jews. In the majority of cases, these involved the risk of great losses, which was the "deal" that generally fell to the lot of the Jews. They were both speculators and gamblers, using the word in its best sense. But they had the courage to risk all, over and over again, when there appeared a chance of their coming out with even a little profit. There is evidence in plenty, however, that in these transactions, they mingled ideals; that always, the hope was cherished of raising their race, and even of returning to their ancestral Palestine.

There had been, in Spain, in England, in Germany, many individually rich Jews prior to the tenth century. They had evolved many of the little principles which now seem so natural in the handling of money. They had at least introduced the Bill of Exchange into European business transactions. Montesquieu credits them, and Sombart has reiterated this, with having invented that little instrument, which today is the backbone of commerce. Mr. Joseph Jacobs, however, who is a respected authority, thinks his race has been over-estimated in this. He thinks it more likely that having discovered the usefulness of the "bill" in his travels in the east, whence we derive our decimal system, that the Jew merely applied it, practically, in his European transactions. The carrying about of money, in quantities, prior to the use of this bill, had been full of risk, and all too often had led to thievery and to murder.

As you read the stories of those early Jewish financiers, you are often struck by the dual aims that occupy them. Their keen quest for money is linked, in almost every case, with a great mournful love for their race. They are subconsciously occupied with a dream of political equity, of freedom, and of raising the race again to a national stature. To attain that end no sacrifice, no risk was too great to be run. It was this indefatigable pursuit of a purpose which gave them their incomparable courage, but which also often brought upon them the antagonism that prejudice had kept smouldering most of the time.

Unpopular with the people in which this animosity was steadily fostered, nevertheless, as financiers, as treasurers, they stood, often at the right hand of kings, enjoying privileges in return for their services in raising money when monarchs needed it. Most of the enterprises undertaken by the sovereigns of the tenth to the fifteenth centuries were promoted by Jewish financiers. Mr. Wells says that during that period, in western Europe, especially in England and France, there sprang up, like flowers, a multitude of very distinctive and beautiful buildings, cathedrals, abbeys and the like, which lovely efflorescence marks the appearance of a body of craftsmen closely linked in its beginnings to the church. Associated with this efflorescence, however, like the forgotten seed from which the tree grows, the Jewish financier almost always was to be found. To cite the case of Aaron of Lincoln:

It was he who raised and advanced the money for the building of the famous Abbey of St. Albans, and the Peterborough Cathedral; and for many others. Jewish money went also to the support of Crusaders; to the fitting out of those heroes. Henry II of England was Aaron's debtor for what now would amount to many hundreds of thousands of dollars. What kings do, their flatterers imitate; and so, many of the smaller knights and barons of England also borrowed of Aaron, pledging their estates in exchange for his ready cash. Upward of four hundred of them were indebted to him when he died, practically the larger part of England being thus pledged to him.

But here enters the curious if cruel comedy in which so many kings have taken pleasure. The laws of England—and those of all European countries were alike in this—permitted the Jew to lend money, sometimes obliging him to do so. They specifically allowed him to charge amazing interest on it only that the crown itself eventually might come in for the profits. It was a sort of *padrone* system by which the Jewish genius did the work and the king took the profits. In this way, when Aaron of Lincoln died, great estates in all the best shires and counties "fell to the crown".

A great deal of vicious fiction has been retailed concerning the "Jewish usury" of those days, the larger part of which, as in the case of late accusations, when brought into the light, prove insubstantial. Instance after instance, however, may be met with of royal cupidity and its ruthless over-reaching of even astute Jewish ministers. Prescott gives a striking one in his mention of Samuel Levy, who served Peter the Cruel as financier. When that sovereign's exchequer was low, Samuel's accruings temptingly large, and Samuel himself giving every indication of having a long life before him, the royal Peter made away with him and took possession of his treasure, which amounted to four hundred thousand ducats. If Jewish wit has grown sharp, it is not to be wondered at, since the Jews have had to whet them upon some pretty hard circumstances. Levy's fortune amounted to four hundred thousand ducats, but this was a mere bagatelle as fortunes went in Spain and Portugal, where many noblemen were in receipt of from forty to sixty thousand ducats annually. These were the profligates who turned to the Jew for loans when their spendings exceeded these fabulous sums.

But new forces entered Western civilization with the coming in of the fifteenth century. Finance was beginning to move in a new and more regular if also more complicated system. The Jewish money-lenders by this time were bankers, even if they had not yet been called so. They were no longer necessary to the Spanish Court, however, for non-Jewish competition had begun, in commerce and in money lending; even the Church had its own usurers. The first bank of deposit and exchange had opened in Barcelona, in 1401, and the city was "booming". In every European State, apparently, minds were busy evolving banking schemes, for providing funds for the building up of domestic and foreign commerce. Evidence of change, enterprise, development meets the eye on almost every page of the histories of that fifteenth century. The scattered, yet cohering Jewish families of Europe undoubtedly even then conducted a kind of primitive chain system of banking. Members of the Mendes family, for example, at the time of the expulsion of the Jews from Spain, or very shortly after, had a house in Antwerp, though the principal home of the Mendes Bank was in Lisbon.

We have said that the tracing of the Jew in finance is like crossing the boundary from the real and entering into the realm of magic. There is vivid romance to be met with in it. The story of Joseph Nasi, for instance, one of the first Jewish financiers of his period, is like turning the pages of "A THOUSAND AND ONE NIGHTS". Nasi was a member of the Mendes family which had long been identified with matters financial in Spain and in Portugal. They belonged to the "Maranos", or converted Jews, who, in order to carry on their work, had outwardly professed a faith to which they did not inwardly subscribe. Francisco Mendes at the head of the house in Lisbon, and Diogo, at the head of that in Antwerp, were regarded as the richest of Portuguese Jews.

Like many of the converts *de convenance* of that

period, their money, perhaps, securing them the privilege, they did not disguise their loyalty to their race, though they had changed their religion. Several members of the family are notable for the sums they contributed for the purpose of softening the miseries of the poorer Jews who had been driven from the peninsula. It was Hector Mendes who, when the king enquired: "And what are your riches?" replied: "The alms I have given away." Francisco Mendes, who was the Mayer Rothschild of his day, loaned vast sums of money to Charles V and other kings.

But out of Portugal, shortly after the expulsion of the Jews, came the youth, Joseph Mendes-Nasi, who was "weary of feigning to be what he was not." He went to Antwerp, joining his uncle, Diogo Mendes, and, shortly, the two combining with another kinsman, formed a great banking house or loan corporation. This was one of the first of the family groups of which so many have since filled the pages of European banking history, that of the United States, and of the extreme East. Joseph, however, was not to remain in Antwerp, or even in Europe. Stories reached him of the sufferings of the Jewish exiles in Venice, and he set out to intercede for them. His journey was not without its stirring episodes, for it led through a continent hostile, almost to a man, to Jews. Unfortunately, he failed in his mission to alleviate the trials of the Venetian Jews, and, his heart infused, as Calderon has described it, with the deadly venom of misanthropy with which the Inquisition had infected the world, he shook the dust of Europe from his feet and crossed into Turkey.

There, in a land which had always been friendly to his people, he cast off his pretences and fearlessly returned to the faith of his fathers. Thereafter his history reads like none other of his time. It was a period in which eventful things were continually happening; in which tragedies were frequent; in which blessing and curses were showered upon the human family. Elizabeth reigned over England, and literature blossomed under her hand; the astute and false Catherine dei Medici ruled France. Political plotters set the European world in an agitation. Nasi knew that world, and in Turkey was soon in high favor with the Sultan Sulaiman, who loaded him with honors and confided many of the interests of his country to his care. He was an astute and wise financier, and so pleased the Sultan in the promotion of all commerce, and by the wisdom of his counsel, that, first made a guard of honor to the ruler, he is next made Duke of Naxos, and presented with the city of Tiberias, in Palestine, together with numerous outlying hamlets. Though he did not attain these honors without exciting the envy of many, yet his star continued in the ascendant.

With the help of the Pasha of Damascus, he now set about the realization of a cherished dream, which was nothing less than that which occupies the thought of the Jewish world today, namely: to re-people Palestine with Jews. He built a great wall about his city, and sent a proclamation to Europe inviting the persecuted of his race to return. To all who would work as farmers or artisans, he offered homes, and free transport on his own ships. While awaiting the coming of the immigrants, he set about the planting of mulberry trees, and arranging for the carrying on of other industries. What the outcome was of this wonderful dream of an eastern financier, who was all but king, is not clear. It is said that one ship-load of immigrants, at least, was captured by pirates and sold into slavery.

The Sultan Sulaiman and his successor Salim presented the Duke of Naxos with the island of that name besides several others; and it would appear that he was not only financier for these rulers, but in charge of the military interests of Turkey, besides conducting the correspondence of State with the sovereigns of Europe. He does not seem to have been beyond the reach of the cupidity of some of these sovereigns, for he is said to have loaned large sums to King August II of Poland, receiving in return special commercial privileges, which, after all, he was debarred from enjoying by the protests of the city of Lemberg. Probably none of his race in modern times ever enjoyed more complete power, or moved in a sphere more important.

In Europe, the Jew's position had been changing. Commerce had passed practically out of his hands, and all his efforts, necessarily were directed towards the making of loans, and acting as general financial adviser. "Court Jews," as they were called, served every king and great man on the continent, and were looked upon, so late as 1800, as indispensable in Germany. Apparently this preference for Jewish advisers roused the anger of the envious, for sometimes it brought a grievous fate upon very innocent persons.

Some time before the appearance of the Rothschilds, who have so affected all banking and transformed it, a great tragedy befell a Jewish financier, which, after events proved, was nothing less than a judicial murder. Joseph Süss Oppenheimer, a notable figure in the financial history of Germany, was the victim. He went through the world almost like a meteor, rising from a very humble beginning and small clerkship at Frankfort-on-the-Main, through a series of widely differing occupations, until at thirty-six he became the confidential man and financial agent of Prince Karl, duke of Würtemburg. He lived in the Duke's palace, and was officially known as the "resident and privy factor," whose duty it was to regulate the finances of the dukedom.

Presently, in addition, he was placed in control of the mint. All he touched seemed to turn to profit for his employer, but in the meantime, the desire to serve his own people, and, perhaps, to have those about him upon whom he could thoroughly depend, was used to his disadvantage by the people, whose prejudices against the Jews made them not only intolerant of the power confided to Oppenheim, but more and more revengeful as it was clear the Duke would hear nothing against him.

Several times in his short career, fearing for himself, as he received from time to time evidence of the harsh intentions of the Würtemburgers, Oppenheimer resigned his office, but each time the duke persuaded him to reconsider. At last, however, his alarm became so deep that, having balanced his accounts, he insisted upon withdrawing. The duke urged him to wait over for a day, and to spend that day with him at his neighboring castle, at Stuttgart. There, quite suddenly, and within a few hours, the duke died.

Before morning dawned, every Jew in Stuttgart, including Oppenheimer, was under arrest. Charges were trumped up against him which, later, were proved to have been baseless, and he was hurried to a gallows and hung before thousands of fanatical people who came from every direction to witness the killing of a Jew! A contemporary engraving of that deed, shows it to have been brutal in the extreme! Oppenheimer had enjoyed the duke's favor for four short years, and paid this heavy penalty for his faithful service at the age of forty.

It is said that the career of the Rothschilds contains the key to all Jewish banking in the nineteenth and twentieth centuries. While they were still unknown, however, there were many notable Jewish bankers whose names still meet the eye from time to time. Jacob Worms served Louis XIV, as Court Jew; Solomon Medina played his part in financing the Duke of Marlborough's plans; Behrend Lehmann at the Saxony Court—the Pintos, Baron d'Aguilar—a long list of men who rose high in the centres in which they operated.

The great Jewish bankers who next come upon the scene, appear to belong to a new and more enlightened era than that which ended with the beginning of the eighteenth century. They lived in an era of different opportunities; and in an increasingly liberal age. They are nearer to us and stand out as familiar figures. The Rothschilds represent a class of Jewish bankers who have "founded a family line" as no others of all who have operated in finance have done. Some one has called it a "close corporation," for, generation after generation, since the time of Mayer Amschel Rothschild, son of Amschel Moses Rothschild, they have married and inter-married with the same exclusiveness as that which obtains among the royal families of Europe. We may not do more here than to trace the rise of this family, from Amschel Moses Rothschild, born at Frankfort-on-the-Main in the first half of the eighteenth century.

Frankfort-on-the-Main may one day be called the cradle of world finance, since the great financiers who have come from that city have been the bankers of the world for now two hundred years. Amschel Moses Rothschild was a "small merchant and money-changer," and it is said that his son, Mayer, who is generally regarded as the founder of the fortunes of the house, often counted change for him, studying the coins he handled, and gaining thereby a variety of practical knowledge which afterward served him in good stead. He, himself, early became a financial agent for the Landgrave of Hesse-Cassel, who was said to own the largest private fortune in Europe. Mayer Rothschild was changing English gold for the Crown Prince in 1794 in quantities as large as £150,000, by which it will be seen that he already had made a princely fortune.

By this time his sons were in association with him. It is said that the branching out of this firm was due to the rudeness received by Nathan Mayer Rothschild, at the hands of a salesman, supposedly an Englishman. At any rate, this son of Mayer Amschel Rothschild was soon established in London, where he had become a British subject, and thereafter we hear of his literally controlling the bullion market. A banking house of Rothschild Brothers was established next at Paris, and little by little, enormous figures become associated with their name. It is said that between 1814 and 1822, this house transferred from England to the continent, £18,000,000. A list of their transactions between 1817 and 1848, in gulden, francs and ducats, amounted to $654,848,200. On two Austrian loans which the German branch of this house negotiated in the first quarter of last century, the brothers' profits were 6,000,000 gulden.

So the success of the house of Rothschild proceeds, building not alone its fortunes but an enviable reputation, even while an army of great competitors in the early part of last century were especially strong. Their history is linked with that of kings of succeeding reigns, with practically all the great railroad construction of last century, and with all the important transactions arising from the late World War. It was Baron James Rothschild who obtained the concession for the Great Northern Railway of France. In the course of time the house obtained control of the Idra quicksilver mine; afterward the Almaden mine in Spain was secured; so that the house of Rothschild now have a monopoly of that metal. They have figured in so many of the large national loans, the great industrial developments, that to enumerate them would fill a volume. By their family affiliations, extending to every part of the globe, they have taught the world's bankers the value of close co-operation between mutually interested groups; and many families have followed their example, of acting unitedly, with, if not equal, at least with marked success. That was notable in the case of the Seligmans, in the United States, and in the later banking house of Kuhn, Loeb and Company.

But it is said by those familiar with banking circles, that nothing could be more erroneous than the idea which the anti-Semites have been sowing so laboriously, namely: that Jewish firms act as a racial unit in their transactions. There are conspicuous occasions on which Jewish firms have not only not acted together, but have frankly competed with each other, and in which they have ended in being injurious to each other. This was observable in the case of the joint-stock principle, which was introduced into banks and institutions like the Credit-Mobilier, the Dresdener Bank, and the Deutsche Bank, which groups were founded mostly by combinations of Jewish firms. The operation of this principle considerably diminished the predominance of the Rothschilds in the financial world, while it increased the general influence of the Jews in international finance. In addition, a financial observer notes the later opposition of such houses as Montague and Rothschild, in London. The Sterns, he also points out, opposed the Rothschilds and obtained the Portuguese loans which the older firm was after.

Some instances are recorded of unusual courtesy between Jewish bankers and their non-Jewish competitors, among them that arising from the Baring failure of 1893, which "brought to an end a rivalry of seventy years between the Barings and the Rothschilds." But here, adds an observer, "the Rothschilds intervened and prevented the utter ruin of their rivals."

The Jewish significance in this field and the contribu-

tions the Jews in it have made to civilization, would have
to be gathered from all corners of the earth.   Primarily,
they have been the discoverers of possibilities; later, the
promotors of the same, thus bringing into reality what
originally was but an idea.

Jewish financiers have advanced money for building
railroads in every country of the world.   Sometimes in-
dustrials of the race have laid the tracks.   The bankers
have financed manufacturers of many sorts in many
places.   If you go down to Cape Town, you will find Jews
who have developed shipping there, and, in time, have
become great ship-owners.   Jews have had a large part in
developing commerce in that part of the world.   They
have founded industries there.   They have invested their
funds in the building of railroads in Russia; in South
America, in the United States, in Canada.   Baron
de Hirsch established the Balkan Railway system.   The
Perières have made local travel what it is about Paris; to
another Jew every traveller south from Paris on the
Chemin-de-Fer-du-Midi is indebted.

Always the Jews adventure their capital in fields of
which others are sometimes afraid.   They are frequently
pioneers, if you will, in opening the way today with their
millions to development and improvement, even as those
modest Jewish travellers who passed between Persia and
Italy and Spain a thousand years ago were pioneers in
the bringing in of education.   Belgium owes her railways
to the bankers Bischoffsheims; the Prussian people owe
their railway systems to the Bleichröders, and so on, one
might list the valuable gifts of the Jews to commerce, to
economic values in every land in Europe, Asia, Africa,
North and South America.

Perhaps the greatest single benefit conferred upon
mankind in the present generation, through Jewish enterprise, is the rescue of miles of territory in Egypt which

for five thousand years has been practically waste land while humanity starved about it. Now, as Douglas Jerrold said of Australia: "You have only to tickle the soil with a hoe and it laughs back in harvests."

Speaking before the Commercial Geographical Society of Havre, General Willcocks, Director of the Reservoirs of Egypt, said of the building of the Assouan Dam: "A few men endowed with *clairvoyance* have been considering for decades what we today all know, namely, the possibility of building such a dam. But none of the group showed more confidence than Ernest Cassel. The project of building the Assouan Dam had been pigeon-holed for years. In 1898 Sir Ernest presented himself with the wished-for capital and accompanied by Sir John Aird, and Sir Benjamin Baker, as consulting engineer, undertook to construct the Dam at Assouan, and also that at Assiout, and to have both finished by 1903. On the advice of Sir William Garstin, the Egyptian Government accepted the proffer, and the work was begun. It was completed by December, 1902!

"Think of the change this means," continued Willcocks, "in a country, flat as your hand; think of hundreds of thousands of acres set out in grain and cotton, and Assouan, with modern hotels teeming with people, where but a few years ago, all was barren, and uninteresting; where, when the river burst over its banks in its annual flooding, the villagers fled for their lives, out toward the desert to escape from threatening death."

To be sure Pièrre Loti has deplored the disturbance of the Egyptian silence; the night skies made to blush by the flare of the electric lights of the city. But in the meantime, a country that was once bare and forlorn, has become seething with life, and health and prosperity abide there. This is the work, the wonderful gift of a Jew of this century, all the more wonderful in that it has not been advertised and indeed has scarcely been heard of by the majority. Heads of world governments know of it; financial manipulators had been made aware of it, and great engineers testify to the marvellous engineering problems that were overcome in the building of the Dam; but other than this, only the waving grain in the fertile fields that now skirt the desert, and the Bedouins that wander into town and recall the old days, tell the tale of Sir Ernest Cassel's civilizing gift to the world.

Crossing Egypt to India, we come upon a notable Jewish banking family of the East. The Sassoons, London and Bombay bankers, have played a great part in building up the industries of the East. They spring from a family of Jews, who fled from Portugal during the Inquisition period, and found a refuge in Mesopotamia. In the last one hundred and fifty years they have become the industrial builders of the East. Their ships are cared for in the great Sassoon docks which are a feature of Bombay. They have built and run canning factories, and what is more, have planted the East with philanthropical and educational institutions. Sir Abdallah Sassoon, who wears the Star of India, is the head of this banking house, which has branches and connections extending to Shanghai, Canton, Hongkong, Yokohama, and numerous points in the East, as well as their Western connections in London.

But we have had, in America, as well, our Jewish miracle-workers. A recent anti-Semitic writer has written of the late Mr. E. H. Harriman as having "helped the banking firm of Kuhn, Loeb & Company by turning the business of Western railroads into their hands." This is a curious reversal of facts, due, it may be, to mere hearsay remarks which have lost their accuracy as they were passed from lip to lip. The Union Pacific Railway and its associated lines, which opened up the great West, were

made possible only through the marvellous personality of
the late Mr. Jacob H. Schiff, a member of the banking
firm of Kuhn, Loeb & Company. When money was
wanting in the United States, when the Government itself
was hard put to it to raise funds for its needs, on the
strength solely of his international connections, Mr. Schiff
was instrumental in raising the needed capital for the
building of those Western roads, from foreign investors.
He thus became the motive power which sowed the Western prairies with cities; which brought farmers with their
grain into ready connection with the great cities of the
continent and likewise with the ports of the country.

By his personal influence with foreign bankers Mr.
Schiff was able to finance the rebuilding of the Union
Pacific Railroad. In the Stock Exchange panic of May,
1901, through his firm of Kuhn, Loeb & Company, it is
said that Mr. Schiff held the financial power of the nation
in his hand. "It was Mr. Schiff's wise action and
moderation," writes a correspondent, "that prevented disaster." What he did to establish community of interest
among competing railroads is known in detail by all financiers. It may be added that it was Mr. Schiff's firm that
was chosen to float the stock issues of the Union Pacific,
those of the Pennsylvania Railroad, of the Baltimore and
Ohio, and of the Western Union Telegraph Company. It
also subscribed for and floated three large Japanese war
loans. During the great World War it was of value to
the Government, to the municipality and to various other
governments in the raising and floating of war bonds.
One who was familiar with Mr. Schiff's great part in the
development of western railroads has said: "Why, if it
had not been for him, the western man who now motors
through the town in his automobile would still be sitting
behind his ox-team. We should have had no trans-conti-
nental service for years. It required a man of Mr.

Schiff's spotless integrity to convince the foreign investors of the worthwhileness of such stock; as to the value of the roads when built; for up to that point the Union Pacific Rail Road was an unproven asset."

Yes; in the matter of the development of the United States in particular, the Jewish race has contributed a mighty quota through its financiers and bankers, as well as through its industrial and mercantile representatives. It has given them great opportunities, to be sure, such, perhaps, as no other country at the same period would have been able to offer; but they have taken advantage of them, and returned their indebtedness with heaping measure.

It is by no means so easy to tabulate a race's good deeds and its worthy citizens as it is to indict it, and them, as a whole. The rise of individual Jews in America, from penury to princely wealth, marks some splendid pages in its history.

There began to arrive in the United States, in 1837, one after the other, five brothers, named Seligman. They opened modest little clothing shops—for their capital was small—some in one town, some in another, and scattered from San Francisco to Lancaster, Pennsylvania, and even to Alabama. They sold clothing; but as their profits came in, they established a banking business. It would seem as if today's international banking on the part of the Jew, of which so much that is invidious has of late been said, was initiated by Joseph Seligman, one of the five brothers, who went abroad early in the seventies to dispose of certain American bonds. His task, it must be admitted, was an easier one than that Mr. Schiff later undertook, for the bonds Mr. Seligman carried to offer in foreign markets were those of the United States Government. He, representing his brothers, was the first to place United States bonds on the Stock Exchange at Frankfort, since which time the firm of Seligman Brothers, impregnable in the esteem of their government and fellow citizens, have been concerned with every issue of United States bonds.

In 1879, when great "deals" were by no means so frequent as in the present day, the house of Seligman, which had practically financed the North in the Civil War, with the Rothschilds co-operating, took over the whole of the bonded loans of the United States, a matter of $150,000,000. This house, since 1876, have been the financial agents of the Navy and State Departments of the United States, and the agents accredited of the Government. No greater history of a family's rise exists in European finance, nor any greater instance of a nation's confidence in the Jews.

About 1847, an emigrant arrived in New York from Switzerland, of splendid industrial worth, though it is probable that few suspected it as he proceeded upon his modest way. He began as a travelling pedlar of stove-polish and glue. Not so very long afterward, he had found a way of making his own stock, and his profits increased accordingly. When these were sufficient, he began to import Swiss embroideries, which for many years were staple attractions in all American drygoods shops. In 1881, at the age of fifty-two, the former pedlar of stove polish and glue was able to turn over to his sons a prosperous embroidery business, leaving him free to launch into a new career. He had invested in a silver mine. It was not long before he discovered that to work this successfully, he must have a smelting plant, and he bought one in Denver, Colorado.

Next he turned all his attention to smelting, and with his sons, who by this time had disposed of their embroidery business, enlarged his smelting operations. Today the smelting properties of this combined family, the Guggenheims, known internationally under the general title of "The American Smelting and Refining Company," are valued at $500,000,000.

Many similar stories might be added of the Jewish fortunes built in and of Jewish worth to the United States alone, as developers of industry, of commerce; as scientific bankers; as international forces which, far from menacing the country, have often stabilized it, and proved themselves to be agencies of special value to the Government.

These will some day be written, no doubt, and will make instructive reading for any who, with honest enquiry, may read them; but always it should be borne in mind that while great fortunes have been made in these avenues of practical life by Jews, the power to accrue great sums of money can scarcely be considered a criterion by which to measure civic or moral worth. This is rather to be arrived at by a consideration of the use to which the owner puts that fortune. It is from this point that we shall next consider the Jew.

CHAPTER VI
The Jew in Philanthropy

"Public spirit was ever a characteristic of the Jew. It has been his special distinction in this country that, while contributing liberally to charitable and benevolent objects favored by his fellow-citizens of different race and faith, he asks from them nothing for the objects which appeal primarily to his own. Hospitals sustained by Jewish contributions make no discrimination in regard to the patients they admit; schools and libraries maintained by Jewish beneficence are open to all who can derive any benefit from them."
(New York Journal of Commerce and Commercial Bulletin)

THE inconsistency has already been pointed out of the attack upon the Jewish race as a money-loving and a money-grasping people, by one, who, having amassed $500,000,000, is himself five times as rich as any Jew in the United States. It becomes even more glaring, as, pressing through the eighty chapters of vituperation for which this capitalist is responsible, you see with what unrelenting prejudice he has caused the Jew's every act to take on a color of unworthiness; and the care with which he has evaded the slightest tribute to or recognition of the finer qualities of the race. It is a matter for amazement which grows greater as one proceeds to an examination of the anti-Semitism of the century that any, however weak their understanding, however mis-employed their imagination, could be hurried by their prejudices into believing that a whole body, or party, whom they do not like, are, therefore, a mere band of traitors and villains. All races, as Professor Commons has said, have their exemplars and defenders, who, as individuals, must be the criterions by which the race is judged.

The attitude of the fanatics of today has been voiced by one of the foremost critics of the Jewish race, when he states that he is "not interested" in the Jew's religion. This at once stamps the character of the complainant. The Jew cannot be understood without interest in his religion. It lies at the base of the Jewish character; it interthreads the every thought of the race. Its special spirit and significance as the mother-religion from which so many other religions, major and minor, have sprung, is interesting the scholars of today as never before. When all is said and done, it is, perhaps, this resolute refusal to be interested in the Jew as a fellow-being, which makes it possible for the malicious to sow broadcast the most baneful libels against him, and to go on propagating from generation to generation, the superstitions which were a blot, upon civilization two thousand years ago.

It is a stain upon that of today that men of illimitable wealth may, unrebuked, turn the force of that wealth to the rousing of prejudice between the peoples of a nation; when they may ward away all who would utter a protesting word in defense of the victims, by ridicule or by the insinuation that money is back of such defense. In other words, by imputing venal motives to those who should be above such suspicion. It becomes a menace to the peace of the nation, when, continuing for two years, eighty chapters and more of hatred-provoking matter may be steadily poured into the public consciousness with no restraining intervention of the law, or counter-presentation on the part of citizens better disposed. There is, indeed, as the result of this propaganda, a "Jewish Peril"; but it is peril for the Jew at the hands of the misled unless the just thinkers in the world shall consent to be interested, to the extent—not of being pro-Jewish, but of being pro-justice.

In all the chapters of *"The International Jew,"* the Jew's better qualities, his actual part in protecting the welfare of even one country, the United States of America, are not so much under-estimated, as deliberately mis-stated, wilfully perverted. Notably is this the case in its malevolent allusions to such a remarkable philanthropy as that of the late Baron de Hirsch. The story has been so manipulated as to be made to appear not as it was, a great, unparalleled example of practical benevolence—similar to but so many times multiplied—the benevolence that brought the Irish famine victims to America in the middle of the nineteenth century—but, instead, as a political move of foreign Jewish capitalists, as a first mighty step toward establishing the ultimate international supremacy of the Jew. To quote one such subversive paragraph:

"When a great block of wealth in America was made possible by the lavish use of another block of wealth from across the seas; that is to say, when certain Jewish immi-grants came to the United States with the financial back-ing of European Jewry behind them, it would be unfair to explain the rise of that class of immigration by the same rules which account for the rise of, say, the Germans or the Poles who came here with no resource but their ambition and strength. To be sure many individual Jews come in that way, too, with no dependence but themselves, but it would not be true to say that the massive control of affairs which is exercised by Jewish wealth was won by individual initiative; it was rather the extension of finan-cial control across the sea."

What is the true story of those Russian Jews who were helped to America in the '80s? This, and this wholly: that thousands were starving in Russia, unable to help themselves in a country which deprived them of oppor-tunity to live as human beings; that one of the same race, Baron de Hirsch, looked on their sufferings, considered his own wealth and set about forming a plan by which to raise the down-trodden. According to all records, he would have had them remain where they were had he been able to make sure that help there was possible. He drew up plans for improving the condition of the Russian Jews in Russia. He offered the Russian Government 50,000,000 francs to be devoted to the education of the Jews there, but the Russian Government would only accept it on condition that it might use the sum as it saw fit.

In view of the hopelessness of the situation, Baron de Hirsch devised the Jewish Colonization Association, with a nominal capital of £2,000,000, which was entirely contributed by himself, the purposes of which association were: "To assist and promote the emigration of Jews from any part of Europe or Asia—and principally from countries in which they may, for the time being, be subjected to any special taxes or political or other disabilities —to any parts of the world, and to form and to establish colonies in various parts of North and South America and other countries, for agricultural, commercial and other purposes." Now, thirty years after this humanitarian work was begun while a sympathetic world looked on, there arises one sufficiently subtle to accuse its originator, by inference, of mere scheming; of having hidden under philanthropic cover a Jewish plan to "seize upon financial control across the sea."

It has been estimated that Baron Maurice de Hirsch contributed upward of $100,000,000 to benevolent purposes, a generous proportion of which has been devoted to the up-building of his race in America. His benefactions took the most practical form of philanthropy, and were matters of personal thought, personal planning. He saw things largely, and nothing more clearly than that the great mass of his race which for thousands of years had been restricted in most of the paths in which other men were free, required moral re-habilitation. This he set about accomplishing by means of education through schools established in many lands.

It is thirty-three years since the de Hirsch Fund was established; since the great de Hirsch fortune was spilled out upon the world, and from it a crop of notable men of the race has already sprung up who are carrying on the work of educating their brothers all over the globe. This is the very realization of the Baron's hope, which was, it is said, that the second, rather than the first generation of his beneficiaries, would demonstrate the value of his thought to the world.

Baron de Hirsch, it has been said, was a materialist, a pleasure-lover, and so adventurous in his business schemes, that the banking firm with which, originally, he was connected as clerk, preferred not to take him in as partner. In fact, until the success of his eastern railways was assured, he was looked upon as a reckless visionary, who might come to grief, and carry others with him. There would appear always to have been in him, however, the humanitarian and philanthropic instinct. Early in his career he established and sustained trade schools in the East. He is quoted as having written: "I never ask whether the cry of necessity comes from my faith or not; but what is more natural than that I should find my highest purpose in bringing to the followers of Judaism, who have been oppressed for a thousand years, who are starving in misery, the possibilities of physical and moral regeneration?"

Baron de Hirsch's practical humanitarianism and not his desire to establish or have part in establishing international power among the Jew in matters financial, was the real and only reason for his great, his far-sighted generosity. It has been said, and truly, that the Baroness de Hirsch, his wife, was his inspiration; that she led him on and directed him in the disposal of his fortune. There is not an atom of reason for supposing that the Baron was influenced by any other motive or personality.

He was a well-derived man, the third of his family to bear the title of Baron.   The Baroness, like himself, came from a family which for several generations had enjoyed political, religious and social freedom, together with great wealth.   She was the daughter of Raphael J. Bischoffsheim, a notable Belgian banker, Senator, and philanthropist, for whom a boulevard in Brussels was named.   She grew up closely associated with her father, sharing with him in the founding of schools and homes for Jewish girls and in the establishing of educational societies.   From her childhood she had been accustomed to study the needs of her race, of human-kind generally. She went into her marriage pre-eminently fitted for the care of the great fortune her husband was to bring her.

As you trace the history of this very remarkable couple, you can nowhere find a suggestion in it of a seeking for political or financial power, nor any of the other menacing qualities which biassed minds would now ascribe to them.   Baron de Hirsch's every utterance in connection with his great philanthropy was that of one concerned only with the moral rehabilitation of a race. So early as 1891 he impressed constantly upon all who acted for him in the distribution of his wealth, his desire to see the Jews return to agriculture and handicrafts.   He hoped to see them: "The sturdy yeomanry of the countries wherein they settled."

The Baron had been identified with Balkan railways, as every financier knows.   He had been brought into contact with conditions in Russia affecting his own people which deeply touched his sympathies.   He had, upon one occasion, sent to the Empress of Russia his check for £40,000 for the relief of this people.   It was the conviction of the impossibility of assisting the race while they remained in Russia that led to the exodus of the Jews from that country between 1880 and the '90s; or, as the

"*World's Work*" has said, to the "dumping of masses" of Jews upon the Atlantic seaboard. Rather inhuman, when you come to look at it, is it not, to describe so the result of a work than which nothing greater has been done for a people since Moses led the early Hebrews from the thraldom of Egypt?

Baron de Hirsch planned, not a concentration but a great scattering of his race. In his planning, he was considerate of other peoples. Foreseeing the possible objections that other governments might make to such a great inflow of foreigners, he devised measures by which to regulate the distribution of the refugees, according to their physical fitness, their industrial equipment, or training. He went so far as to select, as possible emigrants, the best physical specimens of the Russian Jews and those who gave promise of "making good" in agriculture, in the handicrafts, and as moral assets in their new homes.

Of the specific results of that experiment we shall speak in a later chapter. The point here to be observed in this example of Jewish philanthropy, which the justly-disposed will not be inclined to dispute, is that, at every step Baron de Hirsch put ideals, unmixed with mercenary motive, into his benefactions. As he recedes into the past his proportions appear more and more classic. He left no posterity, but made humanity his heir, and his wife as administrator of his fortune. It has been said to have been the intention of the Baroness to give away all her property before her death, retaining only a competence on which she herself might live while sustaining two adopted sons; but this was not to be. She left a rich fortune which went, according to her will, to buttress the philanthropies of the Baron and herself in Galicia, in Argentina, the de Hirsch Trade School and Fund, and the Clara de Hirsch Home for Working Girls in New York

City, and to aid in sustaining the work of the Pasteur and similar Institutes.

The scientific institutions of France have been beneficiaries in many other instances, of Jewish philanthropy. Elie Metchnikoff, of the Pasteur Institute, speaking of the gift to that work of 40,000,000 francs by the Jewish banker Osiris, of Bordeaux, said: "We have come into a fortune which will enable us to carry on our work on a larger scale than ever before . . . By this donation Osiris made himself one of the great benefactors of mankind."

It is said that the Baron de Hirsch was not a religious man, but he was, nevertheless, a man typical of his race in the manner in which he gained riches in the world and gave them back with interest. He was the great modern successor to that other lover of his race, Joseph Nasi, whose story has been outlined in an earlier chapter. That of Baron de Hirsch is less picturesque, perhaps, since he was nearer to our own time, and essentially a modern thinker, living and moving in western civilization; but as an inspiration for future philanthropists, he is the greatest and most humanitarian figure of his own time and race.

The nineteenth century was, throughout, a remarkable one in the history of the Jewish philanthropy. While the poorer among the Jews and the least educated passed through successive hard periods of need, of cruel injustices, of sufferings and persecution in many parts of the world, yet the century brought to light some of the noblest spirits the race has produced in recent times; some of the most brilliant intellects, polished in the great universities of the world; and, as well the most untrammelled opportunities for financial progress and for philanthropic action that had come to them in the present era; this because the race was able to express itself, being politically free as their fellowmen.

Very early in the century Sir Moses Montefiore rises
into prominence, not only as one of the most respected
brokers of London co-operating with the house of Rothschild, but as a powerful factor in the establishing of the
Provincial Bank of Ireland, and as the promoter of great
gas companies which furnished the lightings for the
larger cities of Europe. A financial power in his day, Sir
Moses Montefiore set the standard of Jewish integrity
very high; yet it is as the greatest Jewish philanthropist
of his period that his memory is most cherished today.

Upon retiring from active participation in business
transactions, Sir Moses and Lady Montefiore travelled
extensively, going, seven times in all, to Palestine, the
beloved land of his race. But he visited, as well, the land
of the Steppes, Turkey, Morocco—wherever he had reason
to know the people of his race were afflicted. It is said
that as he travelled he endowed schools and hospitals,
using his own fortune liberally, as well as dispensing sums
which had been entrusted to him to be distributed according to his discretion.

One of his great missions was undertaken in 1840 or
thereabouts, in company with the distinguished Jewish
lawyer, Cremieux, for the purpose of defending several
Jews at Damascus who were being held on the testimony
of the superstitious upon an accusation of ritual murder.
The case was one of the most celebrated of last century;
one in which the Rothschilds, and the bankers Salomon
and Goldsmid, Louis Phillippe, Queen Victoria, Metter-
nich, Lord Palmerston, and Mehmet Ali had part. "The
Damascus affair," as it has come down in history, was
one of the most complicated international cases of the
period. It culminated, after months of the most consum-
mate patience and zeal on the part of Sir Moses and his
associates, in the release of the prisoners, and the awakening of more human sympathy for the Jewish race than

they had ever known.   Clergymen preached for them; in Parliaments men rose to their rescue and pronounced against the treatment theretofore accorded them.   The famous Daniel O'Connell rose at a meeting held in their behalf at the Mansion House and cried out: "Is not a Jew in every relation of life an example?   Is he not a good father? a good son?   Are they not true friends? Are they not honest, industrious?"   And, his emotion increasing, he demanded with great intensity: "I appeal to all Englishmen to raise their voices in defence of the victims of that shameful oppression.   May the appeal go from one end of the British Isles to the other, and if the concurrence of an Irishman be wanting, here am I to testify to it!"

One of the most familiar cries of the present-day enemies of the Jews is: "Beware of them!   They are federated!   Arm yourselves, you countless millions: but, even then, be on your guard! Was not the brave Goliath, armed and in mail, killed by the treacherously flung stone?"   Let us look into the only form of federation that really exists among the Jews, the Alliance Israelite Universelle, and its purpose, while bearing in mind the fact that as a movement, it rose out of the period of "The Damascus case," when such unaccustomed sympathy was shown them as a people.

A historian of their race has called it the period of the re-birth of Jewish self-respect.   The object of the Alliance Israelite Universelle is: "To encourage by all means at our disposal the pursuit of useful handicrafts; to combat, where necessary, the ignorance and vice engendered by oppression; to work, by the power of persuasion and by all the moral influences at our command, for the emancipation of our brethren who still suffer," etc., etc.

It is out of this federation, surely as noble as might be formed, that so many cruel charges have been made within the present century: but it is also the source of the great philanthropies that have gone to the education of the Jews and which, in a surprisingly short time have re-built large numbers, both morally and physically. The attempt at organization has brought the race into harmony with the rest of the progressing world as it has not been in a thousand years. The cry of all sorts and conditions of men since the days of Voltaire, Montaigne, Rousseau, has been: Unite! In union there is strength! United we stand, divided we fall! It has become the watchword of capital and of labor; of religion and of politics; it has spread from social group to social group. How, then, is it possible that the Jews, sharing the common education of the world, should not likewise make a unified effort to help each other toward better health, better education, more complete freedom, whether political or religious? The right to do so should not be questioned in the democratic modern world where it has become a necessity, as well as a right, for mankind in general.

Men of munificent generosity have risen among the Jews in every age. One of the de Pintos of Amsterdam left many millions to be distributed among the needy. He was catholic in his kindnesses, as many others of his race have been, and left money to non-Jewish orphan asylums, to the clergy and the State. Mordecai Meisel of Prague, who died in 1601, was able to amass enormous wealth with which he clothed the poor of his community, giving freely to needy Christians. So high was his reputation for integrity that he was given permission to establish his own mint. His great property, however, was confiscated to the crown when he died, and while his name is still a synonym for wealth untold and boundless generosity among his people, his heirs inherited none of his wealth.

But the constructive philanthropy of the last and present centuries means far more to the Jewish race and to

raising of the moral and intellectual standards of the
world, generally, than all the great gifts of the past.
One of the noblest philanthropists Russia has known, was
the late Baron Horace Günsberg, of St. Petersburg, whose
father before him had invested a fortune in an effort to
raise the standard of life for his afflicted people in that
land.   The philanthropies of Baron Günsburg were too
many and too various to be recalled here; as, too, are
those of European philanthropists of the race, to trace
whom we should have to name every city and country of
that continent.   Joseph Epstein, for example, in Poland
made "heaps of money" in banking.   He won the respect
of non-Jewish associates, and, dying, left the greater part
of his fortune to philanthropic institutions.

Turn to Germany and at random you will find Herr
and Frau Louis Hille establishing a trust of a million and
a quarter for the providing of board and lodgings, for
persons, irrespective of religion or race, who are unable
to earn a living.   A philanthropist in Austria, Joseph
Porges, for the indiscriminate advantage of all, established art and musical institutions; the procession is
endless of Jewish philanthropists who have placed the
human need before the race need.   Sir Ernest Cassel,
desiring to give a memorial to the late King of England,
gave a million dollars to be devoted equally to the needy
Germans in England and the needy English in Germany.

Wherever an educated Jew is found there you will
discover that a principle of up-building of character and
community underlies his giving, whether this giving be
of money or personal service.   This will be especially
apparent as the philanthropies of American Jews are considered, and they began with the first of the race to
arrive in the American settlements.   Early colonial history supplies numerous instances of their public spirit.
The monument that commemorates the Battle of Bunker

Hill also commemorates the philanthropic patriotism of that most picturesque Jewish figure, Judah Tuoro, who, lies now in the Jewish cemetery at Newport, the town of his birth, after having done considerable good in several parts of the world. Tuoro was born of one of the families of Jews who refused to remain in New York when this was occupied by the British, though many non-Jewish folk remained to profit by trade with the invaders. Tuoro and Amos Lawrence were the two patriots who supplied equal amounts for the building of the famous monument on "the hill." He went afterward to New Orleans, where numerous mementoes of him exist and helpful organizations bear his name.

Newport, too, has her memorials to him, among others, the old "Norse Mill" which stands in the midst of the little Tuoro Park, and which he purchased for the city, to save it as a historic landmark. Dying, Tuoro bequeathed fifty thousand dollars to Sir Moses Montefiore, for distribution among the needy Jews of the old world. On Tuoro's tombstone, in the cemetery at Newport, you may still read these words: "The last of his race, he is inscribed in the book of philanthropy, to be remembered forever."

Speaking some years ago of the characteristics of the Jews of America, George Cooper Pardee, then Governor of California, said: "The Jew takes care of his own poor and helps to care for other peoples' poor. He possesses human sympathy and it is backed up by business judgment. When he establishes a charity, it is sure to be well administered." California had had an opportunity of seeing the uncalculating philanthropy of the Jew in the character of Adolph J. H. Sutro. The visitor to San Francisco may well give a thought to one who contributed so greatly to that city's progress.

Sutro was a youth of twenty when his family, ruined by the revolution of eighteen forty-eight, crossed the ocean in one of the sailing vessels of those days, and settled in Baltimore. In those days America was gold-mad, and very shortly Sutro, a young but ambitious engineer, following the example of many others, went west. There, however, he met with unlooked-for obstacles, and, with the tiny capital that was his, he went on to San Francisco and opened a little shop. Prudent, and with a purpose before him, he patiently plodded on until, having a fuller purse than before, he began to look into the subject of mining again, but this time as a practical engineer. Presently he perfected a smelter devised for the reduction of silver ore, which, being a technical success, was shortly a financial one.

About this time the "Comstock lode" was the topic on every tongue, though the difficulties that lay in the working of it were a serious drawback to its success. The great depth of the shaft made the heat intolerable for the miners. There were doubts expressed as to the use of continuing to experiment with it. Sutro, however, set to work upon the problem of a relieving tunnel. When he had worked it out to his satisfaction, he sought capital to carry out his plan. He tried in America, and in Europe, but without success; but, finally, he was able to gather a group about him, and the Sutro Tunnel Company, of which the world was to hear so much, was formed. With the approval of Congress, the work was then begun which resulted, some nine and one-half years later, in the completion of the famous Sutro Tunnel. The main shaft of this is twenty thousand and five hundred feet long; twelve feet wide, ten feet deep, and it lies sixteen hundred feet below the surface.

Upon the completion of this great work Sutro sold his interest in the company and returned to San Francisco.

There, at a period when the future of the city appeared to be negligible, Sutro invested heavily in real estate. It is said that at one time he owned one-tenth of the city, including among his possessions the Heights that now bear his name. To this time his attention had been fixed upon gaining, it may be; but it now turned to giving returns to the city which had given him opportunity. His first effort was to beautify it. He scattered statues through its streets and avenues; next he built a notable aquarium where specimens from the Pacific might be studied. He built public baths, and threw the great park about his palatial residence open to the public. This was the first utterance of munificent philanthropy upon the western coast.

In 1887 Mr. Sutro presented the city of San Francisco with a replica of Bartholdy's "Liberty Enlightening the World," which greets the newcomer in our own bay as he approaches the new world. Finally, he bequeathed his home and park to the city and a two-hundred thousand volume library to the State of California. Who may say that a citizen like Mr. Sutro has not proven one of the finest the country has produced? Who can, conscientiously, take part in assailing a race whose exemplars are such as he? In his day he was the peerless philanthropist of the West. But in the East also the race was identifying itself with good works, and again this was through its recent arrivals. One cannot avoid the thought, when glancing over the many contributions which the American Jews have made to western civilization, of what a pity it is that such strained attention should be devoted to the ferreting out of the Jews' faults when so many of his virtues lie open to the view. It is true that we find what we look for, and what a change might be wrought in public sentiment, what an era of peace and good will might be established, were we to set about it by inaugurating a real effort at mutual understanding amongst the races that mingle in the United States! The list of benefactions by the Jews in New York alone, many of them free to non-Jews as to Jews—how incalculably they outweigh the shortcomings with which the race is so often and so wrongly charged!

In a work of this character one may deal only, according to conventions, with the deeds of the dead; hence, in touching upon the present day Jewish philanthropies scant justice may be done great-hearted members of the race, whose public-spirited benevolence speaks through so many avenues. The names of such men as Joseph Seligman in the past are interwoven with the history of great educational institutions; with movements making for civic improvement. He founded the Hebrew Orphan Asylum. Someone has said of the Jewish merchant: "Of course he rises, because he mingles ideals and hope in all his transactions." Perhaps those ideals are what turn the successful Jew into an especially far-seeing philanthropist; they, it may be, keep the memory of his own struggles freshly before him.

The indefatigable generosity of the Jew during the strenuous days of the war was universally recognized during that dread period; but, lest we forget, we may give here the appraisal of them which has been made by Mr. Herbert Hoover, who, of all others, was in a position to make a just one. Writing from the Department of Commerce in the present year, (1923), Secretary Hoover has said:

"During the nine years that I have been actively connected with the larger American measures of relief to Europe, I have had intimate association with various Jewish organizations engaged in these labors. I have frequently had cause to comment upon the extraordinary generosity and liberality of the American Jews in their charitable contributions. Indeed, their voluntary contributions exceeded that of any other American group, and ranged from the stinted savings of the poorest workman to the full outpouring of those in more fortunate positions.

"During the acute periods in Europe, in order to assure the maximum saving of life and prevention of suffering within our resources, it was necessary to establish the closest co-operation in administration of American relief measures and this co-operation has been given by the Jewish Joint Distribution Committee with unexampled breadth of vision and singleness of purpose. . . . the American Jews have subscribed royally to general funds and in the administration of their own special funds have pursued steadily the broad-minded policy of co-operation in relief of all suffering, and literally hundreds of thousands of non-Jewish peoples were embraced in their efforts equally with the Jews. This broad sympathy so impressed the many countries in Eastern Europe as to shame the persecution of the Jews which during the periods of utter chaos were incipient in many communities.

"Not only has there been this great outpouring of generosity but there has been a great measure of personal service. I have served with the representatives of Jewish groups in joint efforts. . . . . No written appreciation can form adequate tribute to the service these men and women have given so wholeheartedly, so efficiently and at great personal sacrifice. The real appreciation and gratitude to those who gave of their means and services comes from the hearts of the millions whom they have served.

"There is no brighter chapter in the whole history of philanthropy than that which could be written of the work of the American Jews during the past nine years."

The philanthropy with which the name of Mr. Nathan Straus is most popularly associated and generally revered, is the establishment of milk stations in New York thirty years ago, and which are still supported by him; but these represent but one of his many humanitarian gifts to the world. He has helped Christians and Moslems as well as his own race. His motto, as somewhere written, is: "Give till it feels good." He has established milk stations in London; soup-kitchens in Jerusalem, and coal stations in New York, open to all. He has established preventoriums for consumptive children in New Jersey and a Pasteur Institute in Jerusalem. In times of panic he has maintained lodging houses for the needy, and "penny meals" from his milk-depots. A "practical idealist," he has been called, and few can question that this is well-merited.

The music lovers of New York, the art lovers, the students in these departments at various colleges, whatever their race, can scarcely touch life without benefiting by the philanthropy and public spirit of Adolph Lewisohn. His conspicuous gifts to the city in these fields—the School of Mines at Columbia; the great Stadium next the College of the City of New York and many other of his benefactions especially in educational lines, must make many future generations his beneficiaries; make them rise up and call him blessed. Mr. Lewisohn is said to have made his money in mines. So too, was Simon Guggenheim's fortune made, and each has given back a School of Mines to ease the way of future geologists. Mr. Lewisohn has made his gift to his home city, New York; Mr. Guggenheim to the West.

The most interesting characteristic of Jewish philanthropists and one that is clearly common to the race is that haphazard plays no part in their benefactions. They are as constructive as they are various. The race has another remarkable characteristic in that it utilizes anniversaries and celebrates its holidays, even as it perpetuates the memory of its dead, as occasions on which to do good.

A couple in Chicago celebrate their wedding anniversary by the gift of $52,000 for the prevention of malnutrition among children; another pair in New York, upon a like occasion, donates $75,000 to a Denver preventorium for children. In New York, too, Mr. and Mrs. Felix Warburg celebrate their silver wedding by a gift of $100,000 to a local worthy cause. The sum outright of $250,000 is given to Cornell University by Mr. Benny Loewy; Mrs. Mayer, in Chicago, as a memorial to her husband, presents $50,000 to the North-Western University—in every direction, but especially in that of educational institutions, the stream of Jewish philanthropy flows.

None but the initiated could compute the vast sums given away by the late Mr. Jacob Schiff to meet the needs of his race generally, and this to out-of-the-way groups and in out-of-the-way spots in the United States, in Europe, in Palestine. Bearing in mind that according to the information that is accessible to the public Mr. Schiff was not among the abnormally rich of the country, he was, from the beginning of his career, one of the most generous givers. His gifts in the course of the year, scattered in many directions, did not, it is said, amount to much less than a million dollars a year. His philanthropy has had part in the building of many of the best known Jewish charities. He founded Chairs at Harvard and at Columbia Universities; and made annual contributions to such institutions as the Teachers' College. In addition to subscribing regularly to many local Jewish Institutions, he contributed large sums to aid the Jews in foreign lands, in even far-away China.

A mention of late Jewish philanthropy could scarcely be made without reference to the gifts of Henry A. Dix, who but a short time ago made over to his employees a large business which he had built up, together with a working capital of $250,000. He also surrendered his

beautiful country home to the Young Women's Hebrew
Association as a place of recreation for its members. Mr.
Dix is one of that much assailed Jewish group, the Russian. He came here for asylum at the age of forty, and
has expressed his thanks to America in these munificent
gifts to his race.

Taken all in all, there is nothing connected with the
study of Jewish characteristics more fascinating, more
enlightening than to look into the philanthropies of the
race. Money makers the Jews are, but Midas was not of
the race. Nor are Midas traits tolerated where their
ghost even appears. This was made plain at a meeting
held a while ago, at which the plan was being discussed of
opening a new school.

"But" demurred one present, "that will take a lot of
money!" Up sprang one, then, on the instant, "What is
money for if not to be spent for the uplift of humanity",
he cried; and it should be said, perhaps, that the last
speaker was one who has been singled out for special vilification by the Ford author, as "The American Enigma".

But there are other philanthropies that mean as
much, if not more to a people as the giving of monies;
and in no race is the philanthropy of service more highly
rated, more constantly urged than among the Jews. They
look beyond the momentary need of their people; toward
the development of character; of the ideal character that
should express the "People of the Book". Not infre-
quently they give their lives in the same effort. Such a
Jewish philanthropist was Dr. Joseph Krauskopf, who
passed away but recently and who left behind him a will
which every one who would glimpse the inner soul of the
Jew should read. We may fittingly close this view of
Jewish philanthropy with an excerpt from it, in which the
testator addresses his children. Dr. Krauskopf, who was
scurrilously disparaged by the Ford scribe, was an immi-

grant to America, coming from Prussia at the age of fourteen. He died revered and beloved by many non-Jews, and distinguished as "the foremost Rabbi, if not the greatest preacher in the land" in the opinion of his race.

This was his parting message to his children; to the world:

"When, in 1876, I decided to enter the Hebrew Union College of Cincinnati, to study for the Jewish ministry, I knew I had chosen a life-calling, which, even if successful, would yield little more than a respectable living. Experience has proved that I judged aright. Beyond my home, my library and household effects, and the few thousand dollars invested, which sum represents for the most part, matured endowments from life insurance, I own nothing.

"I therefore have no worldly goods to bequeath to you, my dear children. And I would not have wanted it otherwise. I believe I have done my full duty towards you in having afforded you a good education and in having set before you the example of a life consecrated to labor and earnest striving after the higher ideals. Even if Providence had chosen to bestow a fortune upon me, I would have regarded myself as having been entrusted with it solely as custodian for the benefit of others, rather than as a personal possession to be used by me and by my family.

"Too often have I seen a father's fortune become the undoing of his children, and, rather than expose you to such a risk, I rejoice I have no fortune to leave you, my dear children. You have received the necessary education and the home stimulus necessary to enable you to hew out for yourselves a useful career, without the aid of an inheritance. With far less advantages to begin a life's career than you have enjoyed, I was obliged to make my way in life from my twelfth year. And I have, seemingly, been all the stronger for it. The consciousness that whatever fortune you shall have, whatever honorable position you shall occupy is of your own making, will some day become to you a source of supreme satisfaction; and let whatever encouragement I have given you toward attaining that end, be one of my legacies to you."

This is a glimpse of the soul of the race against which we have, of late, been hearing so much that is alarming. Let us turn to a view of the Jew in literature.

CHAPTER VII

The Jew in Literature

"The ancient Hebrew poetry is full of the aptest, sweetest and most impressive descriptions of nature and all her works and of the influence of nature on the spirit of man. 'Canst thou bind the sweet influence of the Pleides?' 'He maketh me to lie down in green pastures; He leadeth me beside the still waters.' 'Consider the lilies of the field, how they grow—' No race has ever surpassed the Jewish descriptions of either the beauties or the terrors of the nature which environs man."

CHARLES W. ELIOT.

(In address delivered in Boston, November, 1905)

WRITING in the last century and in his essay on Greek art, Matthew Arnold remarks that "distinctions of race in the early days were not of the odious and fantastic character which they have been in modern times." But, however odious and fantastic these distinctions were in Arnold's day, the twentieth century has already given proof of the capacity of such distinctions to take on yet more unworthy and sinister shapes. It has arrived at an open, derisive attack upon the Jewish Scriptures. Not only is Mr. Belloc under the impression that no one is interested in Jewish literature, or reads it, nowadays, but Mr. Chamberlain, having strained a multitude of points to prove the contemptible character of the Jews, proceeds to define the books of the prophets as wholly inferior to those of the Greek poets and philosophers. Though impotent to take away the glory which scholars of two thousand years have allowed the Jews as the People of the Book, yet he permits his troubled mind to relieve itself by belittling appraisals of the Writings and their authors, though by so doing he more than once betrays his lack of real ac-

131

quaintance with them, while setting himself in opposition
to the verdict of ages. Scholars of very divergent points
of view have concurred in pronouncing that the Jews in
their Scriptures have provided humanity with the mind
stuff out of which all literature, as we know it has been
spun. Bigotry has fattened on disputing these writings;
controversy has thriven on them, and theologies have risen
from them; poets have been inspired by them; laws
have taken their fundamentals from them; theories of
ethics have been evolved from them; all human conduct
has been affected by them; the great events of history have
been shaped by them; the common speech reflects in its
commonest axioms and even its word combinations, that
of the Book of the Jewish people.

"We continue to 'heap coals of fire' upon the heads
of those who have injured us"; "we eat, we drink and are
merry," even as those early authors described: "how the
mighty are fallen"; "hip and thigh"; "love thy neighbor
as thyself"; "there were giants on the earth in those days";
"the wife of thy bosom"; "a soft answer turneth away
wrath"; "whoso sheddeth man's blood"; "man is born to
trouble as the sparks to fly upward"; "the root of the
matter"; "the morning stars sang together"—in every
phase of speech of today, of thought, where the perfect
expression is sought, back with the instinct of the homing
bird goes the world to those Scriptures.

They are the crystallized thought of present as well
as of extinct humanity; of prehistoric ages, gathered and
treasured and formulated by the reverent Hebrews of three
and more thousands of years ago. Every ancient and
modern poet, every philosopher and scholar, every statesman; even those who would deny the theory of God, and
glory in their unbelief, in the very act of denial have somewhere paid their homage to these ancient writings. Their
aphorisms, axioms, proverbs pop up most unexpectedly in

all modern tongues, so that in English, or French; in Italian, or Spanish—in the Oriental tongues, even, they are the language key to mutual understanding.

One cannot recall a literary work of the present era which does not spring from them. Dante was possible only through them; Milton is a monument to them; while Racine wrote of the Greeks he shaped them from the Hebrew point of view. They inspired Palestrina and the throng of musicians who followed Handel; the art of the Middle Ages was all Biblical. Drama rose from the same source. Few modern works exist which are not born of Biblical problems, Biblical themes. Moulton traces *"Faust"* to the New Testament query:

"What shall it profit a man if he gain the whole world and lose his own soul?" and the Old Testament, with which we have here to do, propounds the same question in other phrase form which had been put to still earlier people.

Some years ago Edmund Clarence Stedman, in a course of lectures delivered before Johns Hopkins University on the *"Nature and Elements of Poetry,"* gave this appreciation of the literature of the Jews:

"It has been said of the Hebrew language that its every word is a poem; and there are books of the Old Testament, neither lyrical nor prophetic, so exquisite, in kind, that I call them models of impersonal art. . . . In the narrative books of the Bible, the good and the bad appear without disguise. All is set forth with a frankness that made the heart of the Hebrew tent-dweller the heart of the world thereafter . . .

"We think of inspiration, and a Hebrew seer glows in the prophetic East; of gnomic wisdom and thought, and many fixed white stars shine tranquilly along the equinox, from Lucretius to Emerson . . . but with Hebrew poetry, that of the Bible, we have more to do since we derive very closely from it. There is no literature at once

so grand and so familiar to us.   Its inherent racial genius
was emotional, and therefore lyrical . . . and of so
fiery and prophetic a cast that its personal outbursts have
a loftiness beyond those of any other literature . . ."

Nor is this all, for, coming to the poetry of the Book,
Mr. Stedman says:

"There is no more wonderful poetry of the emotional
order than the psalms of David and his compeers relating
to their own trials and agonies, their loves and hates and
adorations. . . . Modern self-expression is not so
simple and direct. . . . We feel, in the *naïveté* of
the Davidic lyre, the stress of human nature in its articu-
late moods. . . . This gives to the poetry of the Scriptures an attribute possessed only by the most creative and
impersonal literature of other tongues—that of universality. . . . Technical abandon, allied with directness
of conception and faithful revelation of human life makes
for universality; makes of the Hebrew Scriptures a world's
book that can be translated into all tongues with surpass-
ing effect, notably into a language almost as direct and
elemental as its own, that of our Anglo-Saxon, in its
Jacobean strength and clarity."

The late Lyman Abbott said of these scriptures and
of the Jew in literature: "In my judgment the American
people owe more to the ancient Hebrews than to any other
ancient people; more than to either the Greeks or the
Romans, because we owe to the Hebrews our ethical and
spiritual ideas. . . . I hope the time will come when
the laws and literature of the ancient Hebrews will be
studied as now are studied the ancient laws and literature
of the Greeks and Romans; and when it will be universally
recognized that no man ignorant of the literature of the
ancient Hebrews is a well educated man."

These Jewish scriptures, these many books of the
Jews bound in one, constitute the most widely circulated

literature in the world. The great, peculiar quality about
them, and it is one no other book in the world possesses,
is that their character and composition are such that they
can be and are translated into every known language without their beauty being impaired or their message lost.
Again, far from there being a slackening of interest in
the Scriptures, they are being studied today as never
before, even the unintelligent having become aware that
to remain wholly unacquainted with this ancient and
accessible literature, is to be lacking in the first essential
of modern culture.

Ex-President Eliot of Harvard has emphasized the
worth of these Jewish writings in a way that should stamp
it upon the memory of all who read. He says: "In many
other literatures cosmogonies are found, i. e., accounts of
the creation of the universe; but nowhere can be found an
account of creation so superb and so sound, all modern
knowledge and speculation taken into account, as that
given in the first sentence in the Hebrew Bible: 'In the
beginning God created the heavens and the earth' . . .
The descriptions of the Hebrew literature have never been
equalled and they can never be surpassed.

"The Jewish conception of man's nature as [therein]
set forth, sound all the depths and reach all the heights.
Human lust, cruelty and treachery, and human misery and
sorrow can never be more vividly portrayed than they are
in the Hebrew Scriptures. Neither can the splendor of
human courage, magnanimity and justice, the steady glow
of human love and the incitements of courage and hope
be more nobly set forth. Concerning man the Jewish seers
asked all the fundamental questions which subsequent
philosophers have asked, and answered them better."

A host of other authorities might be cited to prove
how the opinions of the learned and the wise for centuries
have concurred as to the value of these ancient writings;

as to the unassailable literary height of their authors, the
Jews. Mr. Wells speaks of their Book, so full of "glimpses
of the Infinite" as "the most remarkable collection of ancient documents in the world."

Walter Bagehot says the book expresses as no other
ancient book does, the notion of progress. Because of
this characteristic, he thinks it rare in the histories of
humanity. "Savages," he says, "regard what *is* as the
norm. They cannot conceive of change in the past or the
future. As against this, the Hebrew prophets with
splendid indignation, regarded the present condition of
their nation as abominable, and felt a confidant hope that
the divine plan of the universe involved an amelioration
of those conditions, not alone for themselves, but for the
whole world." In that lies the great significance of this
gift of the Scriptures: they are for the whole world. The
literature of a race, it has come to nourish, spiritually, the
great human family.

There is no greater marvel in the world than this
ancient yet modern literature which emerges so richly
full from the mysterious life of five thousand years ago.
It is said it was borne down the stream of that Eastern
people by oral tradition solely, to the days of Hezekiah,
when "literature" is said to have flourished. During
Hezekiah's reign the Proverbs were gathered and perfected and enlarged, this at a time when Rome was but
an infant city and the Greeks were setting out for Sicily.
To that unusual characteristic of the race to which allusion
elsewhere has been made, and which turns so frequently
its disasters to its advantage, is due the written form of
the complete Book as we have it today; for this came into
being in what Mr. Wells calls, "the stimulating atmosphere of the Babylonian world," during the captivity of
the Jews in the kingdom of Nebuchadnezzar. They lost
their freedom and wealth, yet were able to give to man-

kind more than they had ever done, and gained, moreover, a pre-eminent prestige by their literature to which they now turned.

But here it seems to me that Mr. Wells, like many another, though certainly not with a will to do so, has moved into a groove which numerous predecessors have worn rather deep; for he is of the opinion that the Jewish scribes in Babylon, where, however, men of their race had been living in scattered captive groups from a much earlier period than this of the second captivity, "probably" incorporated in their writings the Babylonian stories of the Creation and of the Flood, and even that of Moses in the bulrushes. Mr. Wells may be right. He is safe from being proved wrong at this late day, as are all who undertake to establish history on their own supposition. It is, however, regrettable that "probabilities" are so often advanced by historians when no other means are at hand to support their preferred theories. Conjectures on what mental actions and re-actions took place twenty-five hundred years ago in the remote East are but sorry fictions to hang upon the few known facts. These "probabilities" lend substance to Napoleon's theory that, after all, history is but a fable agreed upon.

It is scarcely likely, Mr. Wells' suppositions to the contrary notwithstanding, that a captive people would employ their leisure in appropriating their captor's traditions and much more probable that the Babylonian kings, boastful to the point of being comical to us, triumphing after centuries of warring over the Jews, whose kings, reign after reign from the time of David, had been so envied, and whose racial pride was well recognized even in that early day, may have gloried in their own power to take over some of those same proud traditions; to claim them. Being victors, they had no reason to refrain from doing this, if they wished to; and, as we read their unblushing boasting, as deciphered from the tablets unearthed at old Chaldea three-quarters of a century ago, the thought more than once presents itself of the contrast between the reverent spirit of the Hebrew records, and the bombastic, theatrical form which the Babylonian braggarts employed.

However, we cannot doubt that in that age, as in our own, there was a good deal of give and take among those little neighboring, primitive peoples. In all probability (if we, too, may indulge in probabilities) the natural bent for writing which has continued to be the characteristic of the Jews, was utilized by their Babylonian captors, as it was by the Church in our own era, and that the Jews did much transcribing for them. It is conceivable, for it brought this about in Christendom, that this ability secured favors for them which softened the rigors of their captivity, and raised them in public esteem.

While they were still captive, while they were beginning to set down their traditions in Babylon, it may be recalled that a great change was operating in the then known world, about and beyond them. Evidence from every side appears to establish a sudden and universally experienced quickening of moral consciousness. In the East, Buddha came into view, and Confucius was preaching. It would seem evident from the researches of archaeologists, that, with these indications of an active spiritual awakening on all sides, the arising would be impossible of such a statement, for example, as that advanced with such infuriate dogmatism by Mr. Chamberlain, namely: that the "Jews took" their monotheistic theories from the Indo-Aryans, and their legends from the Chaldeans. This subject, thanks to the flinging about of such assumptions, to their being caught up and speculated upon by others, is one that might well use up the rest of our available space; we must return, however, to our own of the Jew in literature as he begins his participation in that first literary period, and gathers his material for the Hebrew Scriptures which a world was to inherit.

One of the earliest literary figures we come upon after the greater prophets, and his portrait and biography are amazingly well-drawn, though in pale tones in the Scriptures themselves, is that of Baruch, disciple and secretary of Jeremiah, who transcribed his master's thoughts as he uttered them, and, it may well be, embellished them. He was with the Prophet through most of his travels, devoted to his interests, and zealously eager to be identified with him as Joshua was with Moses; as Elisha was with Elijah. Though in the Bible he is found among the throng rather than in the foreground, Josephus gives him more prominence, and the Talmud and other authorities to the present day place him among the minor prophets. There even hangs about Baruch's story the possibility of his being raised some day to a still higher rank.

Along in years when Cyrus liberated the Jews who had been fifty years captive in Babylonia, Baruch preferred to remain in that land of study under so enlightened a ruler, to returning to Jerusalem. So, too, did others of his race; and he appears to have acted as teacher to many, among them Ezra, of an old and important lineage, whose mind he, no doubt, had part in forming. Ezra was a grandson of the High Priest Hilkiah, who found the Scroll of the Law in the Temple. Baruch's lineage, too, was noble. When the two came together, as teacher and disciple, Baruch was already a venerable figure, but was still profoundly engaged upon the study of the Law, and the manuscripts of the Book of Jeremiah; perhaps upon those works of his own which later caused him to be numbered among the lesser prophets. He made the study of the Law so fascinating to Ezra that, while he lived, that severe young prophet preferred to continue with him to going back to Jerusalem.

An interesting feature of the study of the early world literature, especially at this period, is that nowhere in the product of the many Jewish writers who left behind them notable manuscripts, is there to be found mention of the literary figures of the other near-lying and great peoples of the times, and, similarly, no mention of the Jewish authors in the works of the authors of the Greeks and other nations. Sophocles and Socrates came and went in the outside world while the great literary activity that produced the Scriptures was going on among the Jews in Babylon. Herodotus, the "father of history," was attaining fame as an observing traveller; but from such remains of the time as have come down to us we can only form one opinion: that every little human group looked upon every other human group as little more than curious heathen. A national self-satisfaction was common to them all, as great as that exhibited today, by our modern nations.

Many myths concerning this Jewish bookman, Baruch, grew up after his death and burial in Arabia, where for centuries, his grave was the goal of pilgrims. There came a time, so a legend says, when the king of the country, having heard of miraculous happenings at the spot, decided to have the matter looked into and ordered the grave to be opened. But as his men proceeded to the task, all who touched it fell dead. The king, not to be balked in his determination, at last ordered the Jews themselves to open the grave: which, after fasting and prayer, they were able to accomplish. The story is that the body of Baruch was perfectly preserved in a marble coffin, and that the king shortly afterward became a Jew and transferred the body to its present resting place, a mile away from that of Ezekial.

For centuries it was said that gold dust lay upon the leaves of a plant that grew over this grave. Later the Arabians identify Baruch with Zoroaster, and so, little by little the myths have gathered about him until he is, to most people, an altogether unreal character. But he wrote a book, or one that has been ascribed to him which was for centuries preserved in the Greek, the Syriac, and the Slavonic, and has only within thirty years become known to Western readers through a translation from the Slavonic (and that from the Greek text) which issued through the Cambridge press. The great quality that distinguishes the literature of the Jews is its living interest, which has held the attention of humanity for thousands of years, generation after generation. Baruch, today, may be said to be only now "coming into his own."

We are told that the literary men of Judah were busy upon the compilation and perfecting of their work upon the Scriptures down to 100 B. C., and that at once, upon its completion, they began to form their "Blackstone," or Talmud, or, as it is known, their book of interpretations of the laws as rendered by notable teachers of the race. Their laws, then and today, had and have a greater effect upon their life than any other of their literature. In this writing upon writings, however, in this building upon the original Scriptures, they have set an example that every succeeding school of theology has followed. The most incredible masses of theological literature, as a consequence, have been poured out upon the world. Plato was writing co-incidentally with the compilers and editors of the Scriptures and upon what he wrote many volumes have since been written; but they are as nothing in comparison with the incalculable writing that has been done in explanation, or defence of, or in comment upon "the Book."

That portion known as Genesis, as some one has said, has been the starting-point for innumerable controversies; but so, too, has each succeeding book. And in addition, every classical, and countless far-from-classical works have drawn upon the Scriptures for theme, motive, idea and even plot. But despite this enormous draft upon them, like the widow's cruse of oil, the more they have been drawn upon, the more they have yielded. Twenty-two German and six English speaking Universities have issued commentaries upon Isaiah alone, and each opposes the other in its analysis and conclusions. "Fancy," exclaimed the late Dr. Solomon Schechter, in surveying this merely modern output, "fancy what would happen were the prophet to come back from the dead, and tell us just what he did mean! As he turned over the leaves of those strange works he would probably say, "What an idea! I never meant or said anything of the kind!"

But in treating of the Jew in literature we must avoid the common error of thinking of the literary gifts of the race as having been exhausted in their greatest of all books. The books of the Apocrypha, which by some have been accepted as "sacred Scripture," though their dicta is not supported by others, represent a class of Jewish literary output of decided value to the student. Not that all of the Apocryphal books have been written by the Jews. Many spurious works have appeared which imitated the Jewish style and were pronounced genuine which long ago have been discarded from consideration.

The name Apocrypha is peculiarly used by many. It meant and means today: writings that contain mysteries too sacred to be communicated to any but the initiated. Within a decade or two Apochryphal writings have been discussed as being still in existence, though in all probability the Jews have no connection with these mysterious works.

The Jews as literary people, though the authors' names are in most instances lost, have record of a very varied pre-Christian era literature which includes historical matter, and prophetical, lyrical and romantic, and, as well, tales of adventure. The story of the love of Joseph and Aseneth, daughter of Potiphar, is one of the best known. From the descriptions and cited passages of many of these early works we are led to believe that many of them were highly interesting documents. Joseph, Isaiah, Ezra, Baruch, Jeremiah, even Moses and Jacob, and others of their day figure as heroes, or speakers in these almost forgotten manuscripts; which, however, are being brought to light again from time to time through the researches of Oriental scholars.

By the time the Old Testament pages were closed, civilization had widened vastly, and a new type of Jewish author was coming into view. The Jews in numbers were scattered among the Roman and Greek cities where life presented itself to them under another aspect. Philo Judaeus, the Alexandrian philosopher, appeared about the beginning of the present era, and next, Josephus, the historian, a kind of Bancroft in his day, for he had to do with statesmanship and international interests as well.

Today Philo, like Baruch, is attracting attention again, as never before in a thousand years. He was the predecessor of those theologians who are trying to think out a way of arriving at a universal religion; of reconciling all faiths that spring from a belief in one God. Philo lived when Roman licentiousness and Greek learning had passed their highest point; and in Alexandria, the most active centre of mercantile, moral and intellectual interests in the then known world. He was born a Greek, and disputed and wrote in that tongue; and though the doctors of Jewry disapproved of his liberal theories, he stands out, none the less, as the first notable secular writer to come from his people.

Though it was now beginning to decline in importance, Alexandria for two centuries had been the great meeting-place of the peoples of the world. Its population was as cosmopolitan as that of New York today, and, too, in its day, it was the largest Jewish city in the world, not excepting Jerusalem, as is said of the great western metropolis at the present time. Here Jews spoke Greek, the common language of the community, and had their beloved Scriptures translated into that tongue, the better to hold their own among the controversialists of the time. Philo drank at many philosophical springs in Alexandria and while retaining his love for his ancestral faith, he began to develop that philosophy which afterward became known as "Philonism." It sought, as its main purpose, the reconciliation of the religions of his day, especially that of the Jews, with the Greek and the Indo-Aryan theories. He seems amazingly modern, as one looks back upon that active time of nearly two thousand years ago; for today all thoughtful minds are again turned toward the solving of practically the same problems which he tried to settle.

Greek, Indo-Aryan, and Jewish thought were constantly debated in Alexandria. It is said that philosophical ambassadors from Indian potentates had sojourned in the city, where the first university had been established, and where the most advanced intellects of that period spent their force upon discussions of the diverse God-concepts which existed among the peoples of the world. Greek and Roman, and Indian expounded his own faith and the beauties it contained, and Philo, in turn took up the beauties of Judaism and expatiated upon the wonders of his Scriptures. He stands out among the men of his time, a peace-making preacher endeavoring to prove that the Jewish prophets and the philosophic speculators of Greece, and the dreamers, as well of the East, were striving, after all, for the one truth, however different the outer appearance of their methods of approach.

It appears, however, that many of Philo's ideas, which were later taken on by the young Christian sect, and by the Church as it developed, were rejected by the Jewish theologians of the time, as being Platonian; often, indeed in the spirit less of Jewish than of Greek thought, with perhaps a coloring here and there of other prevailing schools of philosophy, and of those of preceding periods. Philo would be better described, however, as an early eclectic thinker, scholastic in his methods, and withal an early stylist. He is said to have modelled his language upon a close study of works that were already classics in his day. A native Greek, in spirit, too, he has been pronounced thoroughly Hellenic; but in faith he was a Jew of Jews.

Critics speak of Philo's Greek as being mixed with Hebraisms and they note that among his writing one may come unexpectedly upon whole phrases which had been formed previously by other authors; but there is no reason to deduce from this a desire to plagiarize, for one of the points for which his works have been valued especially are the liberal quotations from other authors even then obsolete, but which have been of the utmost service to those who came after him. Such works by Philo as have been preserved, largely by the Church Fathers, consist of Commentaries on the Law, and fragments from other works which Ambrosius and other early writers have incorporated in their texts. It is known that he wrote biographies of many of the Jewish patriarchs, using them as demonstrations of "the active law of virtue;" also a notable work, *"De Vita Contemplativa,"* said to have contained remarkable pictures of a colony of

Jewish hermits who spent six out of every seven days in pious contemplation and study of the Scriptures. There has been a vast amount of pseudo-Philonic literature, which, in itself, is testimony to the important place Philo occupies in ancient writings. Charles Foster Kent says of him that "his work became epoch-making in its influence upon Jewish haggada, Christian dogma, and Greek philosophy."

Flavius Josephus came into the world but a year or two before Philo passed out (in 40 A. D.), and lived on into the next century, having looked upon the scattering of his people, also the mutations of life, from many angles. Descended from the Maccabees, a brilliant general, man of the world, the favorite of Vespasian and therefore envied by Tacitus; a natural diplomat, he was not always approved by the Jews themselves, yet he served them well; for he not only wrote his great *"Antiquities of the Jews"* and his equally notable *"Wars of the Jews,"* but also his immortal defense against Apion, who was the Ford or Belloc of his day, as Tacitus was the Chamberlain, and the originator, as has been pointed out elsewhere, of many of the charges which have been but recently revived.

Nothing that has come down to us from the race, aside from the Scriptures, is at once so simple, so graphic, or so fascinating to the world at large as these stories from the pen of Josephus. He has been criticised as having written wholly "from the Jewish point of view," and praised for having done nothing of the kind. The first named critics prove their point by picking out what they regard as a misunderstanding on the part of Josephus of certain non-Jewish terms; but the examples given of his short-comings in this respect reduce these critics to the position of merest quibblers, of which so many examples may be found among critical writers. The fact is that Josephus left behind him, in these histories of the Jews, both picturesque and absorbing accounts of his people, which rank in the minds of those who read them today with those other fascinating stories of the ancients, Plutarch's Lives. As a whole, they are probably as accurate. They have kept Jewish secular writings on the everyday bookshelves as no other work from the race has done or could do, for now nearly two thousand years.

Written originally in Greek, both the *"Wars"* and the *"Antiquities"* have been translated into Syriac, and Latin, many times into German and French; into Hungarian, and the Oriental tongues, and into English by R. Traill and William Whiston. All along the centuries great minds have paid tribute to Josephus. Joseph Scaliger, a Paduan scholar of the fifteenth-sixteenth centuries was one of the earliest to recognize him in Europe. He said that not only in the affairs of the Jews, but in those even of foreign nations, Josephus deserves more credit than all of the Greek and Roman writers put together. "Certain it is," wrote Bishop Porteus, after quoting Scaliger, "that he had the most essential qualification for the historian— a perfect knowledge of the transactions which he relates; that he had no prejudices to mislead him in the representation of them; and that, above all, . . . he probably continued a zealous Jew all his life." The work of Flavius Josephus possesses the strength of simplicity which was so characteristic of the early Jewish writers, and though an old man when he wrote most of it, his spirit is dauntless, and marvellously virile in its fire and fearlessness; in its power to grip and rouse the reader to sympathy with him.

After Josephus, however, Jewish literary product, like that of the rising Christian sect, seems almost wholly to have consisted of theological matter or of speculative philosophy, until well into the period of the Renaissance. Some fourteen commentaries upon the Talmudic writings and the Law, and upon varying phases of Judaism had been written to the time of Maimonides. Many of these had arisen in the East from among the scholars who were identified with the school at Sora. R. H. Charles, speaking of the great Rabbinical writings of the early discursive and critical Jewish authors of the present era, says without an acquaintance with them the New Testament cannot be understood; and this opinion has been re-stated by T. K. Cheyne and R. T. Herford, all of which authorities are able to note an almost daily increase in the interest in the post-Biblical writing of the Jews. These gentlemen very recently have maintained that an acquaintance with the Talmud, with its theories of religion and its "excursions into the land of fancy" is become an essential to those who would be thought cultured.

One of the most notable literary figures of the tenth century, of any race, is that of Saadiah, who is known also under his Eastern name of Sa-id al Fayyumi, who has been named as the founder of scientific activity among his people. He completed a Hebrew dictionary in 913 A. D., a great work, besides engaging in polemical writings that have become historic. Head of the school at Sora, he ranks, after Philo, as the "great writer of post-Biblical Judaism." But it is said that while Philo's thought was colored by his Greek surroundings, so Saadiah's show here and there the color of his Mohammedan environment. His worth to the modern world of scholars may be gauged by the fact that in 1892 a movement was started for the celebration of the thousandth anniversary of his birth by the bringing out of a complete edition of his works. These were many and various. Saadiah translated the Hebrew Pentateuch, or, the Law, into Arabic. From 1546 to the present day, this scholar has been the delight of the erudite, who have kept him alive by continual discussion of his works. Practically every learned theological work of the present day which includes a tracing and verification of philosophy, cites this Jewish teacher.

The Vatican contains many records of the Jewish writings of those days, so obscure as they seem to the unscholastic mind; among them the martial and memorial poems of Michael Cohen, many of whose pupils rose high in letters; those of Meir of Norwich, who flourished in England about 1260.

The most celebrated traveller of the twelfth century was Benjamin of Tudela, who was the Herodotus of his day, though he exceeded the Greek in the accuracy of his observations. Castro, in his *Biblioteca Española,* says that Benjamin's work had been done into every language in Europe and had (at that writing) passed through sixteen editions. Castro, who "did for the Hebrew literature what a preceding author, Casira, had done for that of the Arabs, gave more than seven hundred excerpts from the choice writings of the Jews of Spain, together with biographical sketches of their authors," which show an amazing erudition and talent among them.

Prescott is authority for the statement, in his "Ferdinand and Isabella," that the Jews, "in the cultivation of elegant letters revived the glories of the Hebrew Muse. This," he continues, "was indeed the golden age of modern Jewish literature, which, under the Spanish Caliphs, had experienced a protection so benign, although occasionally chequered by the caprices of despotism, that it was enabled to attain a higher beauty and a more perfect development in the tenth, eleventh, twelfth and thirteenth centuries than it has reached in any other part of Christendom." . . .

Benjamin of Tudela, whose records show him to have been a man of the highest associations, left Saragossa about 1160, travelled through Greece and Turkey; through Egypt, Italy, Germany and France, lingering long in each country, and writing there his observations.

He left invaluable pictures of the world of his day.   He
returned to Castile only after thirteen years of wandering.
Twenty-five editions of his work are known, and these
in all the modern European tongues; also in Latin.   A
copy of his "Itinerary" is in every National Museum of
Europe.   At least a half dozen of the best known editions
are in Dutch.

A great Jewish author of this period, Ibn Gabirol,
whose work is familiar to many when listed under his
author-name, Avicebron, has been called "unique and the
most noble of philosophers."   His works are among the
treasures of the *Bibliothéque Nationale* of Paris.   That
most familiar to the world is his *"Improvement of the
Moral Qualities,"* which, as an ethical treatise, was edited
and published by the Rev. Stephen S. Wise in New York
in 1902.   But Gabirol was also a poet, and writer "of
metric songs," some of which are used today in the
religious services of the Jews.   Critics have said of him
that he liberated Hebrew poetry from involved expression,
and that in him the liturgical writings and poetry of the
Spanish and the Arabian Jews attained their highest per-
fection.   Late appraisers of his work have called him
"the Jewish Plato."   Literary connoisseurs, and true
amateurs, notwithstanding Mr. Belloc's pronunciamento,
are today, as they have not been in centuries, eagerly
perusing this reviving literature.   We may not linger
over its many great names, since there is as much to tell
of in the story of the Jew in what may be called modern
literature.

CHAPTER VIII

The Jew in Modern Literature

"In their intense, vibrant and infinitely varied literary expression, the latter-day Jewish writers are not excelled by any other race. They rank well as novelists: as dramatists; they are among our best critics, our most virile polemical authors, our journalists. Keen in satire, brilliant in repartee, they often display an ebulliency like to nothing but the vigor of young springs; in their lighter works, to the brilliancy of the sun-touched spray of fountains."

A. S.

MODERN literature properly begins only with the age of printing. But that age liberated literature in all the known languages and fixed immortal works in a form for the use of countless centuries to follow. Most of the Jewish works which this magical invention made available, like most of the non-Jewish writings that were similarly now at the disposal of the world, had to do with theological theory or controversy. One of the first Hebrew works to be printed was Maimonides' *"Guide for the Perplexed"*, a work which, in the course of its history had been burned in the public Square, condemned alike by Jews and Churchmen as heretical, but which became a text-book for philosophers for centuries thereafter, and is still a work of reference and held by scholars to be invaluable.

But Jewish literary output was not all of this serious school. It has been rather clearly established that gaiety, too, had its spokesmen among them though the lighter literature of the race is often found to be fused with that of the people among whom they dwelt. This is said to be so in the case of the *"Thousand and One Nights,"* that delightful collection of Eastern stories which first crept into popular European knowledge in the late seventeenth century. Its composite authorship has always been recognized, but in only a few instances conclusively

151

identified; but some one hundred-and-sixty-odd stories, including that of *Sinbad,* have been pronounced unmistakably Jewish by many of their marked characteristics.

What goes far to establish this connection is that, as we have seen, the Jews were well acquainted with the realm and court of Haroun-al-Raschid, whose adventures are told in the wonderful *"Arabian Nights"* collection. These stories, "so rich, so poetic, so witty, what is more", as Larousse puts it, "and so audacious in painting the gilded slavery of the women of the Harem", have become, as well, the synonym for all that is dazzling, magical, luxurious and Oriental.

In secular literature the Jews have always had their "children of fantasy and sorrow". Mingling with the devotional and semi-devotional Jewish poetry of the eleventh century, are many gay wine songs; many satirical rhymes, many romantic ones, as well as love-songs. One drinking song, famous among the relics of that period is a satire directed against an inn-keeper who charged outrageous prices for his wine, and, notwithstanding, watered it. The theme is by no means outworn in the present day, and the ditty is not unlike similar ones that remain from the English output of the same century.

There was a Jewish poet in the thirteenth century, Immanuel of Rome, who combined "the warm imagination of the Orient with the erotic spirit then rife in Italy" and gave reign to it, probably, being human, in a derisive challenge to those who were inclined to sneer at Jews as hypermoralists. But he paid for his audacity; for his writings were denounced by the Rabbis who forbade their people to read them. At the same time, Immanuel's worth was such that as his work became known he acquired the name of "the Jewish Dante."

A member of a wealthy family, this poet appears to have been active in the city life and to have left a mass of manuscripts behind him. Like all his race he was a wide reader; and he freely used as the subject of his verse the Hebrew writings with which he was most familiar. He wrote in Hebrew and fluently, in Italian. Scholars say he mingled Hebrew idioms with the modern tongue which lent a special charm to it. His writing in Italian would explain his recognition in his own times. He is said to have been an innovator in his Hebrew verse, in that he was able successfully to introduce the sonnet form of Spain into that language, even improving upon it by the introduction of alternating rhyme.

But he was an inveterate satirist, and merciless in his parodies on Talmudic and Biblical stories. These he filled with jests and puns and ridicule of customs very dear to the Jewish heart, and which the leaders of the race openly rebuked him for. In his riper years—he was about sixty at the time—he wrote a *"Vision of Hell and Paradise"*, which many have spoken of in the same breath with the *"Divina Commedia"*; but, while this work was said to be on an expiatory character, and to record his repentance for some of his earlier shocking lightmindedness; to be permeated, too, by a consciousness of sin, nevertheless the old bent toward mischievous gaiety and to poke fun at what he thought outworn and illogical, breaks from him from time to time. In more than one characteristic he would appear to be the literary progenitor of Heinrich Heine.

Immanuel's "Dantesque" work was published in 1491 at Brescia, one hundred and sixty years after its author had passed away; again at Constantinople in 1535, in Berlin in 1796 and at Lemberg in 1870; and, while it has been condemned for its frivolous, even its wanton passages, nevertheless it continues to be regarded with the greatest interest, and to be prized as a relic of the thirteenth and fourteenth centuries' literature. It should be remembered that this author wrote in the spirit of his age, and was, in his way, a pioneer in a field which Boccaccio filled fifty years later, and Rabelais succeeded to after one hundred and sixty years; that his work was written, moreover, in Hebrew in which it long lay untranslated. Because of this, while scholars have given him a high rating, the unlearned in the literature of that age have passed him by as negligible; but from present interest in his work, Immanuel's fame may yet rise in the modern world. Voltaire said of Dante, the beloved of his nation: "The Italians call him divine; but it is a hidden divinity. Few people understood his oracles. He has commentators which, perhaps, is another reason for his not being understood. His reputation will go on increasing because scarcely anybody reads him." To the present Immanuel has had no commentators.

Italy for several centuries continued to be a motherland of many generations of famous Hebrew scholars, among them the Luzzati whence several literary men of note sprang. The Rabbis of Italy were indefatigable writers on theological subjects during the sixteenth and seventeenth centuries as were also those of Amsterdam, and Holland, generally. There is little to note during these years of a general literary output among the Jews. The thought of the world was upon religious controversies; upon the struggle, as someone has said, between faith and philosophy. Out of that struggle the great figure that stands above all others is that of Baruch Spinoza, of the great comprehending spirit; a light-bringer to the world of whom we shall have further to say elsewhere. Moses Mendelssohn, who wrought such an inconceivably great change into the life of his people, began his work in the eighteenth century. He wrote continually and early in life distinguished himself by capturing a prize in a literary contest for which Kant was a competitor. His subject was "Are Metaphysics susceptible of Mathematical Demonstration?"

His friendship with the dramatist, Lessing, and many other non-Jewish literary men of his time, proved a key to the unlocking of the world to Jewish endeavor. He may be said to have set fire to the intellects of his race. Following Mendelssohn came a great increasing army of Jewish strugglers for political freedom; but even before him, the liberation of minds had begun from traditions still to be loved and cherished, but which were henceforth to be made useful to them as a people, rather than detrimental in their contact with the world. Enthusiasts for their people rose up all over Europe. It was the old effort of Philo to reconcile the ancient Laws with the evolution of human thought; but, in the eighteenth century not one but many hundreds were in the struggle and these had printing presses at their command. Moreover, the peoples about them were all in a locked struggle against class rule. The colonists in America, the peasants and working-classes in France, were all in the throes of a vital protest.

To the support of Mendelssohn writers appeared all over Europe; and while these were largely passionate protestors against the limitation of human rights, and their cries seem to us, today, like a confused medley both in purpose and appeal, yet it was, also, the chaos out of which a real renaissance of Jewish literature was to arise. Suddenly the race began to speak in strange tongues, to write in them, what was even more significant; for it brought the Jews into a harmony with the outer world which to that time they had not known; a better understanding of that world and of themselves, and it taught them to raise their bent heads and to walk erect. Now, early in the last century, the propensity of the race to write began to express itself in departments of literature which, previously, had seemed to be closed to them. The young among them took to general literature; to the writing of romances, and lighter verse. Having acquainted themselves with the fiction of the world at large, they began to translate French, English, German master-works into Hebrew and into Jüdischer-German, which is now known as Yiddish. While their scholars still leaned to "heavy" and controversial writing, Mapu, one of the race devised the first Jewish novel form. Within three-quarters of a century a great man of their people was, if not the leading English novelist, at least among *the world leaders* in this field; one who ranks as the creator of the political novel.

Disraeli, or, as he was later to become, Lord Beaconsfield, was a Jew who shed a peculiarly exalted glory upon his race; in connection with which the words of W. W. Davies, in a recent Hibbert Journal article come insistently to mind: "Democracy must be taught to behave itself decently," if peace is to prevail in civilized communities; if we are to have harmony among the family of nations. For how may it be attained if the authors who, Carlisle so truthfully has said, are the real priests of humanity, persist so unblushingly in propagating their personal racial dislikes by means of disingenuous thrusts at the Jews under circumstances which furnish, of themselves, neither basis nor warrant for them? in ways, when all is said and done, which are opened up solely for the purpose of this ill-doing?

The great majority today read these splenetic outbursts without either weighing or discriminating, which, as Lord Bryce has said, "makes them a much greater danger to the world, than were their illiterate ancestors, for they are much more liable to be misled". And there is scarcely anything to wonder at in their being misled, when one considers the *confidence* with which little living men fall upon the remains of dead great ones, with such unveiled determination to make the evil or the weakness, the little human vanities even, which they once displayed, to live after them, while they leave the good unnoticed, to be "interred with their bones".

These thoughts arise, inevitably, upon laying down, let us say, an essay by Edmond Scherer, on a work of Disraeli. It is peppered all over, apropos of nothing, with references to that author's race; to his racial peculiarities. But take them up, one by one, with a predetermination to be fair minded and what do you find? That in each and every case the features complained of are not merely "Jewish" but human characteristics; Disraeli was a dandy in a day when dandyism was the fashionable fad; when non-Jewish dandies were aped and petted by the fashionable. Brummel was quoted as the pattern on which a D'Orsay might be made. Those dandies perfumed themselves and bedecked their fingers with rings, and idled through life leaving behind them only the amusing record of wasted lives, and a load of debts which might or might not ever be settled. Not being Jews, they come off with allowances made for their weaknesses. Their memories are even cherished as carefully as a bit of porcelain because of their very frailty. Let a Jew depart from his air of inscrutable grief or gloom, from his enforced apart-ness, let him betray his vanities and weaknesses; let him, being in dandydom do as the dandies do, even though, besides, he do mighty deeds, and his weaknesses are magnified to obscure his greater parts, and decried as "Jewish traits".

That Disraeli was attacked in life is a tribute to his greatness. Men in high places are subject to attacks; but that he should continue to be so, dying, and in death, and on the score, primarily, of his race, is testimony not alone to the littleness of the prejudiced mind, but to its cowardice as well. Dead Jews, like dead Christians, are at the mercy of any daws who choose to pick at them. Swift said, truly: "We have just enough religion to make us hate, but not enough to make us love each other", and therein is contained the secret of the racial evils that beset the world.

Scherer wrote of Disraeli as "a foreigner, a Jew who raised himself from an attorney's office to the peerage of England and to the headship of his country's government." This is the sort of author who would write of an incomparable Illinoisan—as indeed many have written—"He was a railsplitter, who raised himself to the presidency of a great Republic."

Nor shall we be wasting time to linger for still another moment to glance at the statement: "A foreigner, a Jew"; for these are terms—they are the borrowed epithets which have been applied of late to Jews in America of the second, third, and even of the fifth and sixth generations. Just what new significance has crept into the word that it should be circulated and made to do such invidious service? A foreigner is a person born in another country. Disraeli and his father before him were native-born Englishmen. His grandfather was a naturalized subject of England. He could not, therefore, be either a foreigner or an intruder, but only a true-born son of Britain in fact as he was in act.

Deep-seated prejudice caused M. Scherer, whom we dwell upon as an example of the prejudiced attitude of the literary critic of forty years ago, to see in the premiership of Beaconsfield numerous other "Jewish charactertistics" calculated to reduce in the minds of future readers his stature whether as statesman or author. As for his literary output, Scherer repudiates Disraeli's characters—those in his novels, as "strangers to us", since they are ambassadors and ministers, dukes and duchesses; but this criticism does not hold good. Authors, we are told, should write of what they know best; not of what someone else knows best. Disraeli lived among the class

of which he wrote. He wrote of a class among whom he
dwelt for the greater part of his life; of a class with whom
his critic certainly had no acquaintance, and from the
standpoint of a mind which was capable of directing the
greatest political events of the greatest empire of his time.

Disraeli was twenty-two when his first novel, *Vivian
Grey* was published. Lady Blessington, travelling on the
Continent read it and wrote of it that "it is a wild but
clever book, full of genius in its unpruned luxuriance.
The writer revels," she says, "in all the riches of a brilliant
imagination and expends them prodigally, dazzling at one
moment by his passionate eloquence and at another by his
touching pathos." Walter Scott was less impressed. He
called the work an "odd" one, and clever, but not sufficiently so to urge him to the effort of going upstairs on a
sultry day to get the second volume! The book, published
anonymously at first, met with a conservative approval as
it was commonly supposed to be the work of a known
diplomat; but, Monypenny says, in his recent life of
Disraeli, that when it transpired that the author was
only an audacious boy, it was promptly denounced as mere
"puffery".

We cannot here follow Disraeli as he mounts the ladder as a literary man, raved over by one set, set upon by
another. Of great literary importance to his race, he
pressed on from book to book in a field of literature until
then unassociated with the Jews, and rose to become and
to remain, to the present, a great Jewish author and a high
peak man in English letters. Much of his life reads like
a romance. Monypenny says that Peel and Stanley's successful effort to keep him out of office at a time when his
political aspirations were greater than his literary ambitions, deserves the gratitude of English lovers of literature; for in the retirement to which defeat forced him for
a time, he originated the political novel, producing *"Con-*

ingsby" and *"Sybil"*. These were destined to continue his reputation, to increase it; to carry it down to the present in the company of the most brilliant literary workers of his century.

Writing to Edward Bulwer Lytton, Disraeli spoke of his own nature as being "naturally somewhat indolent and melancholy"; but to others it seemed phenominally active, and alert with nervous energy, and his eye fixed steadily upon a great goal. Some of the racial energy, perhaps it was, that was wakening the Jewish people all over the European world as he began life.

About the time when *Vivian Grey* was the topic of the hour in London, another Jewish figure that was to leave its impress on nineteenth century literature, left Germany to take up his residence in Paris.

In Russell's literary notes there is painted this picture of Heine, "to whom," a poet has said, "poetry was a plaything"; whose career is at once so brilliant and so pathetic. "For several years preceding Heine's death, he was a miserable paralytic. All that time he lay upon a pile of mattresses, racked by pain and exhausted by sleeplessness, till his body was reduced below all natural dimensions, and his long beard fell over the coverlid like swan's down, or a baby's hair. His muscular debility was such that he had to raise his eyelid as best he could with his hand when he wished to see the face of anybody about him. Thus, in darkness, he thought and listened and dictated, preserving to the very last his precision of diction and his invincible humor."

Heine was a poet whom poets love. "The magic of Heine's poetical form" wrote Matthew Arnold, "is an incomparable . . . blend of French modernism and German sentiment and fullness"; but, he adds "No account of Heine is complete that does not take notice of the Jewish element in him. He treated his race with the same freedom with which he treated everything else; but he derived a great force from it, and no one knew this better than he. But he saw his race, as he saw the world, often, from its comic side." Withal, Arnold thinks him an inadequate interpreter of the modern world. Nevertheless, he found in the poet's head "all the ideas of modern Europe were fermenting", and he sums him up as the most important successor to Goethe in Goethe's most important line of activity; as "a soldier for the liberation of humanity."

"He died," Arnold says, "and left a blemished name" and he instances in detail, Heine's shortcomings. Surely, he had them, in plenty, but how could it be otherwise? One of his earliest teachers is recorded solely because of his zeal in trying "to cuff religion into him". It follows quite naturally that he cuffed it out. Then, too, it must be remembered, Heine's mutinous life ripened at a period when all Europe was mutinous. The literature of his times was all decadent. Even Balzac who, by common consent ranks so high, wrote in glee his *Contes Drôlatiques,* in an attempt to outdo Rabelais. Byron and his school were still the talk of the gay world. Georges Sand, in her *"Histoire de ma Vie",* has told some plain truths of the profligate character of the literary thought of her time, which was also Heine's. The poet's "mutiny" but for that cuffing by the "enlightened", might have spoken in a very different key; but, such as it was, it was in accord with the spirit of his times if uttered in his own characteristic cadences.

The poet Stedman found in Heine a natural successor to Byron. "He begins", says the critic, "where Byron left off. His whole song . . . was full of restless changes from tears and laughter, from melody and love and tenderness to scorn and cynicism and again from agnosticism to faith. In youth, and at intervals until his death, his dominant key was like Byron's—dissatisfaction, longing, the pursuit of an illusive ideal, the love of love, and of fame." How free this master critic is from the smallness and racial prejudices which have distinguished so many others! He judged as a man and a brother. Let us go with him farther.

"Heine", he continues, "was many beings in one; a Jew by race, a German by birth, a Parisian by adoption, taste, and instinct for the beautiful, his outlook was broader than that of the English poet;" but "his writing was also a revolt . . . against the age, against contemporary Philistinism; . . . Byron became a cosmopolitan; Heine was born one. In the world's theatre he stood behind the scenes of the motley human drama. He wrought its plaint and laughter into a fantastic music of his own with a genius both sorrowful and sardonic; always like one enduring life as a penance, and suffering from the acute consciousness of some finer existence, the clue to which was denied him." . . .

Heine felt and often avowed that the actual song-motive is a heart wound without which "the poet cannot sing his sweetliest". He mocked, and younger poets mistook it for gaiety, and, as if they, too, meant it, and felt it, they imitated it "without perceiving it to be neither sane art nor true mirth." But Heine himself, who wrote of the man, "whose nerves, like chords of lightning brought fire to his brain," to whom a whisper was a wound, a look or sneer, a blow; and who, as a consequence, felt "more pangs, in years, or months, than dunce-thronged ages know," wrote from personal experience.

In the careless days of his young manhood Heine changed his faith, at least outwardly embracing what was a newer and more popular one in the circles in which he felt he must win his way. It had been impossible to cuff religion onto him; but for policy's sake, and to overcome obstacles (of prejudice) that lay in his way, he assumed that virtue, though he had it not, and no doubt railed at old faiths and new as he did so. Bacon, however, has truly said that "a little philosophy inclineth a man's mind to atheism, but depth in philosophy bringeth men's minds about to religion". So it was with Heine, who ripened in the university of pain, of dis-illusion, wrote as the world receded, his real views of his ancestral faith, and people.

"I have never spoken with sufficient reverence of them", he penned, "and that, of a truth, because of my Hellenic temperament, which was opposed to Jewish asceticism. My preference for Hellenism has since decreased. I see now that the Greeks were merely handsome striplings. The Jews, however, have always been men . . . even at the present day in spite of eighteen hundred years of persecution and wretchedness. I have, since then learned to value them better, and if every kind of pride of birth were not a foolish contradiction in a champion of revolution and democratic principles, the writer of these pages might be proud that his ancestors belonged to the noble House of Israel; that he is a descendant of those martyrs who have given to the world one God and the moral law, and have fought and suffered in all the battle-fields of thought." And they say his cry at last was: "Judaism is not a religion; it is a misfortune!"

It proved so to Heine, even after death; even so late as 1897, when admirers of his work raised money for a memorial for him which, it was planned, was to have been placed in his birth-place in Germany. Permission to do so however, was refused by the Government. The memorial stands in the city of New York, instead, where, at 161st Street and Mott Avenue, it is passed by thousands each day.

Many brilliant young literary men of his own race frequented the Heine circle in Paris, in the first half of

the last century, with whose names contemporary Europe
was familiar, for they were in the very front of the army
of controversialists who strove through the decades that
led up to the eventful year of 1848 to solve the complex
social problems of the times.   One of the foremost of
these was Karl Ludwig Börne who sleeps in Père la Chaise,
and whose birth-place in Germany was long marked by a
tablet commemorating him.   While he lived Börne's ideas
were defended and controverted by opposing parties all
over Europe.   When he died, the sculptor, David, wrought
a monument expressive of Börne's long-worked-for hope
of seeing Germany and France with hands locked in a
friendly clasp.   This now stands over his grave, still to
make its mute appeal.

Alfred Mels was another of this circle, whose first
literary work in Paris was as aid to Alexander Dumas.
He was a constant wanderer to and from all the art centres of Europe, contributing to many of the foremost
periodicals of his day, and writing numerous plays.   His
most famous work for the theatre, performed in 1872,
"Heine's Junge Leiden," is known to have been performed
over two thousand times.   There were and have continued to be very active Jewish writers in Europe throughout all the nineteenth century; poets, novelists, librettists,
among whom might be named Massarani, Lindau, Auer-
bach, Hartmann, Weill, Jung, Leon Gordon, and a host of
less original writers.   All, however, took an active part
in the literary rousing of their people, for they translated
into Hebrew much of the popular literature of modern
peoples, so introducing to them the thoughts of the outer
world, and stimulating them to measure their strength,
presently, with the non-Jewish authors of the period.

Leon Gordon, who put practically the whole history
of the Jews into verse, was called the leading Jewish poet
of his time, and in Russia not only played a great part in

the political education of his race, but was the hero of very exciting adventures. The leader and inspiration of "the younger generation," he wrote a notable call to the people of his race: "Awake, my people, to the life about you!" meaning, to intellectual progress, and to the realities of modern life. This brought attacks upon him from every conservative Jewish quarter. They served, however, only to stir him to satirical retorts, both in Hebrew and Russian.

Gordon was exceedingly mettlesome; but he had need to be: for, an attempt having been made upon the life of Czar Alexander II, his enemies conspired to get rid of him by accusing him of having had a share in the crime. Though he was shortly exonerated, and made "Honorary Citizen" on the score of the services he had rendered in extending a knowledge of science among the Jews, yet the first results of the accusation was that he, his wife and children were thrown into prison, where they were confined for many weeks. Gordon has been described as a powerful satirist, merciless in scarifying the fanatics among his own people, but quick to take up the cudgels in their defense when others attacked them.

In the first half of the nineteenth century every state in Europe held a group of enthusiasts eager to participate in the intellectual emancipation of their race. In the larger cities of Russia in the early part and middle of last century, the eager young Jewish men are said to have hurried, in throngs, to the schools and universities, which, for the time being, at least, were open to them. Hebrew began to disappear as a common medium of speech, and the younger generations to mingle in the general interests of the communities about them. This great movement among the Jews and for the Jews began in Italy and Austria, but presently the centre of activity was changed to Russia, which, afterward, especially in South Russia, continued to be the active Jewish literary centre, until the last twenty years. Latterly this centre has been perceptibly moving toward America.

An outstanding figure in French literary life, Catulle Mendes, rose at that period. A native Frenchman, Mendes displayed a rich virtuosity in a succession of mystical writings of a genuine art worth. He is, perhaps, one of the most widely read among the *dilettanti* of all modern French authors. His works, which are likely to live among their own class, include *"Legends of Parnasse," "Moorish Nights," "The Midnight Sun,"* and *"Hesperus,"* a strangely brilliant imaginative work inspired by his reading of Swedenborg.

Dr. Max Nordau, though an Austrian by birth, has also been associated with literary Paris in the public thought where most of his works have appeared. His activities and status are too well known to require dwelling upon. Like all his race, he is a force, not always a systematic thinker or writer; but original in ideas. His works, *"Parisian Studies," "The Kremlin and the Alhambra," "Paris, Under the Third Republic,"* the *"True Land of Millions," "The Philosophy of History,"* created a furore in French literary circles and have generally been translated into other tongues, as have been his later works.

Georges Brandes, the Dean of the greater Jewish writers of today, is a profound lover of and worker for his own race. His outlook from his first appearance in the literary world, has been especially broad, and his philosophy, born of a deep study of Mill, Taine, and the leading thinkers of his time, has been uttered with a grace and color that stamp it with his admirable culture and charm. He has contributed notable works to the literature of our time, among his latest being his study of Poland and its people, a volume in which there crowd many literary virtues; clarity, keen observation, color and an augmenting interest in his story as it unfolds. It covers periods of impressions extending from 1885 to 1900, revealing the home life of Poland, the literary groups, and political ones, through a panorama of perfectly drawn pictures.

Brandes caught the public attention first in 1871 with his *"Main Currents in Nineteenth Century Literature,"* which, with his succeeding work, *"Danish Poets,"* fixed him as a permanent star among the world's literary men. He has proclaimed himself an aristocrat, an aesthete; but perhaps the best estimate of him was made by a contemporary who called him "the Insurrectionist *par excellence,* who had given the world freedom to build upon, fresh courage to breathe, and a light to lighten our way." Yet this author, within the decade, and even then a venerable figure, was prohibited from entering Russia to fulfill a lecture engagement on the sole ground of his race.

Taken man for man, and work for work, it cannot truthfully be said that Jewish literature is negligible, or that it goes unread. The best energies of the race go today, as they have always done, to the writing of books. They are among the best known playwrights and novelists of Europe and conspicuous in both classes as writers of plays and novels of purpose. Arthur Schnitzler in Austria, and Henri Bernstein in Paris lead the race in the field of drama. Bernstein's plays, *"le Voleur," "la Rafale," "l'Assaut,"* etc., are in book form, as are most of the voluminous works of Arthur Schnitzler. One of Schnitzler's works, which dealt with racial antagonisms arising in medical circles, *"Professor Bernhardi,"* was the occasion of great excitement in Vienna but a few years ago.

We need not say that the novelist, Zangwill, is the ranking Jewish novelist of his own time. A delightful word-painter, he is hailed and valued by the critical irrespective of race, as an author of the first quality, and especially as the one who expresses, and makes it his life's work to express his own race in his own times. His *"Children of the Ghetto"* has been read by everyone who keeps abreast of current literature. His race hail him as "the Master, Israel Zangwill." Certainly he has painted the inner soul of his people as none has done before him and the passionate zeal he has put into his work has been a trumpet call equally to non-Jews whose outlook is just, and who look to a better understanding of our fellow-beings. To them he has "parted the poor garb of the misunderstood dweller in the ghetto," revealing him as a man and a brother.

Someone has called *"The Dreamers of the Ghetto"* "a series of biographies of struggling souls." A bit of Zangwill's own aspirational soul may be quoted from his proem to *"Italian Fantasies."*

"I, too, have crossed the Alps, and Hannibal himself had no such baggage of dreams and memories, such fife-and-drum lyrics, such horns of ivory, such emblazoned standards and streamed gonfalons, flying and fluttering, such phalanxes of heroes, such visions of cities to spoil, and riches to rifle . . . palace and temple, bust and picture, tapestry and mosaic. My elephants, too, matched his; my herds of mediaeval histories, grotesque as his gargoyled beasts. Not without fire and vinegar have I pierced my passage to these green pastures; *'Ave Italia, regina terrarum!'* I cried, as I kissed the hem of thy blue robe, starred with white cities.

"There are those who approach Italy by other portals, but these be the true gates of heaven, these purple peaks snow-flashing as they touch the stainless sky; scarred and riven with ancient fires and young with jets of living water. Nature's greatness prepares the heart for man's glory. . . .

"I have stood by the tower that gave a smile to Dante; and by the low-hung wall of Padua's university whence Portia borrowed her plumes . . . and have left a footprint on those wind-swept sands where Shelley's mortal elements found their fit resolution in flame. I have lain under Bocaccio's olives and caressed with my eye the curve of the distant Duomo and the winding silver of the Arno. Florence has shown me supreme earth-beauty, Venice supreme water-beauty; and I have worshipped Capri and Amalfi, offspring of the love-marriage of earth and water . . . O, consecration of the purifying dawn, O flame on the eastern altar, what cathedral rose-window can replace thee? O trill of the lark soaring sunward, O swaying of May boughs and opening of flower chalices, what tinkling of bells and swinging of censors can bring us nearer the divine Mystery? What are soul liturgies but borrowed emotions grown cold in the passing and staled by use!" . . .

Many sweet singers of Israel have written in the past fifty years whose contributions have a fixed if minor place among the literature of the world. Living members of the race are striving, even now, for recognition in the world of letters, and doing worthwhile work in every department of literature; but we may well rest here upon the presentation given of the Jew in literature and turn our thought to the work of the race in other departments of human progress.

CHAPTER IX

The Jew in Art

"The Jew, so recent an arrival in the domain of art already has spoken in fine work whether by brush or chisel. He ranks high as a draughtsman and colorist, and has seized, all at once, the implements of art and handled them with a natural skill. Two centuries ago none considered his potentiality in a field theretofore foreign to him. Today the first fruits of the racial genius in marble or on canvas, fill the niches and adorn the walls of the choicest galleries in the world."

A. S.

MUCH capital has been made in the past, and continues to be made in the present by the unfriendly of the fact that the Jew "appears to have no art history"; that they have "neither a past nor a present art status." Usually this assertion is added: that the race lacks art sense. Contrasts are made between Judea, of whose ancient architecture nothing remains but word-painting, no art indications, pictorial or sculptured relic to attest her rank, and Greece, "Mother of Arts and Eloquence," which has left so many priceless records in stone of her past glories. Even such pottery as has been identified as Judean, is of such simple character that, at most, it consists of a flat band of crude color about a vase which is of unmistakeable Phoenician contour.

It is, of course, within the probabilities that some day it will be discovered that all is not ancient that is worm-eaten in the relics of other races, and it may be true, as a modest member of the Jewish race has written, that early Hebrews may have been deficient in form and color sense. It cannot be said truthfully, however, that the Jew of today suffers from any such deficiency. His participation in art, though belated, has been so brilliant; talent has sprung up among them so vitally and from so many differing national groups, as to make argument as to their lack in this field impossible, and also as to indicate as the more logical explanation of their earlier art inactivity, that the barrier that has separated them from it, has lain in the orthodox attitude toward "the graven image or the likeness of anything that is in the heavens above or in the earth beneath," etc.

The Art we know today came into the modern world under the aegis of the ecclesiasts of the Middle Ages, who regarded beauty, color, rhythm as conducive to the devotional spirit. Though Mr. Chamberlain declares it sprang wholly from Greek and Indo-Aryan inspiration, which he regards as so much more lofty than Christian or Biblical concepts, this would seem to be no more capable of being substantiated than are certain other of this Germanophile's claims and utterances. The art of western civilization, like each other feature of it, is a composite thing; a something that has arisen from the crucible which Europe was in the Middle Ages. There is, indeed, in some of the most ancient remains of the early Italian artists, likenesses both in drawing, and in the use of color to the Egyptian, and to other defined Semitic work.

However, there is no gainsaying that the Jews were not identified with the art, or, so far as we can learn, with the fostering of it in any direction. The Jews neither carved nor painted their gods, as one writer has put it. The second commandment was against it. Every effort was made to keep from their synagogue anything that, to them, savored of the ways of idolators. In every land they knew in those old days, gods in the shape of man, or strange beasts, were worshipped. From time immemorial their prophets had preached against the introduction into the synagogue of decorations that might attract the eye and divert the mind from the worship of God. On many sides beauty, which might so well have attracted them, and which tempted them, no doubt, was seen to be steeped in depravity. Presently, as in the case of the later Puritans, Seventh Day Adventists, and certain Baptist and other sects, the revolt of the Jews against the beautiful, as we regard it, became marked, and the austere piety of the teachers continued to ban painting, and statuary, and all worldly allure, for thousands of years.

The more we examine into the Jewish character and into the vicissitudes of the race, the more sharply are the Jews revealed as fundamentally a simple people, and far from the mercenary folk the prejudiced would have us think. In so far as their worldly well-being is concerned they have been woefully shortsighted. Against unpopularity which has cost them their blood, they have adhered to their traditions, though many of these seem to the non-Jew to be outgrown; to their religious forms and customs, with an unparalleled tenacity. Not that theirs is a history clean of backsliding. On the contrary, this has been frequent. That is where the human qualities of the race become so marked. They are forever climbing toward the heavens, and falling or slipping back to the earth; a type race, if you will, as you trace its history, which brings to mind John Bunyan's Pilgrim, making his slow progress toward self-conquest.

For hundreds of years prior to the destruction of Jerusalem, the Jews had been reacting from a period of earlier luxury and general moral laxness, which roused the prophets to repeated denunciation and warning. Their voluptuousness at that period comes in for some violent condemnation from Mr. Chamberlain, who scathes the race for its lapses, its licentiousness, though a few pages farther on he tells us that though Byron was licentious, it "makes us love him." A matter of race, it would appear, decides who may or may not indulge in vice.

In the days of the Jews' worldly splendor, they appear to have indulged at least in a lavish use of art. So early as 624 B. C. all the groves and high places about Jerusalem, even as the groves of Athens, held their carved and molten images. One of the most colorful word pictures in all Jewish literature is that of the boy-king, Josiah, who might have served as model for D'Annunzio's *"Saint Sebastien."* Taught by the austere priests, and filled with the clean zeal of the young, you may follow him, as, intent upon ridding his kingdom of idolatry, he passes through the groves, beating the brazen statues to powder, and breaking down the altars which recreant Jews had set up to false gods, and whom they were worshipping in imitation of the fashions which other nations followed. What they did, in those days, we do today.

No more stirring example of the keen religious conscience of Jewry is anywhere extant than this of Josiah. The wonder is that none of the latter day artists of his race have chosen this boyish, kingly zealot as the subject for a painting. From Josiah's time we hear no more of brazen statues to gods among the Jews. And from these days a kind of recoil, on principle, from art is noted in the Jewish race. Grotius, quoting Tacitus, says: "The Jews look upon every attempt to represent God under the appearance of human form as a profanation of his heavenly nature."

When the Renaissance in literature, art, and science began in Italy and France, united as these countries were through the Medicean alliances, the Jews had been wanderers over the broad face of Europe for a thousand years. If they gave any attention at all to the increasing art activities which were going on around them, it was probably disapproving. There is evidence that the painted and sculptured saints which met them on every hand, appeared in their eyes but another form of the idolatries from which their ancestors had fled. There is nowhere to be found a record of Jewish painter or sculpture in those days; yet Jews, as mathematicians, at least, drew, if they did not paint. A mapmaker of renown lived in Mallorca in the fourteenth century, who seems to have been, in his way and day, a celebrity. Such other skill as the Jews may have had with pencil or brush, or other instrument of the time, was chiefly exhibited in the illuminating of manuscripts, which, even after the discovery of printing, continued to be prized for some time.

The ban of their law tied them, however, from the greater fields of art. They enter into them first in the eighteenth century, when the spirit of revolt, which Schiller has recognized as the spirit of art, began to spread through the modern world. Rousseau, Voltaire, revived and intensified Montaigne's earlier pleas for toleration for all peoples. On every side the hampered cried out for freedom. Personalities as inflamed for their cause as were the early prophets, began to attract the attention of the world. Some spoke for the Jews, so long politically handicapped. Lessing was first among these. Then the Jews began to speak for themselves, not alone as against their political restrictions, but also against hampering, obsolete traditions. A new perception came to many of the race, of the need for being of the world as well as in it, if they were to rise to the height they were capable of as men. Jewish love for the beautiful began to assert its right to express itself.

Quite suddenly miniaturists and portraitists of the race begin to appear in Denmark, in Italy, in Austria, in Germany and England. Among the first names of note to appear in the early eighteenth century is that of Israel Mengs, of Denmark, a miniaturist of worth and distinction. Denmark has since had other native-born Jews who gave value to her art reputation. Karl Bloch, Ernest

Meyer, David Monies, and latterly Geskel Salomon as *genre* and portrait painters are all represented in her galleries.

The Thorwaldsen group, in Rome, so catholic in its attitude toward all who felt the thrill of art accomplishment stirring them, was one of the first to throw open the doors of the democracy of art to Jewish students. Soon they were coming from the north of Europe; from Germany; and a notable figure among the first comers was Edouard Bendemann. But for the real rank to which he rose Bendemann's wealth might readily have kept him classed as a mere rich amateur. He is one of the many examples to be found among the Jews who refute the charge of their being solely material and mercenary.

Bendemann turned from a mercantile career that promised rich rewards, and from an income at hand, to take a chance with fortune with other Berlin lads less fortunately born. With a quartette of others, non-Jews, generally, he started for Rome to take up an art career. No doubt the fact that he was one of the group of whom Moses Mendelssohn was the leading light, accounts for his aspirational surrender of ease, to take up the life of a poor student. He spent many years as such; but when he returned to Berlin, it was to meet a fame that was to go on increasing throughout his career, whether as draughtsman, or colorist. Like so many of the artists, littérateurs, and musicians of his race and day, Bendemann chose his themes from Biblical stories. His many canvases are still to be found in the noteworthy galleries of his native land.

Nor did his reputation end with his life. His greatest work, concerning which much has been written, was *"The Jews Mourning in Babylonian Exile,"* a majestic composition, involving a multitude of figures, each one of which is delineated with remarkable detail, and each of which may be said to be a complete study in itself of grief, of despair, of submission; of accusation, too, as a crowd surrounds the prophet Jeremiah, the central figure of the picture, reviling him as the cause of their tribulations. While preceding them by a full quarter of a century, perhaps even more, this great canvas resembles, in grouping and coloring, the canvases of David, whose later vogue in Paris was so great.

Bendemann was the most widely known and famous Jewish painter of the eighteenth century. The great sought his canvases. On commission for the Crown Prince he decorated several rooms in the royal palace. On all sides, social as well as artistic, he was recognized as a force for the elevation of his people. Rudolph Bendemann, his son, also attained high rank among the mural artists of his day.

From this time on, Jewish artists play an important part in German painting. Moritz Daniel Oppenheim was one of the favored Jewish youths who were able to secure their art education in Rome. He spent years there acquiring a technique, which afterwards brought him fame. He was one of the first Jewish artists to be taken up by the fashionable of the early nineteenth century, and the rich atelier he was able to establish at Frankfort-on-the-Main became a center where the notables of all races met. Oppenheim made the ghettos of Rome familiar to northern people; he undertook also to express with his brush the beauties of the Jewish family and synagogue worship.

Felix Possart, who lived well into the beginning of this century, did notable work with Spanish subjects. His interior of *"the Alcazar, Seville,"* the view of *"the Alhambra from Darrothal,"* the *"Moorish Baths in the Alhambra,"* etc., made him one of the famous painters of Europe.

So early as 1750 Austria had produced at least one

Jewish artist, Raphael Mengs, whose portraits and historical studies stand out. Thereafter she has found her native Jew continuously illuminating the art world. Lájás Bruch, long a resident of London and Paris, first attracted attention in the Salon of 1876. Soon examples of his work were eagerly sought after by critical collectors from Europe and America. Philip Szenes, less known, it may be, in America, has done some of the choicest work produced by the painters of Austria-Hungary. His canvases hang in the Budapest and Dresden galleries, and are to be found principally in the famous private and royal galleries of Europe. None who possesses them regards them as other than enduring contributions to art and civilization. Austria has elevated a German Jew, Friedlander, to the nobility, giving him the new name of von Malheim. His canvases, many of which are Swabian studies, hang in the Imperial galleries at Vienna. His best-known work is his famous *"The Pawnbroker's Shop."*

There died in 1902 a Jewish Hungarian sculptor, who reflected the greatest glory upon his people and upon his native country. The story of Josef Engel reads like an episode of the Michael-Angelo period. Apprenticed in early boyhood to a wood carver, he had the good fortune to find in his employer a man of sympathy and vision, who, perceiving his young helper's ability, assisted the lad to gain entrance to the Academy of Art. We may not follow his progress step by step, but with his first exhibited work he gained unusual recognition. *"The Fighting Amazons,"* the title of this first work, so charmed Prince Albert, the consort of Victoria, that he purchased it at once, paying 600 sterling for it. Thereafter Engel was enabled to spend twenty years in Rome, perfecting his knowledge by an industrious study of the Vatican sculptures. One of his works, *"The Parsee,"* done on commission for Sir David Solomon, Lord Mayor

of London, has attained a world-wide celebrity. The most
notable example of his work in Hungary is the famous
Szechenyi Monument in Budapest, which was unveiled
in 1880.

Now, from quite another direction, we come upon
what in some respects is the most amazing of all the work
done by artists of the Jewish race since their recent entrance into the art field. Russia has been a name
synonymous with unparalleled persecution of the Jews.
This was continuous under the Czars. Nor have matters
actually changed for the better under the so-called Jewish-
Bolshevists' regime. Yet, notwithstanding her reputation, no rulers in the world have been nobler in their recognition and encouragement of the gifted artists of the
Jewish race. Russia has been one with her sons in the
field of art. She certainly has reverenced it and has
looked upon its exponents as "favored of the gods." She
has been generous in the bestowal of honors, and even of
more substantial appreciation upon her painters, her
sculptors, her dramatists, her musicians.

One of the greatest of the Russian artists is the sculptor, Mark Antokolski, a native of Wilna, a city which
has given birth to many Jews who have distinguished
themselves in letters and in the higher professions. In
the beginning Antokolski had not only to battle with poverty, but also against marked racial animosity. Eager for
the aid which associated groups interested in the same
subjects can give to their members, he made application
early in life for membership in the Russian Academy of
Art. He was barred solely because of his race. However, the time came when, having carved some notable
small pieces in ivory, he attracted the attention of the Czar
Alexander II. These pieces have since become very celebrated. They were *"The Jewish Tailor"* and *"The Miser
Counting His Money."*

In recognition of the beauty of this work, the Czar bestowed a pension upon him, which made it possible for him to proceed to the working out of what proved to be his later triumphs. His colossal figure of *"Peter the Great,"* shown at the Exposition in Paris, attracted the attention of the critical of the world. It was followed by another colossal group, *"The Death of Socrates."* This not only won the highest prize for sculpture offered by the Exposition, but also a verdict from a jury of the greatest art authorities in the world, to the effect that the group was the most notable piece of sculpture of modern times.

It is interesting to observe that after this great acclaim Russian art circles developed marked eagerness to overlook Antokolski's race and to welcome him among their members. But their approval was no longer necessary to him. His statue of *"Ivan the Terrible"* caused the Czar personally to name him an Academician. Notwithstanding the odium his race often brought upon him in the beginning, Antokolski took a genuine pride in his origin. His art, however, as the work of great artists should be, is catholic and universal.

A lesser Russian sculptor, who left behind him notable busts of celebrities, was Leopold Bernstamm. He did numerous statuettes, setting a vogue for miniature sculpture among the fashionable art patrons of Paris. Bernstamm made busts of Flaubert, Ernest Renan, Victorien Sardou, François Coppee and many others of the *literati* of Paris, where he occupied a unique position. It is said that the unveiling of a bust by this sculptor was looked upon as a genuine art event. Perhaps, when all is said and done, it will be found that Schiller was right, that art and not the Jews, is the real force operating in the world today for the internationalizing of the human groups.

Nor has Russia been lacking in great painters. Isaac
Lyovich Asknazi struck a high note in his *"Woman Taken
in Adultery."* He has been a prolific painter of Biblical
themes. It has been said that his work is the most Jewish
in spirit of any that has come from the painters of that
race. Asknazi has become identified with domestic types
and Jewish family scenes. One of his canvases, *"A Jewess
Praying,"* attracted attention at the Columbian Exposition, and has since been placed in the St. Louis Museum
of Art.

From Russia, too, came Isaac Levitan, who, though
he ultimately enjoyed a most unusual acclaim throughout European art circles, yet for years he suffered
the extremest poverty and never attained what people,
generally, regard as comfortable circumstances. His
Russian countrymen looked upon him as an artist-
poet. "He knew how to interpret Nature and her mysteries as none other could," said Count Lyov, as he stood
beside the simple grave into which the poet-artist was
being lowered in 1900; and he added: "Levitan's pictures were not mere paintings; they were something more.
We not only saw them, but felt them."

Twenty-five of Levitan's canvases are hung in one of
the notable galleries of Russia. It is said that between
1887 and 1897 he produced about a thousand paintings.
Notwithstanding the fact that he, with other Jews of
Russia, suffered greatly during the '80s, and '90s, an anti-
Semitic paper wrote of him, after his death: "This full-
blooded Jew knew, as no other man, how to make us
realize and love our plain and homely country scenes."
Levitan's pictures, some of which were shown at the
Columbian Exposition, have been appraised as singularly
faithful to the Russian spirit, though marked with sadness; but this is a quality that has often been remarked
in Russian painting, literature and music. It remains a

feature of Jewish expression in the same land. London's great Chief Rabbi Adler has said that the Jewish *scherzo* in fact is little more than an *adagio*.

France, the artistic Mecca of the modern world, has numbered distinguished Jewish artists among her native-born. Albert Lévy has won an enviable reputation for his studies of life in Algiers. Gerôme, Dagnon-Bouveret and others combined to recommend Alphonse Lévy for the Cross of the Legion of Honor. He was prize-winner at the Beaux Arts and at the Paris Exposition and a Member of the French Academy. Jules Worms, a French Jewish artist, took a Salon medal for three successive years, winning it again some years later. American collectors have shown great eagerness to obtain examples of this artist's work.

England, which has produced so many Jews distinguished in statecraft, and which has opened channels in which ability of every kind might express itself, has not, strange to say, numbered very great painters or sculptors among her native-born Jews. Felix Moscheles, son of the musician; Solomon J. Solomon, a Royal Academician, and S. A. Hart are among the most prominent.

And yet the half has not been told of the accomplishments of these but late-arrivals in the free world of art. It would be interesting, though it is not possible here, to trace to its source the stimulus by which the race has been, one might almost say, hurried into this artistic promised land. There were representative Jews, we know, in Florence, Sienna and Pisa and other Italian cities from the beginning of The Renaissance. They must have been aware of the work of Cimabue and Giotto. As a people they were numerous in the Italian cities in the century that gave Titian, Michael-Angelo, Raphael and Leonardo da Vinci to the world. Da Vinci was a great mathematician, as we know, and it is well within the probabilities that he had commerce with the Jewish mathematicians of his age; but nowhere is there any indication of a benevolent association between any of these great artists and the Jewish people.

Perhaps, aside from Rabbinical objection to painting, the social lines may have been too closely drawn to permit of an opportunity for the encouragement of art among the Jews, even had these masters thought of offering it. There can hardly be a doubt that many Jews of that period had art gifts latent in them. Notable rings, made by Jewish industrial artists, still exist in the foreign museums. A tale is told of the fiery Cellini, that most cantankerous of men, finding asylum in one of his only too frequent flights from the law, in the house of a goldsmith, one Raphael del Moro, who must have been a Jew, if we accept the testimony of his name. But the line of early connection between the Jew and art is too pale and indefinite to trace further.

Very different conditions arose, however, in Amsterdam, which proved such a haven to Jews in the sixteenth and seventeenth centuries. In the course of time we find Rembrandt so interested in the race, that he fixed his residence near to the Jewish quarters and there made immortal studies of some of the best types among them. As he painted, his human interest in them increased. He became the friend of Manasseh ben Israel, who afterward was the ambassador between his people and Cromwell and ultimately the instrument by which was secured a readmission of the Jews to England after the banishment of several hundred years.

It would look as though a growing feeling of comprehension of the Jew as a man and a brother began at this period to operate among the nobler minds. Thought breeds fast, whether of good or ill. The portraits of many of the scholarly Rabbis and Jewish men of affairs of

Amsterdam, so sympathetically painted by Rembrandt, went abroad into the finest museums and most notable private galleries of the world. It would seem to be a significant fact, that within a hundred years, every country of northern Europe was claiming more or less notable Jews among her artists. Certainly something of very real importance came to the race through the stimulus of Rembrandt's art and sympathetic comprehension.

In the present day a great Jew has renewed the glory of Holland as an art center. Josef Israels, perhaps, furnishes the most emphatic refutation that could be cited of the charge that the Jews are materialists who care for nothing but the getting of money. Israels was born to money, to quantities of it. His atmosphere was well calculated to stir him to the acquisition of more. His father, a prosperous banker, desired nothing better than to have his son follow in his footsteps. Indeed, it is said, he went so far as to compel the youthful Josef to serve him as bookkeeper, in order to instil business principles in him.

However, he soon had cause to excuse the young man from this task, for he discovered his ledger pages to be decorated, not with figures such as he desired, but with fanciful sketches, which were more to his progeny's taste. When he could no longer withhold his consent to his son's entering upon an artistic career, the elder Israels gave it with no good will, but cut him off with the merest pittance of an allowance. The youth, however, stuck to his resolution. He travelled, he studied Delacroix, Diaz, Millet. He studied, in fact, all schools of art which were in vogue in the middle of the last century. Presently he created his own, incomparably soft in atmosphere yet firm in draughtsmanship and exquisite in color and modelling. So prepared, he returned to Holland to make his immortal studies of the peasants and fisher-folk of Amsterdam.

Israels has been summed up by world-famous connoisseurs as having attained the extreme of realism in depicting life's sober side, its toil and sacrifices. He has contributed as none other of his time to the glory of Holland, and it may be said, without fear of contradiction, to the culture of the world. He has received more medals and decorations than we may here enumerate. Though he has recently passed away, he has left treasures in canvases which stand as landmarks in the art of the nineteenth and twentieth centuries and are represented in every notable collection in the old and new worlds.

In the eighteenth century there were Jewish as well as non-Jewish painters in America. Modest, most of them, none have left work behind them of more than sentimental value; but it may be said that when artists of worth began to paint here, the richer members of the Jewish population were among the first to encourage such painters as Stuart, Sully, George P. A. Healy, Charles Wilson Peale, Jeremiah Theus, John Wesley Jarvis and others. One of the most beautiful of the Gilbert Stuart paintings was of Mrs. Solomon Moses, who was sister to the famous Rebecca Gratz, and herself a lovely type of her race. Rebecca Gratz has been identified as the model from whom Scott drew his inspiration for the Jewish maiden in *"Ivanhoe."* Miss Gratz and her father were both painted by Thomas Sully, the canvases being now in Montreal, in the collection of Henry Joseph, Esquire.

By the beginning of the nineteenth century admirable work was in sight from American Jewish artists; and, as the century advanced, we find the two Rosenthals, Max Weyl and others attracting the attention of the critical. Henry Mosler, H. N. Hyneman, and George deM. Peixotto, all have contributed important service in the building up of art interests in the United States, and their lists were soon to be swelled by the names of Albert

Sterner, Koopman, Meilziner, and numerous *genre* painters, portraitists, water colorists and etchers, many of whom have established reputations abroad as well as at home.

The most distinguished craftsman of his race which America can as yet claim is the *genre* painter, Henry Mosler. His is a permanent position in the world's art roll. Mosler exhibited his canvas, *"The Return of the Prodigal Son,"* at the Paris Salon in 1888, and it was almost instantly purchased by the French Government for the Luxembourg. Within a year he received the Salon Gold Medal, and the Gold Medal of Carl Ludwig of Austria. In 1892 France made him a Chevalier of the Legion of Honor. Four years later he won the Thomas B. Clarke Prize at the New York National Academy of Design. Two of his notable works went into the collections of rich amateurs of his own race, *"The Wedding Feast"* being purchased by the late Jacob H. Schiff, and *Invoking God's Blessing,"* by the late Henry E. Seligman. Albert Sterner's beautiful watercolors and notable book illustrations rank high among the pictorial products of the time. Peixotto has attained a position of value through his portraits of such notable men as the late President McKinley, John Hay, Sir Moses Montefiore, Cardinal Manning and others.

When we come to consider Moses Ezekial we reach a representative Jew who has given to the world the most distinguished sculptures of which his race in America can boast. Born in Virginia, Ezekial was knighted by the King of Italy and by the Emperor of Germany. Always proud of his American birth, however, he never relinquished his citizenship, though he spent many years in other lands. He was a lad when the Civil War broke out. At fourteen he was fighting in the ranks with the Confederate Army. When the great struggle was over,

Ezekial turned to the study of painting; but we soon hear of him as a sculptor in Rome, where he settled after a period of study in Germany. His statue of "Eve" was placed in the Emperor's Palace there. One of the first works from his chisel to attract American attention was the colossal bust of Washington which stands in the Cincinnati Art Museum. His heroic figures of Phidias, Raphael, and other artists fill the niches of the Corcoran Gallery at Washington. La Chapelle de la Charité, at Paris, and St. Margaret's at Westminster, both contain specimens of this sculptor's work, and others adorn many cities in the old and new world.

From the lesser countries of Europe, and from South America, Jewish artists are coming into view. Excellent work which hangs in galleries at Adelaide and Melbourne is from the brushes of native Australian Jews. One of the first institutions to be established in Palestine is a school for instructions in the arts.

This record of Jewish contributions to the art of the last and the present centuries is incomplete; yet it should be sufficient to indicate the Jew's large share in late additions to the culture of the world. But let us turn to his part in another field, that of music.

CHAPTER X

The Jew in Music

Jubal was already acknowledged as "the father of all such as handle the harp and the organ" in 3,875 B. C. The Jew was the first to recognize the pathological value of Music. When Saul, about 1100 B. C. having ceased to commune with God, was troubled by an evil spirit, his servants begged him to permit them to seek out "a man who is cunning with the harp; for it shall come to pass that when an evil spirit is upon thee, he shall play with his hand and thou shalt be well." When permission was given, they besought Jesse to allow his son to soothe the king. "And it came to pass that David took an harp and played with his hand; so Saul was refreshed and the evil spirit departed from him".

A. S.

(See Genesis 4.21; and I Samuel, *16.* 14-23)

TO get an approximate idea of the influence of the Jew in music, it is necessary to glimpse the history of this youngest yet most ancient of the arts before we reach its remarkable and so recent revival and expansion. Its origin is lost in the remote past. Goethe said of music that "it stands so high that no understanding can reach it, and an influence flows from it which masters all and for which none can account. Hence, religious worship cannot dispense with it. It is one of the chief means of working upon men miraculously." Ergo, from the beginning all religious rites have had their musical elements. Before arriving at its present forms, it has passed through many vicissitudes, enjoying periods of favor in alternation with those of reprobation. It can hardly be said to have attained the stature of modern art until within the past four hundred years. The Jews have shared in its development scarcely more than a hundred years.

When we take into consideration the great Opera Houses of the present day, the innumerable concert halls;

the hosts of persons variously gifted who find their place
in life in the entertaining of others by music; the armies
of instrumentalists, soloists, and group singers; the
teachers for the training of these hosts; the schools, the
conservatories; the choral societies and orchestral bodies
that are now a feature of every city of size in the world;
the numerous instrument-makers and publishers who supply this world of music, it is difficult to grasp the fact that
music only began to attain its present social and commercial as well as art significance in the sixteenth century.

Fathered by Palestrina, "Prince of Music," but
grandfathered by the magnificent Lorenzo of the Medicis,
whose May Songs are the notable relics of his day, it
branched into its present form, its present scales, phrases,
and contrapuntal complexities, in Italy, where Jews were
many, and artists flourished there as never before. A
careful reading of the literature of those and anterior
times would lead to the supposition that the Jews, though
apart from the Christian world, nevertheless may have
been healthy supporting influences in the developing
period of the art. There is scarcely a doubt that their
enforced international character had a most useful part
in the work. Even as the Crusaders, in passing back and
forth, carried from place to place melodies from Spain
which, in turn, had come through the Arabs, so the Jews,
wherever they travelled, in addition to their treasured
tunes from old Judea, bore with them such pleasing folk
airs as they might catch up as they passed. Such airs,
hummed or strummed, first by this and then by that group,
soon formed a link between group and group—a sort of
international bond of interest.

It is a tradition among the Jews, but one which historians of music dispute, and with some show of reason
in special cases, that the tunes used then and continuously
even up to the present time in their orthodox services,

have come down in their exact original state from the period of the dispersion. There are even said to be extant and in use tunes which were used by David. These moot points we shall not attempt to clear up here. The important fact is that the Jews religiously preserved, from generation to generation, their early synagogue music. None but a race in which music was inherent would so reverence it.

In post-Biblical days they seem gradually to have discarded instrumental music in their worship, though prior to the destruction of the Temple it had been an important part of its ceremonies. Many instruments were kept in the Temple at Jerusalem, in order to have them ready for the priests when required. This custom evidently was continued in the Turkish synagogues to a late day; for it is recorded that in the twelfth century a deposit of ancient instruments was found in an upper room of a synagogue at Bagdad.

To diverge for a moment: The upper rooms, and the inner ones, of the old synagogues often concealed for centuries relics of the utmost importance. It was the custom to use them as depositories for outworn Temple accessories, which sentiment forbade them to destroy. It was due to the renovation of the Temple that Hilkiah, the High Priest, forbear of the Prophet Jeremiah, looking among such discards, came upon the Book of the Law, the last work of Moses, upon which all later Jewish writings have been based. In a similar way the late Dr. Solomon Schecter, while still attached to Cambridge University, came upon the priceless deposit of scrolls and manuscripts in an upper room of a Jerusalem synagogue, which are now to be seen at the Jewish Theological Seminary in New York City.

So far as has been ascertained, however, these manuscripts reveal nothing of the Jews in music in the

present era. It is said that in the eleventh century the folk
airs of other peoples had begun, to the great indignation
of the orthodox, to affect the Jews' traditional melodies.
One of their historians has noted that "the Rabbis began
to observe with alarm spirited lovers' songs applied to holy
psalms."   To them this was nothing less than sacrilege.
They protested vehemently, but without lasting effect.
Change, though operating with them so slowly as to be
almost imperceptible, was in the air.   Several years later
we come upon a gifted musician, a contemporary of Palestrina, one Israel Najara, a Rabbi of Gaz, who published in
1579 six hundred Hebrew lyrics, set to the choicest melodies of Arabia, Spain, Italy, Turkey and Greece.   Even he
was frowned upon by the orthodox Rabbis, whose rule
was "that the traditional must not be varied in any place,
even in the matter of melodies to which the people are not
accustomed."

But if we may trust the incidents which early
romancers have woven into their stories—those which
elaborate the D'Annunzian poetic dramas, which, however adorned by that author's incomparable imagination,
are generally regarded as historically accurate—there
were Jews skilled in music who went about from country
villa to country villa, singing to and teaching the ladies the
songs that were the latest fashion in Florence or in Rome,
and making an honest penny in that very pleasant way.
Those who were domiciled in these cities, however, do not
figure in the musical records of those times.   It may be
that in this field, as has happened in some others, notably
in literature, they have lacked historians, and, consequently, some of their just dues.

In 1622 we find them publishing music in Venice,
where Solomon de Rossi, regarded as "The Father of
Modern Synagogue music," began what was spoken of as
"the regeneration of Zion's songs."   He seems to have

been supported by a number of progressive Rabbis, who, like certain Methodist clergymen of a later date, had waked up to the mistake of "letting the devil have all the pretty tunes."

Rossi introduced perfected counterpoint and polyphonic music into the synagogues. A critic of the time has said that he brought into his music a wonderful homogeneity and the echoes of many lands and peoples, together with a new and surprising dramatic quality. However, he appears not to have been sufficiently popular to maintain the new music against the steady opposition of the traditionalists, or to attract the attention of the non-Jewish world.

It should be said, however, that the orthodox Rabbis were no more opposed to the innovations that were being introduced into their music than were sundry Christians who threw their energies into opposing the development of the same art. Those who had to do with it, came in for abuse or derision from many such quarters. In England, in 1579, Stephen Gosson felt such scorn for musicians and all who dallied with them that he wrote a book entitled: *"The Schoole of Abuse conteining a Pleasaunt Invective against Poets, Plaiers, Pipers, Jesters, and Such like Caterpillers of the Commonwealth."* His work is a monument to the estimate placed by some upon music in the great Elizabethan age. When Gosson wrote, Shakespeare had not arrived to define music as "the food of love."

It may be added, as time went on, far from softening toward the new and multiform instrumental music, the orthodox Rabbis, as it became increasingly a feature in the Church's services, held more and more rigidly to their rule of excluding it. Even today the organ has no place in their Temples. In New York, in the twentieth century, its use has been preached against. In 1815 a notable instance occurred of Jewish determination to keep a feature so profane from desecrating their services. By this time the thought of emancipation had begun to operate in a large part of the race. It was not an emancipation from the spirit of their Laws, but rather from the letter that bound upon them forms and phrases that were obsolete. Their worship became, if anything, more fervent than it had been, but they sought to relieve the austerity of, and to beautify the synagogue ceremonies. A new edifice was built in Berlin and a distinguished Rabbi invited to dedicate it. An organ had been installed, but when the clergyman saw it, he recoiled with horror. He denounced it loudly, and carried his complaint to the King, with the plea that the synagogue be closed. It is interesting to learn that his prayer was granted. However, three years later another attempt was made by the Hamburg progressives, and this time, by means of a compromise the organ remained, a non-Jewish organist being brought in to play it.

It will be seen that the entry of the Jew into this modern art field was no easy matter. On the one side religious traditions bound him; on the other, there was the opposition of non-Jews. For centuries the musical guilds, unions, societies, had put up barriers against admitting Jews to membership, even as the artisan guilds and unions throughout Europe had barred them. How marvellously they have broken down prejudices, how triumphantly they have taken rank in the new art will be seen by glancing over even an incomplete outline of the story of the last century.

Co-incidentally with their appearance as composers, interpreters, music begins to enchain the interest of all classes. Examine the records of it for the past hundred years, and you will find that through educational, municipal, religious and other agencies, it has superseded both painting and sculpture in the ordinary life. Musical instruments in some form, though it be only mechanical, are to be found in every household, in every public gathering-place. Because its pathological value has been definitely ascertained, it finds a place in every hospital and public institution. The insane are soothed by it, and prisoners made more readily amenable to the authorities under whom they are placed. Children are drilled to it at school, and at home entertained by it. You dine with it in public places, pray with it in church.

The universal application of music, its progress step by step, may be traced to the time of the appearance of the Jew in the modern musical world. This, very naturally, calls up the question as to how far the race is responsible for bringing about this condition. Have they done anything besides popularizing music, and if so, what? This question was put to one whose income is derived from a Jew's enthusiasm for the art. His answer came with a glance in which there was at least a shade of indignation, and unmistakable contempt.

"What have they done?" he asked, with an accent on the "have" which held a sting. "They claim a lot, but have they produced a Liszt, a Wagner, a Gounod, a Paganini or Paderewski?" Now, counter-questions of this sort—hurled so suddenly at one who is not a specialist in an art so crowded as music—being in the nature of a "poser," they brought a reply that began tentatively:

"Possibly not—and yet—" But here courage returned—"Yet, when you come to think of it, it is not more than a century since a musical career became possible to the Jews. In that time they have given the world a Moscheles—"

"A Moscheles"—this with a shrug of the shoulders, and a glance of pitying amusement.

"True, his vogue may be passing; but in his time he not only composed fine scores, which are still heard in modern repertories, but he was among the first Jews who made themselves acceptable in the art to critical London. It hailed him as the conductor of its greatest Philharmonic Orchestra. Besides, he taught and inspired many greater musicians. Mendelssohn-Bartholdy was one of these, who in his day, as composer, conductor, and pianist, 'literally carried all before him.' Marchesi, in her memoirs, says that 'London worshipped' Mendelssohn. His *'Songs without Words,'* his *'Walpurgisnacht'* music, his *'Elijah'* and *'St. Paul,'* etc., etc., are surely true art products. When Judah spoke through Mendelssohn-Bartholdy, it was with a heavenly voice that still charms the world.

"There is Meyerbeer, creator, as Liszt called him, 'of Cyclopean melodies.' He dazzled his contemporaries and after-generations as well with his splendor of imagination. In return for his contribution to art, in *'L'Africaine,'* *'Les Huguenots,'* *'Le Prophete,'* etc., he was rewarded by medals and other distinctions from every civilized government. His bold operatic pictures, theatrical, if you will, undoubtedly stimulated Wagner for the great work he was to do. It is said that Wagner 'had no use for Jews,' yet he accepted with no *ill-will* substantial aid when necessary from Meyerbeer, who was the son of a rich banker.

"The race has given Rubinstein to the world, not only a great composer, but one of the three great pianists of the last century, the others being Liszt and Carl Taussig. Taussig was a Jew from Poland, whose Jews of late have been very bitterly denounced, in one instance, chiefly because the orthodox among them wear beards and gabardines. Beards, by the way, have not so long been out of fashion in America. All the great heroes of Lincoln's day wore them, and a study of Watts' portrait of Burne-Jones will show that that most aesthetic of the artists of the period had been at pains to acquire a thoroughly Jewish hirsute adornment. Apropos of Carl Taussig; it was he who devised the plan by which 300,000 thalers were raised for the building of Wagner's Bayreuth Theatre—"

But here the interlocutor, uncomfortable, remembered an engagement. We may dismiss him and consider farther the part the Jews have had in music. Elsewhere it is suggested that the art movement among the Jews nearly a century earlier may have been due in a great part to Rembrandt's sympathy and understanding of the race, of whom he made so many studies. He certainly revealed them to the world in a dignity theretofore unknown. In considering the sudden recognition of the Jew in musical art, there would appear to have arisen another very different, yet even more powerful force in his behalf in the person of Handel. In so far as is known none has inquired into the effect upon the public of his day of that master's musical treatment of Biblical themes. They were entirely new music-forms. Their stories were emotional appeals for the Jew, whom they raised immediately into prominence. They held up the race's heroic, its noble, and its pathetic past in a manner altogether electrifying. They put the Jew into the art thoughts of the world; into the one art of all others which could lift the human being from the sordid and mean of the daily life, to higher concepts of mankind.

We are told that Handel's Oratories, for almost a generation, met with every form of abuse. There is reason for supposing that some of this arose from his exaltation of the Jew, who, then, even more than at present, was a "problem" which everyone was thinking of, talking of, writing of; but the encroachments of rival composers from Italy, at first glance, had more to do with Handel's innovations. He was confronted with competitors who threatened his popularity; but he was the last man to give ground in such a struggle.

The greatest musical figure of his time, Handel may be said literally to have forced his works upon the London public. He did so at a time when Moses Mendelssohn, in Germany, was beginning his great mission that was to lead the Jewish people to their present political freedom by way of the University and general education. Mendelssohn in Berlin, through letters, and Handel, working through the emotions and imaginations in London, each had part in affecting a change in that variable quantity which we call public opinion.

Mendelssohn worked with a definite and high hope in view. In all probability, Handel had nothing in mind beyond the downing of Italian rivals, whose operas were proving more to the taste of Londoners than his own. He was probably an unconscious instrument acting under the directions of the great Maestro, but he went to his work with a will. As is known, he was naturally catholic in his attitude toward mankind. He drank his beer with equal satisfaction in the company of the dyer, the artist or his own secretary. He refused to differentiate between man and man, on the mere ground of race or religion.

When he set out with his Biblical compositions in their new oratorio forms to defeat the Italians who had superseded him so successfully with their more frivolous operas, all the cliques in London opposed him. He ceased to be fashionable—for a time. Horace Walpole said that since foreign singers would not sing for him, Handel hired all the farce goddesses and variety-hall singers in town to give voice to his great *"Hallelujah Chorus."*

But little cared Handel for Walpole's satire; or anyone else's. *"Samson," "Joshua," "Israel," "Susanna," "Judas Maccabeus"* poured from him, one after the other, an inexhaustible stream from an inexhaustible source, which was to have its part in stimulating a race through its emotions to a new self consciousness; for it is impossible not to think that the Jews, who turned out in numbers to hear the new Oratories, who bought their scores, and studied and discussed them, did not feel in those stirring emotional pictures, a great inward thrill of new possibilities in them. Similarly, it is impossible to avoid the thought that the very tradesmen of the city, who thronged to hear the new music—they could do so and easily, since admission to it was to be had for the payment of a shilling; real "pops" these performances were— looked thereafter upon their Jewish neighbors with a new interest, a new enquiry.

A great many forces now began to work to open the way for the Jews in music. The statesmen of the day were all discussing the advisability of removing "the disabilities" under which the race lived among them. Jewish men of family were admitted, if somewhat tentatively, into the German Army, on equal terms with other men. Voices more potent than those of Statesmen or pamphleteers began to utter their plea to the common mind, for brotherhood among men. Schiller wrote his *Ode an die Freude,* which moved Beethoven, the artist of artists, who "had the gift to feel and understand his Maker's presence," to speed, through his music, a message of universal brotherhood in his *Ninth Symphony,* which was to roll on through the centuries. Shubert sings his *"Hagar's Lament"* and his *"Bonds of Humanity";* everywhere, art, through her many agents, begins the melting away of the fetters which prejudice and the cruelty of creeds, greed and politics had welded about the Jews for a thousand years and more.

Suddenly, in a paean of grateful joy, the race breaks into melody. Moscheles comes from Bohemia to London, young, ardent, with concertos and sonatas in his hand, of such quality that the world turns to examine him. One of his first offerings was his *"Homage à Beethoven."* He, preceding and also surviving his pupil, Mendelssohn-Bartholdy by many years, in many respects was a pathfinder for his race. The hours of delight, of exaltation, which Ignatz Moscheles, as an artist, and through his greater pupils, provided for the modern world, form a contribution of immeasurable value to civilization. At twenty-four he was teaching Mendelssohn-Bartholdy. A few years later we find him, succeeding Sir Henry Bishop, as conductor of the London Philharmonic Society. His Concertos in *G Minor* and *"Pathetique"* were in high vogue, as they are among today's musicians. Moscheles was to be followed, however, by a long line of Jewish musicians, who were, if not to obscure him, at least to overshadow him by the brilliancy of their talents. They were destined, indeed, to illuminate all musical history.

Mendelssohn-Bartholdy, his pupil, has been summed up as one of the most electric and original musicians who ever lived. Grandson of Moses Mendelssohn, one of the world figures of his day, fortune, birth, circumstances, all combined to give aid to Felix Mendelssohn's genius. Volumes have been written about him (some by Moscheles and his son) and about his compositions. As an instrumental composer, he ranks nearer to Beethoven than any musician of his century, and that a wonderful century for its chorus of masters, minor and major. Ferdinand Hiller was not one of the least of these. Liszt, who knew them both and who has painted an immortal pen picture of a group gathered about the chair of the declining Chopin, of which Hiller was one, said of Hiller, that whether as a pianist or composer for the piano, he was allied, at least in spirit and technique, with the Polish artist.

Halévy—in whose veins ran blood that might be traced back to the most glorious days of Spain, and thence into the ancient line of Levi, wrote, besides many lesser operas, his masterpiece, *La Juive*. Like Moscheles and

Hiller, he also taught, and among his pupils were many who outshone their master, Gounod, Bizet, and Bazin among them. Nor was the race to derive its glory in music through the instrumentalists only. Famous singers came from their ranks, John Braham (abbreviated from Abraham) among others, who held for three decades the first rank at Covent Garden; directors and impresarios—numbers of them, began to appear, who were to prove powerful distributors of music, promulgators of it. Otto Goldschmidt, though he walks in the shadow of his incomparable wife, Jenny Lind, was not only distinguished as "a gentleman of the highest general culture," but as an accomplished musician, co-worker with Sir William Benedict in the development of music in London, and in the founding of the Bach Society. He directed some of the greatest musical festivals of his time.

Liszt is said to have caught up the Jewish child prodigy, Anton Rubinstein, clasping him in ecstacy as he declared: "He shall be my musical heir!" As the genius of Rubinstein grew with his physical growth, he, presently, was hailed as few pianist-composers have been hailed, in all corners of the earth. It is said that the Czar was so proud of his Jewish subject, that he addressed him, smilingly, as "your Excellency". When under the charm of music Russia has always forgotten her tendency to racial discrimination. She was proud to number her Jewish geniuses among her great and in innumerable instances her Czars have smoothed the way for them. So late as in the great world war, Efram Zimbalist and Micha Elman, great among living violinists, were excused from military service, that they might be secure to the art world. Karl Goldmark was another of Russia's distinguished Jewish sons, whose *"Queen of Sheba"* was first presented at the Metropolitan Opera House in 1885 by Anton Seidl. Other of his notable work was the writing of the score for the poetic Indian drama "Sakuntala" by Kalydas.

Nor may we omit Jacques Offenbach, whose lively burlesques have put gaiety into the heart of the world. Had Offenbach been a poet, he would have been a parodist. As it was, he created that form of music which we call burlesque opera, or, *opera comique*. Having first set his muse to work upon parodies of la Fontaine's fables, he shortly thereafter met with success as the composer of music for de Musset's "La Chandelier". Afterward America came to know him through his later works, *"Barbe-Bleu" "La Grande Duchesse de Gerolstein"; "la Belle Helene"* and others.

France cherished many Jewish musicians, among them in the later days, Saint-Saens, and the director Edouard Colonne, (in private life, Jules Juda). In whatsoever line you follow them, the contributions of Jewry to music, is endless, and inestimable. The great violinists, Wienawski, Joachim, Joseffy; the most famous directors and impresarios—a volume might be devoted to them. Max Maretzek, one of the pioneers in this field to spread a taste for opera in America, conducted in New York in 1848, and "made opera fashionable" as it had not been before in the young republic. He dared much in the way of introducing new works, many of which have become permanent in the repertories of great Opera Houses. He introduced his child sister-in-law, Adelina Patti to America; also Piccolomini, Minnie Hauck, and Lucca, and himself wrote the opera, "Hamlet". "One of the most lovable of men", as he was called, he lived to celebrate his "golden jubilee", in which the greatest musicians of his time took part.

Maurice Grau, Alfred Hertz, a list too long to be given here, all in turn have made their contributions to a world which forgot under the charm of their genius to think of race or creed.   Again, few musicians have had so great a part in educating the American public to an appreciation of the profounder elements in music than Dr. Leopold Damrosch, founder of the Oratorio and the New York Symphony Societies, and notable as the musician who established German Opera (in 1884) in the Metropolitan Opera House repertory. Dr. Damrosch, whose degree came to him through Columbia University, not only gathered the first German company to be heard at the Metropolitan, but himself conducted them.   He was esteemed the greatest conductor of his time; but, what was more, as one has written, "no man, unless, it may be, Theodore Thomas, has contributed so much as he to the cultivation of good music in America".

In view of even this fragmentary telling of the Jews' contribution of music to the world, can any ask the question today: What have they done for civilization?

CHAPTER XI

The Jew in Mathematics; in Physics

*"In the achievements of science there is not only
beauty and wonder, but also beneficence and power.
It is not only that she has revealed to us infinite space
crowded with unnumbered worlds; infinite time peopled by unnumbered existences; infinite organisms
hitherto invisible, but full of delicate and iridescent
loveliness; but also that she has been as a great Arch-
angel of Mercy, devoting herself to the service of
man. She has labored, her votaries have labored, not
to increase the power of despots, or add to the mag-
nificence of courts, but to extend human happiness, to
economize human effort, to extinguish human pain.
. . . She points not to pyramids built during
weary centuries by the sweat of miserable nations, but
to the lighthouse and the steamship, to the railroad
and the telegraph . . . She has lengthened life;
she has minimized danger, controlled madness, tram-
pled on disease . . ."*

ARCHDEACON FARRAR.

NOTWITHSTANDING the honor which the world
of scientists yields to their Jewish confrères, the
Messrs. Michaelson, Bergson, Einstein, and a host of
lesser men, who, nevertheless, have made and are making
continually, great discoveries toward improving conditions of life for humanity, there have been published, and
recently, a vast amount of deliberate mispraisement of the
Jew in science as in other departments of life, and ingenious
arguments, the purpose of which is to minimize his present-
day worth, and to deny his race a position among the
pioneers in the field of physics. It is not surprising if the
uninformed, overwhelmed by the dogmatic positiveness of
such a rabid foe to the Jews as Mr. Chamberlain—who
angrily deplores that "Walhalla and Olympus became de-
populated because the Jewish priests wished it so"—

should take on similar prejudice and beliefs; or that they should accept his violent assertions when he declares that it was the Jews' scorn of science which long retarded the spread of knowledge along scientific lines. Nor is it to be wondered at if the uneducated, seeing in a news-sheet a belittling allusion to the uselessness of star-measuring should find themselves repeating such idle estimates of the scientific seekers, especially in connection with the measuring of Betelgueuse.

Mr. Chamberlain's statement is an interesting admission in more ways than one. It ascribes to a people strictly "inferior", and he so names them over and over again, powers which only a distinctly superior people could possess. This contradiction is a common characteristic, as has been pointed out in another connection, of the resolute anti-Semite; but few so often display it as does the writer just referred to. He pronounces the Jews "mentally sterile", and presently shows them to be the most mentally active people in the world, dangerously creative in fact; he undertakes to prove them the most money-worshipping race in the world—by means of a characteristic with which he invests the matriarch Rebekah—and denies them wit enough to invent numerals.

To prove their stupidity he says that in sharp business transactions "one Armenian is a match for three Jews." He resorts, as well, to quoting Apion's time-worn accusation—ascribing it to Wellhausen—that "the Jews never invented anything," and he attaches a deal of indexed learning to prove that the race has never even been near to "grasping the eel of science"; to prove, as well, that all the Jewish people knew—they with a known history of three thousand years, and a traditional one of many thousands more—they borrowed, he says, from their young neighbors, the Greeks, who came into existence 800 B. C.

The reconciliation of divergencies of this sort, however, is a task for the archaeologist. The modern individual is scarcely concerned with them. The reasoning individual by this time is pretty sure that "the manifold structure of civilization" necessarily must have been erected by the common effort of a multiplex humanity. Common facts in science known to the early peoples can no longer be traced to a single human group. The dwellers by the waterways learned to make their primitive water-crafts, as those on the plains made their caravans, simultaneously, necessity being the mother of invention. The Chinese, with a long sea-coast, (the Phoenicians, similarly, later) are said to have been the first to guide their craft by a given star; the first to devise a compass, which, as Locke has said, has done more to increase the production and invention of useful commodities than the building of factories.

Chinese navigators probably traversed the Indian ocean, directing their way with a compass, at a time when the Grecian and Phoenician fleets, propelled by cautious oarsmen could but crawl along the shore save when the polar star was visible to guide them. The Greeks, we know, were still regarding the sun as a great fiery torch in the heavens, a something lighted and extinguished each day, long centuries after the Hebrew patriarchs had recognized it as a something that "marched in the procession of heavenly bodies"; a work of God, and part of a great system. Long, immeasurably long before the writing of the book of Genesis—for science led and did not follow literature, as Francis Bacon has made clear—men from China to the Assyrian plains, thence on to Palestine where the stars still sparkle and glow incomparably in the bosom of night—men whose names we shall never know, searched the spangled depths above them in awed curiosity. Who they were, nothing is left to tell save the precious traditions of the Jews; but one of them, looking into the night has left his immortal impression of the wonders he beheld there. "The Heavens declare the glory of God and the firmament showeth His handiwork." "When I consider Thy Heavens," wrote one of the early psalmists, David, or another, "the work of thy fingers, the moon and the stars which thou hast ordained; what is man that thou art mindful of him?" These observers of the skies, who lived approximately about 1000 B. C. make notable allusions to all manner of living things, showing that natural philosophy was making its appeal to them, as well.

Jewish tradition, at least as reliable as any other, and given to the world not by a careless scribe, but by the scholar Josephus, of priestly birth and instruction, indicates that under the Pharoahs the Jews were already acquainted with simple mathematics, for they built city walls, cut river channels and made dams "to restrain the river"; and, the historian adds, they even had part in the building of the lesser pyramids, all of which feats required knowledge of a high order, which was surely not possessed by a mean people. But this Mr. Chamberlain ignores and pictures the Jews in this wise:

Having analyzed the race from many angles, and found them, as Semites, to be lacking in all fine qualities, he proves conclusively that they were not full Semites, but half Syrians, which race, to this point he has praised highly. But, having proven the Jews of thousands of years ago to be half-Semites and half-Syrians, he proceeds to show that *they had also a large admixture of Indo-European, with possibly Sumero-Accadian blood in their veins!* According to the reports from the latest excavation fields, this is going farther back than even the Jews claim to trace their ancient origin. It also supports their claim to a very early culture, bearing most favorably upon the race as being connected with the developing science of the Sumero-Accadians, who, as predecessors of the Chaldeans, are credited with being the most advanced people in that early world; for Abram, the acknowledged father of the Jews, is also identified as having come out from the city of Ur in the land of the Chaldeans.

Abram, who lived considerably more than 4000 B. C. as Josephus tells us, was a wise and sagacious man "when he discoursed on any subject he undertook; and this not only in understanding it, but in persuading other men also to assent to him". He argued religious points with the Egyptians, and "was admired for his wisdom"; and, "he communicated to them arithmetic and delivered to them the science of astronomy; for before Abram came into Egypt they were unacquainted with these parts of learning; for that science came from the Chaldeans into Egypt and thence to the Greeks also". We have it from the same source, that the family of Seth, placed by the Oxford authorities at about 4004 B. C., were the inventors "of that peculiar sort of wisdom which is concerned with the heavenly bodies and their order. And that their inventions might not be lost before they were sufficiently known . . . they made two pillars, the one of brick and the other of stone, and they inscribed their discoveries on them", their hope being to preserve them for future ages. These pillars, however, have long furnished matter for furious disputes among contending scholars, as, indeed, almost everything related by the ancients has done. We shall find it, then, more profitable to continue our tracing of the Jew in science, even to that of today.

Whether "Pan lent his pagan horn to Moses" as Pope has it, or Moses threw his torch of wisdom to Pan will probably never be discovered; but the odds are in favor of Moses, if we may trust, as age upon age has had to trust, the treasured manuscripts of the Jews, which were surely the work of intensely serious students of the mysterious skies and their wonders. The Book of Job, which dates from about 1520 B. C. refers to "Arcturus, Orion and the Pleiades and the chambers of the South"; showing that these orbs were already distinctly identified. Already in the narrative of Genesis, shadows had been noted, and the division of time was already begun into days and months and years. Observations were early made on the "vapors" that arose from the fields, and metals were early worked, so that at every step in the Writings two things are clear: that natural philosophy interested that young Jewish world; that it unfolded its secrets to them responding at every point as a reward to the God-seeker. This was not only true in connection with the findings of the early Hebrews, but, as well, as time went on, with such enlightened scientific men as Aristotle, for he recognized and looked for, back of all, the "immovable Mover" of all things.

The type of mind that has gone angling into the depths of antiquity for matter with which to besmirch the modern Jew is sufficiently courageous, as has been said, to declare that the early Hebrews stole their knowledge from (1) the Babylonians, and (2) from the Greeks. But none of the many who have picked up and repeated this statement appears to have examined it. The written record of the Greeks begins only about the fifth century B. C. That of the Babylonians, thus far has not been traced further back than about 650 B. C. at which time the Jews were recording in their own defined and formed language, their traditions of long ages. From the arrowpoint language of the earlier Sumero-Accadians of which the world has only recently become aware, it has been possible to confirm the general idea of historians that science first unfolded in the East and to opine that the zodiac came from the Phoenicians, but little more. But the Jewish peoples, descendants of

the Sumero-Accadians, the occupants in remote ages of
Chaldea, afterward Babylon, knew much of the starry
heavens, and had other names for the planetary bodies.
There would seem, all things considered, some reason for
looking into the question of how the lusty young Greeks
and the still younger and as lusty young Romans came to
affix their names to the stars for which earlier peoples
already had names. This grafting of Greek names, and
Roman ones on the planets, befogs the common mind, con-
veying to it the idea of precedence in discovery. It may
be that some future Chamberlain, rather than to allow the
honor of the discovery of Uranus, (which so long bore the
name of Herschell, its discoverer) to rest to the credit of
a Jew-descended scientist, may find a way of tracing a still
earlier acquaintance with this body to Greek, or Roman,
or Teuton.

This much we may be sure is reliable of all that oral
tradition and writings have brought down to us: that
science, coming from the East, the Jews had their laudable
part in developing it; that while that grandam of today's
science, Astrology, draped every new light that came with
superstition, the Jewish voice was the first of which we
have record, to protest against it. Isaiah, some 712 B. C.
is both satirical and derisive in his attacks against the
star-gazers and astrologers whose counsel the weak in
faith seek. Look to them, he says scornfully; let them
now "stand up and save thee from those things that shall
come upon thee."

While the Chaldeans and Babylonians multiplied superstitions in connection with their observations of the stars,
and appear to have been content to rest there, the Jews,
essentially a people of contemplation, were seeking truth
through the revelations of the heavens. This is established
by Daniel who was one of the captive children brought
into Babylon with Jewish hosts by the victorious Nebu-

chadnezzar about 600 B. C. He says that this King sent for a selected number of the bright children of the captive people . . . "such as were skilful in knowledge and who understood science", for the purpose of training them in the Chaldean tongue. But this surely gives warrant for thinking that he wished them to speak it also, in order that he might learn the secrets of the Hebrew knowledge and science. This testimony, rather than any other of the time, proves that the Jews were advanced in these things, else how might it happen that even the children of the race were instructed in them?

The Roman Pythagarus was living at this time, of whom we know extremely little and that all hearsay, brought down orally, even as the Jews' traditions had been carried down, by those who studied their teachers' wise sayings. But in the next century writings begin, in every direction. They are heard of as suddenly as books were, after the discovery of printing nearly 2000 years later. Nomadic wandering is superseded by planned travel and observant travellers began to write down their impressions of what they had seen and heard, and had learned from the people and priests of strange lands. Herodotus comes into view about this time. The history of astronomy, which is called the mother of all sciences, begins to take form here. Pythagoras is said to have taught and to have been the first to recognize that the earth and the planets turn about the central and immovable sun; but from this time on scientific investigation would seem to have languished, probably over-shadowed by the immense development in commerce and conquest among the countries of that little ancient world. However, mathematical studies were being carried on here and there throughout that world, and though they are often involved with theological interests, yet wherever notable discovery occurred, the Jew was near.

After Pythagoras, astronomy languished. Dr. Johnson says with his usual crispness that "the human mind
was not yet ready to receive his truths". The honor of
the revival of the science, as a thing of vital worth, belongs
to the Kings of Egypt, the Ptolomys, whose reigns have
left heritages to the present day which all civilized peoples
share. During those reigns mathematics, the science
which "contemplates whatever is capable of being numbered or measured", was developed, while Greece was still
measuring the divisions of the day by shadows. Proctor
tells us that Egypt and Mesopotamia are the places of all
others in which astronomical studies are to be made, since
the beauty alone of the heavens there was and is sufficient
to inspire worship and investigation. Layard has left some
rare descriptions of the Mesopotamian night skies. Proctor believes that the Greeks, who so constantly admit their
indebtedness to the Egyptians in scientific matters, give
them an exaggerated reputation "largely because they
have always boasted that they were descended from them".
George M'Arthus says that "the sober belief of the Greeks
was that the sun was a torch which, with the stars was
lighted and extinguished daily.

From this Ptolemaic period it becomes difficult to
trace the Jewish part in scientific development, as it would
seem because they, too, were mingling in Roman and Grecian life, and mathematicians who bear Hellenized or
Roman names, may well have had others of Hebraic form,
as was the custom of the day, and as it became an enforced
custom in the older European cities a thousand years
later. Fashion forced this in Alexandria as fanaticism
later compelled it in Spain and in Rome.

There were Jews in Greece when Aristotle taught;
when Euclid formulated his immortal rules on which
civilization has gone on building for twenty-two hundred
years; rules which, for the first time, we are told, are now

being challenged by the recently advanced Einstein theory, and which, if definitely proven, may be upset. Jews were in Egypt and in favor there when Hyparchus, "the illustrious founder of astronomical science, and Prince of Astronomers" attempted to catalogue the stars with a view to observing the changes that might occur to them and in their positions. They surely were about when Apollonius advanced his theory of conic sections; and when Eratosthenes, that wonderful man, who, wearied of his long life, deliberately starved himself to death at eighty-five, made his remarkable measurement of the earth's size which came within fifty miles of its true diameter, though geographical knowledge was still so rare and at best, vague.

That the Jew as a figure in scientific fields disappears about this time and is seldom heard of for centuries, is not at all strange. The dispersion of their people, in 70 A. D., followed by their wanderings in the East, principally, and the settling of groups in Italy and in Spain; and presently the settling over the European countries of the shadows of The Dark Ages, blurs all scientific traces. But, after all, it would seem to have been the Jews who saved science to the later civilization that was to recreate the old world. It is during this period, when the perplexed fathers of the young Church repressed scientific investigation as a dark occupation likely to be at variance with their revealed knowledge; when alchemy and numerous spurious spawns of the scientific thought of earlier ages absorbed the minds of men, that the Jews begin to take on the character of middle-man, whether commercially or intellectually, which so long distinguished them; and, passing to and fro among nations which offered small permanent hospitality to them, they disseminated, as their forefathers had done, knowledge of invaluable kind in the sciences, for which everywhere, the serious were eager.

In opposition to the animadversions so persistently heaped upon the Jews' enlightenment, it is interesting to note a point made by R. A. Proctor. He says in the Encyclopedia Brittanica, that while India has been hailed as the cradle of all sciences, and of astronomy, in particular, there are other authorities, equally reliable, who maintain that India got her arts and sciences originally, through the visit of Pythagoras, made in the sixth century B. C. But he goes farther, and speaks of a third opinion, that exists, in several reliable quarters, that astronomical knowledge was *probably carried into India in the ninth century of our era; probably by the Arabs.*

This was the period of Haroun al Raschid, when the Jews, the Arab's kinsmen, are known to have been the intermediaries between western Christianity and eastern Mohammedanism. The more these times and the personalities of the times are examined into, the greater the probability grows, that during them the Jews played a great part in the founding in those days of the structure on which modern astronomy was to rise. They brought scientific works, in Arabic forms into the European ken, and translated them for the Europeans. Toledo, Naples, each held groups of Jewish scholars. Not for gain but from pure love of learning they translated scientific, theological, and philosophical works of all lands.

Aristotle and other ancients reached Europe through the Jews; and by common consent it is agreed that they brought knowledge of the decimal system from Arabia, and geometry from India. They brought into use the astronomical tables of the Eastern peoples, and the knowledge of map-making, together with medical knowledge which was to be of vast service to the European world. The Jewish translators of those days were benefactors in a dark world, and rich men with a bent for knowledge, took them, frequently under their protection, making secretary-authors of them. There is warrant in plenty for stating that many of the greater translations of those days, though they bore the names of non-Jewish scholars, in fact were the work of erudite Jews.

Roger Bacon, who never balked at truth-telling against those he did not like—that great mathematician who could, in the thirteenth century, deduce that in time we should have "ships propelled without rowers . . . so that great ships, guided by one man may be borne with greater speed than if they were full of men. Likewise cars may be made so that without a draught animal they may be moved with inestimable speed . . . and flying machines, that a man may sit in the middle and by turning a device fly like a bird—"; Roger Bacon speaks of the erroneous translations of his time, and says: "When a great many translations on all kinds of knowledge have been given us by Gerard of Cremona, Michael, the Scot, Alfred, the Englishman, Hermann, the German, and William, the Fleming, you cannot imagine how many blunders occur on their works. Besides, they did not even know Arabic. . . . Michael Scot claimed the merit of numerous translations; but it is certain that Andrew, a Jew labored at them more than he did, and so with the rest."

Leonardo di Pisa, who founded his text-books on Indian arithmetic, geometry, and trigonometry, did so through the translations of John of Seville's *"Algorism"* and Plato of Tivoli's *"Liber Embadorium"*, both translators being Jews. Plato of Tivoli was one of the most important intermediaries between Mahommedan science and the Christian world, and, in addition, the author of original works on *"The Form of the Earth"*; a *"Calculation on the Courses of the Stars"*; and, among many others, his *"Book of Intercalation"*, which is accounted the oldest Hebrew work on the calculation of the Calendar. This was published in London, in 1851, about seven hundred years after the decease of its author.

From this time on Jews are identified inextricably with the progress of modern science. They had part, at least, in the making of early astronomical tables, and were famous as instructors in mathematics and astronomy. Tables of this character made by Zacuto, a Portuguese Jew, written in Hebrew, but translated into Spanish and Portuguese by a pupil of the author, were carried by Columbus on his wonderful quest for a Western short-cut to the East. Prescott says of the Jews: "Whatever may be said of their success in speculative philosophy, they cannot reasonably be denied to have contributed largely to practical and to experimental science"; and, again, "We meet with Jewish scholars and statesmen attached to the courts of Alfonso X, and Alphonso XI; of Peter, the Cruel, Henry II and other princes. Their astronomical science recommended them in an especial manner to Alfonso the Wise, who employed them in the construction of his celebrated tables. James I of Aragon condescended to receive instruction from them in ethics."

Levi ben Gerson, an astronomer and mathematician of the thirteenth-fourteenth centuries, (he died in 1344) and who is also known, as Leon de Bagnols, has been called one of the most remarkable men of his time. He is credited with having discovered the *camera oscura,* and was the inventor of "Jacob's Staff", which served the purpose of a quadrant to ascertain the right ascension of the sun. This instrument was used by the noted navigators, Martin Behain, Vasco de Gama, Magellen and Columbus, and its use continued until Hadley introduced (in 1731) his Quadrant. A "Quadrant Judaicus" an improvement upon an invention by Robert the Englishman, and which was evolved by the Jew, Jakob ben Maker, was long in use among mariners.

In Prague, associated so closely with historic events and personages, the resting place of David Gans is a point of interest to all Jewish visitors. Gans was one of the first German Jews to become known as a scientist. He translated for Tycho Brahe the famous Alfonsine tables (from the Hebrew into German) and took part in the observations made at the Prague Observatory by Brahe and Keppler. He wrote valuable works on cosmography, on geography and mathematics, and was among the enlightened scholars of a day which boasted Galileo and Bacon, but which, at the same time, opposed, fought, and, where it could, reprobated the bolder scientific leaders.

Science was not then esteemed the blessing we now know it to be. It held its own only by contesting for its every step taken. Important enemies to it regarded it as a too bold system of enquiry; a something contrary to God's laws and to those of the theologies of the day. Roger Bacon, and, indeed up to the days of Francis Bacon, many scholars ventured to pursue their studies only under conditions of the greatest secrecy; and to record their discoveries in codes and in anagrams calculated to balk inquisitorial searchers. But, despite this, modern science came into being in the 16th century, and with but little to block its way has gone on from triumph to triumph to the present.

In retrospect, and in considering their part in modern progress whether as scientific teachers, or as translators to the European world it would seem not possible not to perceive in the Jew one of the primal forces that spurred Copernicus (who made the first analysis of the movements of the heavenly bodies), that guided Kepler and Galileo, whose new science of dynamics was to produce such important results. Great discoverers the Jewish race did not at once produce, but while Galileo worked in his observatory, Jewish geographers were making authoritative books on both mathematical geography and astronomy; medical scientists were doing notable things, and in every field thereafter, the Jewish scientist, even against great hindrances, political, religious, social and always fanatical, begins to appear more and more frequently in the list of those who have accomplished fine scientific deeds. As chemists, as mathematicians, as physicists, as active astronomers—wherever the avenue is open, or to be opened for the seeking of the "knowledge of causes and the secret motion of things", there, today the Jew is to be found, "standing upon the frontiers of human knowledge" and looking into the unknown for a sight of that which their eyes cannot yet see, but which mathematical calculation tells them is there; for, as Lord Kelvin has said: "nearly all the grandest discoveries of science have been but the rewards of accurate measurement and patient, long-continued labor in the minute sifting of numerical results."

It is nearing one hundred and fifty years since the son of Jewish parents, William Herschell, who to that time had been but the modest organist of a little chapel, electrified the world with his discovery of the planet now known as Uranus and was hailed by the scientists of that day, as the most remarkable discoverer since Galileo. At once raised to the post of astronomer of the British King, Herschell continued upon a course of unparalleled discovery and opened wide worlds for those who were to come after him.

A partial list of his "etherial discoveries" shows that Herschell fixed the positions of some twenty-five hundred nebulae which, previously, were unknown. He identified two hundred and nine binary stars, of the existence of which none before him had suspected. He determined the elements of Saturn more conclusively than any predecessor, and was the first, as well, to show the relation of the

Milky Way to the universe in general. "When William Herschell discovered a new planet," some one has said, "and this beyond the orbit of Saturn, he doubled the boundaries of the solar systems known to even his most notable predecessors. All the activity of his race seemed concentrated in him in his pursuit of the astronomical mysteries."

At the time of this wonderful occurrence, general interest in astronomy and in science at large can scarcely have been great, for Johnson's dictionary, a fairly enterprising piece of work, dismisses both magnetism and electricity with the briefest possible comment, saying: "Philosophers are now endeavoring to intercept the strokes of lightning."

Since Herschell, an army of notable Jews have made their names known in the most important departments of science, among them Ricardo, in mathematics, early in the last century, and James Joseph Sylvester, whose influence in the development of mathematical science rests primarily upon his investigations of the "Theory of Variants". Three men in the last half of the nineteenth century have been ranked as mathematical geniuses, Sylvester, his friend and co-worker, Cayley, and Hamilton. To non-scientific students the theory of variants may seem abstruse and aside from the common needs of life; so, too, does an analysis of the air; yet, to the initiated scientist, who seeks the fundamentals, Sylvester's accomplishment ranks with those of the highest importance. Speaking of it Macmahon says: "The theory of invariants sprang into existence under the strong hand of Cayley, but that it emerged finally, a complete work of art for the admiration of future generations of mathematicians, was largely owing to the flashes of inspiration with which Sylvester's intellect illuminated it."

The University of Cambridge was obliged to withhold

from Sylvester his degree, because, as a Jew, he could not subscribe to articles at variance with his faith, though Cambridge, as one has said, was his "natural intellectual home"; but this circumstance carried him to Johns Hopkins, where, for seven or more years he was a notable light among a distinguished faculty. Reckoned among the mathematical giants of modern times, Sylvester took the Copley prize in 1880, and at his demise was a member of the most serious and progressive scientific associations of the world. Thereafter, the Royal Society established in his memory, the Sylvester triennial prize. This is but one of many instances of the non-Jewish world conferring post-mortem honors upon Jews, who, through life have met with a cold tolerance, when an encouraging sympathy was due them. Nothing raises the Jewish man of science so high as his power to proceed upon his studious way and to press toward his high calling, notwithstanding the blows which the narrow and ignorant, and the prejudiced deal him; but it is none the less deplorable that, in the face of the moral heroism of the Jewish race, displayed again and again in every generation, that non-Jews, beneficiaries the while of his work, should continue to perpetuate prejudices which is more degrading to those who sow it than to those who are the victims of it. To return to the Jew in science:

A predecessor of Sylvester's, Moritz Jacobi, was not only a discoverer of note in his day—he discovered, among other things, *galvanoplasty,* a method of coating metals by galvanism, which has had a large commercial value since it has entered even into the making of kitchen-ware of our own generation—, but also a prolific writer on the topic of galvanism, in association with machines; on galvanism and electro-magnetism and their application to the operation of machines.

Otto Wallach, who has but recently passed, was a

notable figure among organic chemists. None in his day has to his credit more valuable findings in the chemical field. His work on terpenes, and camphor, its related substance, is appraised as a classical example of chemical research. The list of men of the Jewish race of the last century alone who have added, by invention or discovery in the scientific field, to the enlargement of knowledge, and to the improvement of comfort in life, is far too great for commensurate attention here.

Science, year after year, "is busy", as Dr. Faunce has said, "in dissolving matter into more spiritual forms"; and, he might have added, in seeking to bring into visibility, that which in previous eras, has been the invisible, the unattainable; and none of all who have pursued her secrets make a greater showing than do the Jews. Herschell revealed a universe that had been undreamed of in the history of the human race. Beer, in the first half of last century, from his own observatory, penetrated unknown secrets of Mars, and made out the landmarks on the moon. With an associate, Maedler, he made a map of that orb which today is consulted and relied upon. Look where you will, however, you will find valuable scientific contributions by the Jews. Gabriel Lippmann invents the capillary electro-meter, and besides, numerous instruments in connection with photography, writes valuable works on Optics and Acoustics, and serves as professor of Experimental Physics at the Sorbonne.

One of the most pathetic figures in the history of science is that of Otto Lilienthal, of whom F. A. Talbot, in his *All about Inventions* said: "He paved the way for the realization of the flying machine as we know it today. He built a machine comprising a rudder and wings . . . with which he indulged in sailing flights. He approached the problem from the severely scientific point of view, discovering new facts and new data for himself. . . . By starting from an artificial hill one hundred feet in height he was able to sail over distances up to one thousand feet. . . . While testing a new steering apparatus which he had designed, he fell from a height of forty-five feet, broke his spine and died from the effects of it in August, 1896. . . . A. M Herring, while associated with Octave Chanut of Chicago, built an exact copy of Lilienthal's machine within a month after the inventor's death, and made a hundred successful glides with it; but, he gave up the machine as being, perhaps too dangerous. Chanut", Mr. Talbot continues, interested in the Wright Brothers' experiments, "extended the fruits of his experience to the Wrights" while they were at work upon their gliding machines."

With the University of Chicago, presiding over the Department of Physics, Albert A. Michelson, one of the greatest scientific figures of his age has been identified for thirty years. Very early in his career Professor Michelson's abilities began to declare themselves by his search into the methods of improving the determination of light. The Morley-Michelson experiments in this field are landmarks in the progress of modern science. They not only fixed this scientist in history, but brought him to the attention of the contemporaneous scientific world which, in a few years was to name him "the foremost scientist of America". It would seem to be Michelson's star-measuring feats which called forth a line of flippant contempt from Mr. Ford's author.

Professor Michelson might fitly be called the wizard of the air. How else, indeed, may we describe the mind that sets out to determine such impalpable problems as to whether there is ether in space, and to determine the value of "certain interference" means of measuring that which, to the eye of ninety-nine out of every hundred, is not? Michelson has succeeded by this same "interference method of measurement" in ascertaining the diameter of a star three hundred times larger than the sun: the great Betelguese, of the Orion constellation. Nor has he stopped there. He has measured, as well, the diameter of Antares, in the Scorpio group, which is now found to be some four hundred and twenty million miles; or larger, by one-third than Betelguese. The first great astronomer citizen of the Western hemisphere, Michelson is also one of the five American recipients of the Nobel prize, the others being Messrs. Theodore Roosevelt, Elihu Root, Woodrow Wilson, and Alexis Carrel.

As each new ascent in knowledge is made possible by the plane attained by our predecessors, so it has been said that the Morley-Michelson experiments are the starting-point whence arises the Einstein theories on Equivalents and Relativity, which latest discovery of the Jewish mind, though yet to be proven, have been greeted by the scientists of the age as "probably the most profound and far-reaching application of mathematics to the phenomena of the material universe that the world has ever known"; one which "takes us behind our present ideas about space, time and matter to the primitive reality out of which we have built up those ideas". Professor Thomson says Mr. Wells had a pretty clear idea of it all before Einstein's theory appeared; but, he adds, Einstein takes us a big step farther. He asked a question which nobody had asked before him: "Is the space and time interval which separates two events the same for everybody"?

It has been said that Albert Einstein was introduced to mathematics through an uncle, an engineer, to whom the youth propounded the question: "What is algebra"? "Algebra", the uncle is said to have replied, "is the calculous of indolence. If you do not know a certain quantity, you call it x and treat it as if you do know it; then you put down the relationship given and determine x later." Out of this grew the interest of the young student (until then described as a dreamer), which today has set the world of science agog; which threatens to overturn the mathematics that have stood the test of twenty-three hundred years, and to relegate Euclid and all that he stood for into what Mr. Cleveland so picturesquely described as "innocuous desuetude".

The Einstein Theory, while still, in part, under experiment, nevertheless has already solved problems that had worried great mathematicians for generations. To test it, England sent out an important expedition, for the purpose of photographing the stars whose light passed near the sun, when it was in eclipse. The "Theories" stood the test; more, strikingly verified them. "Einstein's Theory", say the editors of "The Outline of Science", shows, further, "that there is something in the nature of an ultimate entity in the universe" though even yet we know nothing intelligible about it; but, these authorities believe it will presently be made clear through the Einstein discoveries that the whole universe has been . . . created by the mind itself.

To what insignificant proportions do fanatical critics shrink before the blaze of scientific accomplishment which haloes the modern Jew, and this, not alone because of his exploration of the spaces of the sky, not alone for setting back of the horizon to take in undreamed of worlds, but because, too, great men of the race, regardless alike of fame, and of profit, work on in the secret quiet of "Science's holy cell", seeking tirelessly and often finding panaceas for the relief of humanity's ills!

But, great as are the findings of the race in the broader fields of physics, to the individual they are of less instant value than are the mysteries of life which chemists, physicians and other scientists of the race may be credited with. At these, too, we will now glance.

CHAPTER XII

The Jew in Medicine

"The Jews cannot reasonably be denied to have contributed largely to practical and experimental science. They were diligent travellers in all parts of the known world, compiling itineraries which have proved of extensive use in later times . . . bringing home hordes of foreign specimens and Oriental drugs, that furnished important contributions to the domestic pharmacopoeias. In the practice of medicine, indeed, they became so expert, as in a manner to monopolize that profession."

WILLIAM H. PRESCOTT.

(In "The Reign of Ferdinand and Isabella")

IN the past fifty years alone thousands of books have been written and printed that purport to record the history of the human family, many of which specialize on the world's progress in this or that particular field; but if you are a careful reader, and are seeking knowledge, let us say, in connection with the Jew's part in it, you will be amazed, as you turn the leaves of a work by this or that "authority"—even those whose reputations might recommend them as fair-minded,—to observe the scant mention, and this grudging, or derogatory, in connection with the discoveries and contributions of the race in the field of medicine. This has been admitted by one of the most recent Anti-Semites to disseminate his evil suggestions among the reading public. He goes so far as to say: "We dare not or will not teach in our history books the plain facts of the relations between our race and the Jews. We throw the story of these relations in the background."

To prove the truth of this confession, you have only to cast your glance back to the schoolbooks from which you were taught history. With the exception of a book

223

here and there which tells that the Jews crucified Jesus,
and were from that time on the objects of persecutions,
the authors have not "dared" or wished to apply the principles advanced by Jesus, of considering the Jew as a fel-
lowman and a brother. Such historians as have not been
willing to appear as uninformed allude to them, but, generally speaking, they have hastened over the topic as
negligible, unless, by chance, they have happened upon
some reprehensible thing of which some member of this
long-tortured race has been guilty. Then they have let
down the floodgates of their eloquence, though "It is a
poor and pusillanimous sport," as Mr. David Lloyd
George has declared in his recent book. But the work
goes on, and will go on undoubtedly until people think for
themselves; until they examine into the spiritual credentials of those who would saddle every new generation,
whether by carelessness or design, with the hatreds and
malice of past and ignorant ages.

This system of elimination of the Jew extends even
to the field of modern scientific writings. A recent work
of two volumes which deals with medicine and science,
solely overlooks the participation of this people in both
lines, though it devotes innumerable pages to Hippocrates,
who, the author notes, "knew so little of physiology that
he did not know a vein from an artery; nor could he distinguish a tendon from a nerve." Yet there is every
evidence that in the Biblical times—in those times in
which the Scriptures were first assembled, which preceded
Hippocrates by a hundred or more years—Jews were at
least enquiring into and observing physiological facts, and
concerning themselves with the very questions that today
occupy the scientific mind, namely, of how to prolong
life, how to improve health, and to assuage pain, and this
not by magic, or by pagan rites, but by their laws
of health. This is revealed in Exodus, Leviticus, and

Deuteronomy.   These laws may not be set aside as something borrowed from the Greeks or the Babylonians who had not yet appeared in any notable instance, as physicians or law-makers.

We have, on the other hand, corroborative evidence that very important dietary laws were understood and obeyed by even the Jewish children, who astonished the learned in Babylon by their adherence to them.   The case of Daniel again may be cited to illustrate this.   He was one of the four children selected by the officers of Nebuchadnezzar, who were to be fattened at the King's table and afterwards instructed in Chaldean.   Though he was lean as were the others, captives in the city, yet Daniel "would not defile himself with the King's meat."   He seems to have caused considerable discussion; but, ultimately he was given permission to demonstrate that a simple diet would nourish him better than the King's varied table. When, after ten days' experiment on a diet of pulse and water, the children were brought into the King's presence, he was astonished at their fair countenances and clear minds; for, "in all matters of wisdom and understanding . . . he found them ten times better than all the magicians and astrologers that were in the realm."

Today, when science has unlocked so many secrets concerning the human body—though life itself, and the mystery of it, as Sir Oliver Lodge has pointed out, even that of the common housefly, still eludes her—we know the body to be a physical and chemical system, an animal organism which the scientists regard as a mechanical marvel.   The metaphysician knows that back of all this marvel is the still more marvellous mind; that the state of this mind makes or mars the condition of the physical body; yet nearly three thousand years ago the Jewish fathers knew it and proclaimed in their proverbs that: "a merry heart doeth good like medicine."   Herbert Spencer merely proclaims this truth anew when he tells us that laughter at meals aids digestion.

Who really searches these Scriptures, doing so not in a spirit of seeking to find support for a concept and opinion already definitely established on accepted precepts —those accepted without enquiry—those who seek in the spirit of unprejudiced desire to know the right, cannot fail to be amazed at the manner in which the knowledge possessed by those early Jewish people tallies with or fore-shadows that of today. For example, nowhere in their book will you find such remedies as the learned Greeks of two and even three hundred years later were still resort-ing to in their treatment of the sick. Galen notes (as one instance) a way of making "digestive oils" by boiling whole foxes and hyenas, alive or dead, in oil: and if he and Pliny may be taken literally, Xenocrates and others employed commonly the practice of blending human blood and entrails in the manufacture of their medicines. The probability is—for it became a proverb that when Hippoc-rates said "Yes" Galen said "No"—that Hippocrates approved these cures, since Galen did not.

Galen had been rated as the greatest anatomist of antiquity; very recently, at a Congress of Medical sciences met in London, his knowledge of muscular anatomy was gravely discussed. But glance through the Jewish writ-ings, book after book, and you will meet with a surprising succession of references to the human anatomy, made generations before Galen's time, which point conclusively to the Jew as being already an observant physician; which show that he was able to identify and to study human organs and their illnesses, and that he knew and sanely applied sane remedies. It is true that in the later Jewish writings occasional cures are described that are but a trifle less absurd than those devised by the learned Greeks; but as these are not recorded or hazarded by Jews until after their intermingling with the Greeks, it would seem at least a fair conjecture, a reasonable one that evil communications had corrupted the Jews' better understanding and obscured their earlier light. On the other hand it may also register a spirit of liberal desire on their part (for which they have never had credit) to investigate and not reject without experiment, the ideas which other nations were acting upon. Maimonides showed this breadth of spirit fifteen hundred years later when he drew on some of the early theories of Galen, which had to do with the more perfect production of the species; but he drew only from the most rational and not from those which the simplest today must smile at, as worthy of the deepest and darkest ages of mankind.

Galen was a great man in his generation. He lived when scribes were numerous and easily available for the recording of the results of his researches. He was, as someone has said, seventeen centuries ahead of his time; yet he believed in the efficacy of the blood of a bedbug to remove the hairs of the eyebrows, which many, in his day considered as disfiguring, and sought to get rid of. Bayard Taylor in his famous trip to the east, noted the plucked eyebrow as a standard of beauty which still obtained there in the middle of last century.

"To stop a cough," one of Galen's prescriptions reads, "wear the tongue of an eagle as an amulet." Was a cure necessary for a sty on the eye? "Catch flies," wrote that great physician of the Greeks, "cut off their heads and rub the sty with the rest of their bodies. "A cooked black chameleon," he adds, "performs the double duty of curing a toothache and killing mice."

Pliny left records as worthless; but Galen, Hippocrats, Pliny—all those ancients left layers of worth-while observations on which future medical men were to travel farther and farther. The weaknesses of those early investigators are laughable, but who laughs at them? Their strength, their successful investigations are dwelt upon, and properly, by medical and general historians, as landmarks in scientific progress. The opposite course, however, definitely, clearly and deliberately is followed by all but the most occasional historian when it comes to facts that connect the Jew with this progress. Nevertheless, he, too, is honorably identified with it at every step. As the laborer is worthy of his hire, so, too, must it be acknowledged that to the Jew belongs credit for his part in the dissemination of knowledge of medical science and of general knowledge even, while the Dark Ages were silencing the voices of Greece and Rome. The Jew was the first to be identified with the colleges and hospitals established by the Califs of Asia Minor in the seventh century, and, as will have been seen, was at least an assisting force in translating into European tongues such Greek and Hebrew lore as was available. Nor should it be overlooked that their ancient Scriptures, at that time known to all scholars, but through the Greek, mainly, were considered as Greek documents by many non-Jews. Because of those peculiar conditions many things that would seem to have belonged to the Jews, of right, have somehow changed hands.

The Arabs are credited with the translations of Galen and Hippocrates which lie back of all European medical practice up to the sixteenth and seventeenth centuries; but there were many Arabian Jews, and many translators and scholars among them, and they were teachers, passing on their knowledge then as the race does today. If the unfriendly eye may build his propositions against the Jew upon suppositions, and probabilities, the truthseeker, availing himself of the same privilege, will be warranted in assuming that the dividing line between the Jewish and the Arabian Light-bringers of those days is extremely hazy.

Among that Eastern culture, the Jews had a short period of prosperity and peace, but their fate, even under Haroun-al-Raschid, was to teach others, to bring the schools of Bagdad to a flourishing condition, and then to be thrust out of the position they had filled, to make way for their pupils, and begin again elsewhere. Their first restrictions came when they were prohibited from teaching any but Jews. Next, they were restricted to the practice of medicine among their own race; but soon we come upon an edict prohibiting them even from studying medicine. As a result, the highly gifted among the race were soon wending their way westward toward Arab Spain where the young schools of Toledo, Seville, and Cordova were just coming into existence.

Jewish scholars also made their way, but in fewer numbers, to the Italian cities, and to those of northern Europe, and from this time on they are heard of as teachers or as practicing physicians in all the western centres of learning. Medical and scientific writings of that period are still extant from the pen of Isaac Israeli, a notable Jewish physician and oculist who left many pupils and descendants who were later to attain a high standing in the medical activities of their day. Israeli served the Fatimite Calif at Kairwan as personal physician. His work on fevers, like those of the later Maimonides (on foods and on diet generally), were long current in Latin form, and are still consulted by the curious in medical lore. The names of many scientific and scholastic Jews of those and succeeding centuries have been lost owing to the compulsory change of faith (which was accompanied by a change of name, also), which so often took place at a time when there was practically no choice between this act and the most cruel persecution. Comparatively re-

cently a non-Jewish medical historian has identified Aven-
zoar, theretofore listed as an Arabian, as a Jew; but Jewish authorities, even more conscientious, find no ground
for accepting him, notwithstanding the distinction which
attaches to his name.

A few such leading names as Israeli, Maimonides, and
Levi ben Gerson represent the truly scientific seekers for
truth who may be identified between the ninth and the
sixteenth centuries and all of these are associated with
medical practice. Ordinary doctoring by non-Jews as well
as Jews, was a matter of healing through the fantastic
prescriptions of the ancients; through magical brews.
Much of it was in the hands of "leeches," who appear
frequently to have combined the functions of barber,
apothecary and physician. It was not until the sixteenth
century that the medical scholars, perceiving medicine to
be a real and not (as it was then rated) a pseudo-science,
succeeded by bringing pressure upon the governments, in
establishing a better standard. The more highly equipped
Jewish physicians at this time were found in attendance
upon potentates, in the east and in the west. While these
and the Popes, as well, were continually issuing decrees
restricting the activities of the Jews as a people, nevertheless a great number of them retained Jews as their personal physicians—a singular testimony to the complete
trust reposed in their skill, but, above all, in their
integrity.

Romance and drama associate themselves with the
careers of many of the Jewish physicians of the Middle
Ages. You will come upon stories of potentates com-
pelling them to administer poison to those of whom such
royal persons would be rid without incriminating a Christian in the unholy deed; and of others, who, summoned to
do the miraculous in the healing of a king, have lost their
heads for their incapacity to do it. They were unques-

tionably skilful in the chemistry of their day, and there is
no reason to doubt, since it was a merciful act, that they
sometimes prepared such draughts as Friar Laurence persuaded Juliette to drink. They had a hand, at least, in the
making of the cosmetics and unguents which the fashionable beauties are said to have used so lavishly in the
Middle Ages; for of these and the secrets of perfume-
making they had known in the East.

It has been noted that practically all the luxuries enjoyed in Europe in the ninth, tenth and so on to the fourteenth centuries were brought there by Jewish travellers.
This was not only true in the case of fine stuffs for the
fashioning of wearing apparel, but especially so in the case
of drugs. Syrups, nitre, cubebs, borax and alum, senna
and laudanum, camphor and medicinal mercury, mace and
musk, aloes and asafetida, and innumerable remedies
known today in every family pharmacopoeia were practically unknown in the early Middle Ages, to any but the most
progressive medical practitioners. These are the little
things, which meant so much, however, for which the
modern world is indebted to the wisdom and enterprise
of the Jew. They were introduced by him when his every
step was opposed and rendered difficult by sporadic persecutions, begun, often in mere cruel caprice but ending
only too frequently in tragic suffering for him.

Among the Jewish physicians whose names are
associated with what may be called the pre-scientific
period of the modern world, Bonet de Latis may be noted.
When his people were expelled from Provençe in the last
part of the fifteenth century, he was called to Rome to
attend Leo X, whose personal physician he became. He
had there an opportunity which he seized, of stoutly defending his people during some especially cruel times for
them, and which are designated in history as the Pfeffer-
korn persecutions. Jacob Mantino was physician to Pope

Paul III. He appears to have been a diplomat as well as medical man, for he acted as ambassador, on behalf of Charles V at Venice.

From fifteen hundred on, the list grows of important members of the Jewish medical world. They are to be found in every Court in Europe, generally serving the King and sometimes able, because of the esteem which their worth had brought them, to alleviate the condition of their people. Marie dei Medici was attended by Elias Montalto, for whom she held such high regard that at his death, she had his body embalmed and sent to Holland where he had desired to be buried. They tell a story of Francois I, who, though debarring Jewish physicians from practicing in France, nevertheless when ill insisted upon being treated by one.

In Germany, where very few Jewish physicians appear to have practiced previous to the sixteenth century, these and their successors appear earliest in what approximates to an actual scientific study of medicine. They were receiving college degrees in 1700, but not, however, without experiencing many difficulties in attaining them. Frederick William prohibited them from practicing without diplomas, and thereafter hostility erected innumerable barriers to prevent their securing them. Pamphlets by the Belloc and Chamberlains *et al* of those days, protested indefatigably against admitting Jews to practice. These more or less seriously retarded Jewish medical progress for a century. Nevertheless none of Germany's native-born sons have added more glory to her scientific history in the past hundred years than those of Jewish race or derivation.

The first Jewish physician to be allowed to fill the position in Prussia of *privat-docent* (lecturer or teacher, but not upon the regular paid staff), was Robert Remak, who was already famous for his discoveries in electrotherapy, embryology and neurology. Since his time monuments have been raised in Germany to physicians of his race, and a hundred names shine out among the scientific lights of the present age; Ludwig Traube—"Father of Experimental Pathology"—was one of the first practitioners of his time and left a legacy to the medical world of valuable monographs on thermometry, digitalis, and diseases of the lungs. Karl Weigert, also a pathologist, and one of the faculty of Leipsic University, made discoveries of value and wrote much upon the subject of the staining of bacteria in microscopy.

Julius Bernstein, whose day is scarcely passed, was a noted anatomist and physiologist, and not only has written valuable works on the nervous and muscular systems, but also presided over the Physiology interests at Halle University.

The brothers Richard Liebreich, in ophthalmology, and Oskar M. E. Liebreich, distinguished throughout the medical world for the many new remedies he has added to the modern pharmacopoeia, have done conspicuous good to the human race in their time. Richard Liebreich, long associated with St. Thomas' Hospital in London, made a special study of the influence of school-life on the eyesight, and invented two opthalmoscopes which are in universal use, besides improving upon certain inventions of Helmholtz. Oskar discovered the narcotic effect of chloral hydrate, and demonstrated the anaesthetic effects of ethylene chlorid and butyl chlorid. He introduced platiniridium cannulas for the hyperdermic syringe, and the use of hydrargyrum in the treatment of syphilis. The healing properties of lanolin, since become a household remedy, were discovered by him in 1885. Nor do these begin to number his many discoveries; creosol, tolipyrin, formaline, metheline blue and many drugs now regarded as

indispensable in medical practice are due to his research
and experiment.

Benedikt Stilling, whose medical researches were
made in every country and in almost every University of
Europe, and who became celebrated as one of the first
anatomists and surgeons of his day, was one of the first
to introduce ovariotomy into Germany. His writings on
the nervous system, and its central organs, especially the
brain, which are rated as standard works, brought him
honors from the French Institute.

The city of Frankfort-on-Main, famous for the
number of unusual financiers she has produced, has been
no less remarkable for sons gifted in medicine. Among
them is Albert Frankel, nephew of Ludwig Traube, and,
like him, notable in experimental pathology. Moriz Schiff,
from the same city, a leading biologist of last century,
occupied the chair of physiology at the Institute di Studii
Superiori at Florence and afterward a similar chair at the
University at Geneva. He collaborated with Lucien Bonaparte on a work on South American fauna, and ranked
high as an authority on the construction of the nerves.

Wherever the Jewish scientist is found there a
teacher is to be found, following in this twentieth century
the same course his forbears followed, of passing on his
knowledge. Moriz Benedikt, a Hungarian neurologist,
occupied the chair of neurology at the University of
Vienna. A master in electrotherapy as well, he became
famous throughout the medical circles of the world for
his many-sided abilities, and was a notable pioneer in
modern criminology. Many of his works have come
through into English, notably his studies of the brains of
criminals.

Dr. Cezare Lombroso was one of the most dazzling
medical figures of last century. Known to the non-pro-
fessional English-speaking peoples principally through

his *"Man of Genius,"* to the medical world his meaning was vastly greater. From him, as an authority on criminology, a Lombroso School rose for the study of crime and criminals, many of the students of which have attained great fame, in some instances to world-wide renown, such as Ferrero, Enrico Ferri, Zerboglio, Carrara, etc., etc.

Lombroso began his career as Professor at the Pavia University, where he taught without pay for some years, finally attaining a second professorship which yielded him the munificent salary of $400 a year. Throughout his teaching career he suffered extreme want, and often went without the very necessaries of life; yet he added to the opportunities for study which the University offered by observations in a nearby insane asylum to which he also gave his services gratuitously. While he was still a student, he was writing on the insanity of the ancients, and making his deductions as to the relation between insanity and genius. He deduced two theories with which his name is associated; the first, that genius is a "peculiar psychical form of larvate epilepsy;" and, second, that "there is a degenerate class of human beings distinguished by anatomical and psychical characteristics, who are born with criminal instincts, and who represent a reversion to a very primitive form of humanity."

This Jewish physician, however, performed a greater service for humanity in a very different department of science. While at Pavia, he made a study of pelagra, a peculiar skin-disease which long had ravaged the people of Northern Italy. He discovered its source. It was the result of eating mouldy corn, the only available food for the agricultural poor of the land. He no sooner made the results of his investigations known, however, than all the rich landowners in that part of the country rose against him, viciously. Their purses being threatened, they represented to the Government that Lombroso was a mad man and demanded his removal from the University of Pavia. Years afterward, Lombroso's theories were adopted by the medical fraternity the world over.

Another psychiatrist, Max Leidesdorf, of Austria, who made a study of many years in the insane asylums of that country, was regarded as the leading alienist of his time. He was one of the medical group to examine into the mental condition of the dethroned Murad, and, later, into that of Louis II of Bavaria. He is an authority whom authorities quote.

To do even scant justice in listing the debt of civilization to the scientific Jew would be a gigantic task. Gabriel G. Valentin, long a leading pathologist of Europe, left notable works on the circulation of the blood; on toxicology; on digestion; and on the electricity of muscles and nerves. Gluge, a Belgian by adoption, was one of the first physicians to examine the diseased tissues of the body under the microscope. In special microscopic researches he discovered a curious parasite in fish which thereafter was given the name of *Glugea microscopra*.

Julius Cohnheim, of "Cohnheim's areas" fame, who, until his death was professor of pathology in the University of Leipsic, was the first to use the now "universally applied idea of freezing fresh pathological objects for examination." He was the first, also, to demonstrate "nerve determination" in "Cohnheim's areas." Cohnheim began his career with Virchow. He was a pioneer in applying the "theory of inflammation" which now is generally accepted, but which new departure was the result of his researches in the field of pathological circulation and the causes of embolism.

Haffkine of Calcutta, famous as a bacteriologist; Marc Sée, Lucian Dreyfus-Brisac, Gabriel Lippmann and Max Nordau, all of Paris; Salmonson, of Copenhagen; Arnold Pick and Siegmund Meyer, of Prague; Richard Willstäter, occupying the chair of chemistry at the University of Munich and winner of the Nobel prize for his researches into the chemistry of chlorophyll; Robert Barany, of Vienna, and Paul Ehrlich, of Berlin, winners, both, of the Nobel prize for medicine—what a list in this department of human achievement alone, to refute, to contradict the statements so insistently reiterated by our literary Jewbaiters of today! "The Jews have never achieved anything at all in any field of human knowledge or activity." So Mr. Chamberlain has written.

The layman, it is said, links the name of Dr. Ehrlich with his famous "606," an arsenical cure for a dread disease; but this is but the climax of a long career of valuable medical "finds" for which practically every government in Europe has honored him. But, it is unnecessary, after all, to go abroad for examples to prove the work that has been and is being done by Jewish physicians, Jewish men of medical science, who have contributed and are contributing greatly to the welfare of the new world. One of the first physicians to practice in the United States was Jacob Lumbroso, who set up his sign in Maryland in 1639. He is said to have been the only Jew of that quiet little Maryland group of whose faith there is indubitable proof, and who furnished the nucleus for all knowledge that exists concerning the early Jewish settlers in that State. Practically every Jewish community after his time had its own physician. We may not here stay to trace those earlier medical men, who, in all probability were obliged, as were the Rabbis, to add to their incomes in other than professional ways.

In the last century America's Jewish physicians have risen to positions as lofty as any in the world. They have been second to none in their activities that have to do with the public welfare, scientific research and progress. Many

have achieved a world reputation. Many fill the chairs of
Pathology, Chemistry, Bacteriology, Hygiene, and so on
in the leading Universities of the United States and
Canada. There are today approximately one hundred
and thirty scientists of this race in the United States and
these of first quality, who are devoting their skill to the
investigation of such scientific branches as zoology, horticulture, anthropology, hygiene; some ninety chemists, and
about one hundred and sixty physicians and surgeons,
besides numerous earnest workers who have not yet done
the thing that takes them above their fellows.

One of the most interesting figures in the medical
history of New York was the late Dr. Abraham Jacobi
who, in himself, was a living denial of the many denuncia-
tions that are hurled against the passionate young Jew
in foreign lands. There, under goadings and lashings
which cannot be understood in these United States of
America, he has been in rebellion against the legalized
cruelties which again and again his race is called upon
to endure, we hear of him only as a rebel. Were Dr.
Jacobi to arrive in America today, someone would be
pretty sure to attempt to bar him from landing, on the
score of two years spent in prison, on the charge of high
treason. Yet he was but twenty-three years old when he
came to New York where he was destined to rise to the
Presidency of the Academy of Medicine, and to become
one of the best loved as well as most famous physicians of
his time. His studies in Europe had been interrupted by
his participation in those revolutionary uprisings in which
half of the young men of his time were involved; but upon
his arrival in America he at once entered upon a course
in the New York Medical College, where he shortly is
found holding a professorship in the children's department. This he retained until he went to the College of
Physicians and Surgeons of Columbia University, in 1870,

where he remained for twenty-two years. Dr. Jacobi was
the great authority of his time on the therapeutics of children and left important works on this topic.

Dr. Carl Koller, the opthalmic surgeon, long associated with Mt. Sinai Hospital in New York, has won a
permanent place among the great discoverers in medical
science, by the introduction (in 1884) of cocaine as a local
anaesthetic in eye operations. This feat, which led to the
general adoption of local anaesthesia in operations in practically every branch of surgery, has been adjudged one
of the most merciful blessings conferred upon mankind in
recent years.

There are Jewish medical scientists established in
many parts of the United States whose reputation is coun-
try-wide; Dr. Bernard Sachs, alienist and neurologist, of
Baltimore; Dr. Milton Joseph Rosenau, Sanitarian, who
is Professor of Preventive Medicine and Hygiene at Harvard Medical School and director of the School of Public
Health of Harvard University. Medical progress on the
western coast has been promoted by Dr. Abrams, a widely
valued pathologist of San Francisco. Professor Jacques
Loeb, at the head of the division of general physiology at
the Rockefeller Institute for Medical Research since 1910,
is a world medical figure, as is Dr. Simon Flexner, an
American-born Jewish physician, formerly of Kentucky,
and today director of the laboratories of the Rockefeller
Institute. Dr. Flexner attained great fame in connection
with his monographs on Infantile Paralysis and on the
serum treatment of Epidemic Meningitis.

Nor does this, by any means, exhaust the list of
Jewish contributions to the physical well-being of the
modern world in this and other scientific departments.
The Jews have been taxed with lack of participation in
the agricultural problems of the present. Let us look
next into this complaint, and see how it tallies with facts.

CHAPTER XIII

The Jew in Agriculture

" 'So far from the colonies and colonists [in Palestine] draining the countries of its resources, they have created resources which were previously nonexistent; they have planted and skilfully cultivated desert sands and converted them into fruitful vineyards and orange and lemon orchards; in other parts they have created valuable agricultural land out of what were previously dismal swamps producing but diseases. They have not shrunk from the tremendous work and the heavy sacrifices required. Some laid down their lives over their work; the survivors went on bravely, draining swamps, planting Eucaliptus trees by the hundred thousand so that at last the swamp became a fruitful garden and the desert once more blossomed like the rose.' "

DAVID LLOYD GEORGE.

(In "Where Are We Going?")

THERE is a complaint which is commonly repeated against the Jews which shows either lack of information concerning them, or a desire wilfully to mislead the uninformed. This concerns the Jew in agriculture. The statement is made and continually repeated that he will take no part in producing, but only in consuming the world's supply of food. The accusation is not confined to one, for in all quarters every prejudiced voice finds another to echo it, and so this, with other disquieting messages, circle the world. The massing of immigrants in large cities, at first glance would seem to support this charge; but as to all questions there are two sides, so, in this case, two exist. An examination of conditions will show that it is not only the immigrant Jews who mass in the cities, but the native born citizens, who are forsaking the farming districts—this needs no proof for it is a readily ascertainable fact. Until very recently, indeed until the great movements among the philanthropic Jews for the education of their people in things agricultural, nothing was heard of but "deserted farms". Pleas have been uttered continually for a return to agricultural life. These were uttered, too, among the Jews for many decades ere the public heard of a "back to the farm movement" among non-Jews. That movement instituted through the efforts of A. B. Ross in 1907, who pleaded for the establishment of a Farm Bureau that would inform farmers on the latest scientific aids to farming, received, and deservedly, the warmest support; but for many years the Jews had been at work upon the same thought, and their people in scattered groups throughout the world, were struggling back to the farm, wherever a reasonable hope was held out of an ultimate independence; for this is the fundamental hope of all men, irrespective of race, in whatsoever line of occupation they are to be found.

Agriculture loses its appeal to the great majority when cheap labor ceases to be available. The cotton-growing sections of the United States suffered lamentably for decades after the abolition of slavery. When it was abolished in the Danish West Indies, now the Virgin Islands, the agricultural interests that had flourished on St. Thomas, died at once. Its harbor was one of the finest, and held out a continual invitation to commerce; but without cheap labor to assist, its commercial interest withered; and the same thing has happened repeatedly in connection with the histories of many ports and commercial centres. But the onus for this falling away of interest in the farm, in agricultural pursuits, does not lie upon the shoulders of the Jews, since, until within a century, the race has not been allowed, in any land, the opportunity to return to the farm on any fair terms; on any that would tempt non-Jews in this truly money-ruled age.

They have been ruled out from land-owning, in many instances even from land-leasing, for thousands of years, long enough to eradicate from any race the love of husbandry that early was a characteristic of them. No country has encouraged or permitted them upon an equal basis to till its soil. True, a short-lived caprice has seemed to hold out here and there such opportunity; but usually under such conditions as to be tantamount to allowing them to "make bricks without straw". But there can be no gainsaying that they were agriculturists even as they were herdsmen in their old home in the east, in the days when they were permitted to hold homes of their own. They cultivated fruits; they were experts in viticulture long before they were pedlars or merchants. They were notable winemakers; they cultivated the mulberry tree and the silk-worm in Greece in the early centuries of the present era.

Long ages before, the Writings bear witness to the agricultural bent of this people. They abound in references to the staff, in all lands the herdsman's companion; to the grass in the field; to the wayside bushes even, and to harvest and the sowing time.

All over Mesopotamia, age after age, little groups have been noted of Jewish farmers, clinging with unparalleled tenacity and devotion to the land of their fathers; planting and reaping from it generation after generation. Bayard Taylor was deeply impressed by them, and by the sight of a tattered parchment of the Law which tradition traced back to the ancient days, but to the reading of which, Sabbath after Sabbath, these farmers lent a reverent ear.

In his recollections of *"The Land of the Saracens"*, he describes the Jewish farming communities in Palestine as he saw them in the late 40's of last century, resting in "a sea of bowery orchards". Abundant streams, he notes, "gurgle through thickets of orange and fig trees; through pomegranates and rosebowers; and then the masses of wild vines and the olives! We continued our way", he writes, "through gardens of almonds; and apricot, prune and walnut trees growing along the mountain sides were bound each to the other by great vines whose heavy arms they seemed barely able to support." And, he adds, as his rapture and reverence increases over the beauty and luxuriance of the historic landscape: "We rode for miles through a sea of wheat . . . the tobacco in the fields about Ramleh was the most luxuriant I ever saw and here the olive and the fig attain a size and lusty strength wholly unknown in Italy. . . . Except in Asia Minor, no portion of the Levant is capable of yielding such a harvest of grain, silk, wool, fruits, oil and wine."

This description was written more than seventy-five years ago, before any thought of the introduction of modern ideas of agriculture had begun to penetrate to that historic land. It was still a patriarchal country, to go back to which had been the dream of the scattered Jewish people for eighteen hundred years. Benjaman of Tudela, whose travels are elsewhere referred to, visioned a revival of Jewish life in Palestine, the hope of the race; and he and others noted so early as 1170, small settlements, all agricultural groups, scattered through the land. Sixty Jewish families are recorded as dwelling in the neighborhood of Gaza in 1485, who were practical farmers engaged in the raising of cereals and grapes and in wine-making.

It is believed by today's scientific investigators that Palestine was the original grain and cereal producing country of the world, and those in correspondence with the Departments of Agriculture of the various modern governments within a decade have become aware of Palestine, as a land to which the human family is likely to turn for at least a portion of its breadstuffs in the comparatively near future.

Joseph Nasi, that picturesque lover of his race, and predecessor of the great philanthropists of the nineteenth and twentieth centuries, was moved to begin the re-building of Tiberias, in the hope of providing a sanctuary for his people where they might have a fighting chance for an undisturbed life. He pictured them as leading the pastoral life of their forbears; of raising flowers, and breeding silkworms; as occupied with the culture of bees and the production of the famous honey of the Levant. Tiberias was not only dear to him and to Jews, generally, as the home of his ancestors, but as the shrine where the remains lay of Maimonides, the second Moses of his people. Despite the materialism of which the Jews are so persistently accused but which, in another race would be called practicality, they have been at all times the most uncalculating idealists in these dreams for the betterment of living conditions for the weaker members of their race.

So early as 1845 plans were again made, tentatively, for the restoration of the land of Palestine to the Jews. This was especially recommended by Sir Moses Montefiore after his tours of observation in the east. Both he and Cremieux, his fellow-ambassador to Damascus, were convinced of the feasibility and desirability of such a plan. In the early sixties the first association of rich Jews was formed with the object in view of relieving as they might the less fortunate of their race in Eastern Europe from the hardships they suffered in many lands.

By the seventies they had succeeded in getting the assistance of the Sultan of Turkey to the extent of a grant of a tract of six hundred acres for the establishing of an experimental school in agriculture for Jewish youth. The graduates of that school, and their descendants are today residing on their own farms in Palestine, or attached to other institutions of learning as instructors and demonstrators in the various departments of agriculture. From that time on agricultural colonies, weaklings often because of the poverty of many of the would-be farmers who were comprised in them, have come into being in many of the districts of Palestine, and slowly, ever so slowly it may seem, and fostered for nearly two decades almost solely by the devotion of Edmond de Rothschild, progress has been made toward the rebuilding of that Holy Land.

De Rothschild furnished the farmers with silkworm stock in the hope of re-establishing one of the ancient industries of his people. He built wine-cellars and substantially encouraged viticulture. By this time many others were helping in the work, but were beginning to see that much more intensive preparation was necessary in the way of modern and thorough instruction in agriculture to the new arriving colonists, the majority of whom at no time had had the opportunity to practice even the simplest planting and sowing. But the eve of the great Russian exodus was at hand. Some of the first to emigrate from Russia sought the refuge of the colonies in Palestine. Baron de Hirsch, who had been concerned for some time over the pitiful plight of his people in the East, now began to visualize their rehabilitation through an organized effort to help then industrially. How this great project has been deliberately maligned, has been indicated elsewhere. It may be said, none-the-less, that this philanthropist's example has generated among his people a true passion for the regeneration, not alone of the Jews of the east, but for those in remote corners of the earth.

The de Hirsch philanthropies not only embraced assistance to the Jews desiring to colonize in Palestine, but the vastly less circumscribed plan of aiding them to emigrate to newer lands, where they might grow up with the country. They included the idea of self-help through industrial and general education, especially in the useful trades and in agricultural pursuits. His was not a thought of charity, or the development of paupers; but one of redemption for a race hampered and held down for a thousand years, until its best qualities of body and of mind were often all but extinguished by the humiliations and hardships it had been called upon continually to bear. It was his explicit wish in connection with the American Fund which he (later) established and which is administered by the most representative American Jews, that it should be used to teach immigrants, especially those from Russia and Roumania, trades; to take care of them, if need be, while learning them; to institute colonies for them where they would be free from the horrible experiences which had followed them in their earlier homes, and to furnish them with the necessary tools for the carrying on the trades acquired. Above all, they were to have inculcated in them a loyalty to their new homes, and to be taught the language of the land they dwelt in.

This philanthropy, the more it is examined into is more and more clearly to be recognized as the greatest and most constructive gift to mankind that was ever made. Nominally it was to the Jewish people; but it is, in fact, a contribution to the welfare of mankind that is felt in every corner of the earth, and for the reason: It has set the Jews to work in the field of agriculture, side by side with non-Jewish agriculturists, at a time when skilled agriculturists are more needed than ever before. Sir William Crookes, an authority in many lines of scientific enquiry, stated in 1908 that the bread-eaters of the world had increased by 101,000,000, though the raising of wheat had by no means kept pace with its consumption. Bread is chiefly consumed by the white races, and with humanity increasing at its present rate, its position as a staff of life makes it more and more necessary that agriculture be

speeded up. So late as 1918 reports from the Agricultural
Experiment stations throughout the United States support
that of the older scientist. One of these, at hand, states
that "extraordinary conditions now prevailing in the national life are affecting the production and distribution of
food. The rising prices of food on the one hand encour-
ages production; but, on the other, the high price of raw
materials and particularly of labor required in agricultural
work, limits it. The breadstuffs grown in the State", it
adds, "fall far short of the normal requirements."

These questions may not have presented themselves to
Baron de Hirsch as he sent his agents—Emanuel Vene-
ziani was among them—in a search of the world for countries in which the Jews might be colonized without fear of
further persecution. But it is significant that one of the
first countries in which he purchased land for them was
Argentina, the great bread and meat market today of the
Western hemisphere. Argentina's history since that
colonization began, has provided ample proof that given a
man-to-man chance, and reasonable equipment for sustaining himself during the period of adjustment to his new
surroundings, both the Jewish immigrant agriculturist and
his children will give as good an accounting of themselves
as any who have had to do with the agricultural up-building of North and South America.

Many Russian Jews, also others from eastern Europe,
entered into the industrial life of Argentina. At the outbreak of the World War some twenty-seven thousand Jewish immigrants were established there, of whom nineteen
thousand were engaged in agricultural occupations. Notwithstanding those drawbacks against which the farmer is
helpless, drawbacks which are legally termed "visitations
of God", such as plagues of locusts, overlong rains and
overlong droughts; in some parts, even of seismic disturbances now and then to terrify them, these Jewish agricul-

turists have produced excellent crops; raised great herds
of livestock including thousands of milch-cows, and have
established thriving creameries and dairies in many locali-
ties. By those who have visited their Argentina farms it is
said that at the bottom of the success of the Jewish farmers
lies the fact that they have been met by other races with
an amity and understanding that has relieved them of the
double effort of fighting down prejudices while building up
the interests of the country.

Baron de Hirsch did not live to see all of his hopes
materialize, but such reports as reached him from South
America fortified his belief in the ultimate success of his
colonization plans. He died sure that his people if given
an opportunity, a fair one, would turn willingly from
crowded cities and acquit themselves in occupations that
were connected with the soil. His own words will best
explain this faith, his views, his hopes. He wrote, in the
Forum, in 1891:

"In the countries where Jews have been permitted to
acquire land, where they have found an opportunity to
devote themselves to agriculture, they have proved to be
excellent farmers. For example, in Hungary, they form
a very large part of the tillers of the soil; and this fact is
acknowledged to such an extent that the high Catholic
clergy in Hungary almost exclusively have Jews as tenants
on mortmain properties, and almost all large land-holders
give preference to the Jews on account of their industry,
their rectitude and their dexterity. These are facts that
cannot be hid and that have force; so that the anti-Semitic
movement, which for a long time flourished in Hungary,
must expire. It must do so because everyone sees that so
important a factor in the productive activity of the country
—especially in agriculture—cannot be spared. My personal experience has led me to recognize that the Jews
have good ability in agriculture. I have seen this per-

sonally in the Jewish agricultural colonies of Turkey; and the reports from the expedition that I have sent to the Argentine Republic plainly show the same fact. These convictions led to my activities towards bettering the unhappy lot of the poor down-trodden Jews; and my efforts show that Jews have not lost the agricultural qualities that their forefathers possessed. I shall try to make for them a home in different lands, where, as free farmers, on their own soil, they can make themselves useful to the country in which they dwell."

The Baron de Hirsch Fund has greatly advanced the agricultural and industrial status of the Jew in the United States, but prior to its establishment there had been displayed in many States and at different periods several movements toward the farm, marked and highly significant efforts here and there to enter the agricultural field. In the Colonial days, a Portuguese Jew, brought the first mulberry trees to Georgia, and planted grapevines there. There were Jewish cotton planters, as well, in the days before the Civil war. So far back as 1837, when Jewish immigration was a scarcely mentioned incident in the life of the United States, though the Jew in Europe was meeting with various ill-treatment that seared his spirit, a handful of Russian Jews arrived here and attempted to establish a colony for farming in Ulster County, New York. A dozen families yearning to found a "refuge for the Jews", to have a place they might call their own, settled in Wawarsing, in that county.

Unfortunately they were better idealists than they were practical agriculturists, and five years later they had lost their little capital, and, what was worse, their courage to proceed; yet forty years later when the disgraceful pogroms against the Jews were launched in Russia, when Austria refused to harbor the fleeing refugees and Baron de Hirsch stepped forward with the *Alliance Israélite;*

(which he had so largely financed) when he, with the help of co-workers in the United States made it possible for the better-trained Jewish agriculturists to come to America, the town of Wawarsing came to life again, and shortly became a centre for a great colony of Jewish farmers, who today are in the highest degree, prosperous. Throughout Ulster, Sullivan and Rensselaer Counties in New York State farmers of this race own, free and clear, large areas of fertile country, which, by their diligence and intelligent agricultural enterprise has become known the nation over as one of the most prosperous farming regions in the Empire State.

Each farming community in these counties has its own centre, in such towns as Monticello, Centreville, Nassau, Tannersville, besides the many thriving villages that have grown up, each of which has its own Jewish School. Each may follow peacefully its own home customs; each has its own physician and special religious leader. They raise grain and poultry; vegetables, fruits and berries for nearby markets. They are energetic in Jewish agricultural movements, indeed this is characteristic of all the active agricultural centres which are being developed by Jewish farmers. They are of their time and are organized for mutual help and co-operation, the country over. Is a discovery made in horticulture or agriculture—a something of value in the care and raising of cattle—their excellent farming papers carrying the news from one end of the country to the other. Men of the same traditions, the same past sufferings, they have perceived the value of such organization and of the educational advantages they offer, and they work unitedly for the improvement of farm labor and farm life. Between these and other agricultural communities, too, a Jewish Farmer's Exchange has been established which plays a valuable part in solving many of the difficult problems that confront the detached farmer from time to time.

But Onondaga county in the alfalfa belt of New York State, has also a large Jewish farms area. Some of the most successful dairymen in the State are Jewish and reside here contributing to the supply of milk which is daily carried on to New York City. On Long Island are to be found many Jewish farmers engaged in raising vegetables and fruit and poultry for the city trade. But it is not possible to confine the refutal of the charges against the Jews in agriculture to instances gathered from a county or two in the Empire State, since they are farming today, and successfully, in practically every State in the Union.

What is regarded as the most prosperous Jewish farming settlement in the country lies about Hartford, Connecticut, where great dairy farms and rich herds of choice cattle are to be found, and also tobacco plantations as rich as any on the western hemisphere.

Professor Cance of the Massachusetts Agricultural college has rated this community most highly, and describes its growth as having been made possible through loans from the Jewish Agricultural Aid Society, which lent not only money to the immigrants who were equipped for farming, but also its practical knowledge and counsel in the matter of purchasing and equipping the farms. This important Jewish farming centre is not yet twenty years old; and, though mill workers have left their benches with their savings and purchased there, yet the bulk of the farmers are again those Russian Jews against whom so many vicious attacks have been made in the last year or two.

When the Jewish farmers began to enter Connecticut, in 1902, there were many "abandoned farms" available; farms abandoned by non-Jews who could not endure the hardships of farm life, and were not disposed to cling to the soil their ancestors had tilled for generations at the expense of further sacrifice. No reverence for past associations held them. Some of those farms today, by the thrift and scientific farming which their Jewish owners are applying, are yielding as high as $6,500 annually on their tobacco crops alone.

There are Jewish farmers developing land in Michigan, growing fruit there, raising poultry and cattle. In the arid belt of Nebraska, where few others would have the courage to attempt it, Jewish farmers have taken up government land and are growing with the country. There are colonies of Jewish farmers in Utah; in Missouri; in North Dakota where, though they were obliged to go through periods of great want, they are nevertheless triumphing, and in many departments of farming, prospering. Compelled in their early days in this territory, to live as did other pioneers, in dugouts, in any shelter they could get, since 1905, they have been able to erect frame houses, comfortable barns, and supply themselves with the best and latest farming implements.

It has been said that the Jewish farmer colonists in the United States and in Canada which countries were the first to receive the de Hirsch Fund Colonists, soon grew weary of their struggle and went back into petty commerce. Upon examination into facts, however, it would appear that their courage held out a little longer, fact examined upon fact, than that of non-Jewish (and therefore entirely unimpeded), farmers in parallel situation. Some fifty or more Jewish farmers, coming direct from Russia went in 1881 to Louisiana, where, assisted by loans from the de Hirsch Fund, they were enabled to settle on the Island of Sicily in the Mississippi and purchase the needful farming implements. With diligence and enthusiasm they set to work. Success seemed smiling at them when without warning, (as one of their people describes it tersely) "one of the Mississippi floods swept everything away;

houses, cattle, implements and first crops". It can bring
no criticism upon those farmers that they fled, in despair
to take up what they could to gain their bread.

Another little colony in South Dakota, their crops of
rye and flax, of wheat and oats ready for the harvesting
find it suddenly destroyed by the Hessian Fly—a pest
which devoured the substance of Jew and non-Jew, and
made as many of the latter despair as it did of the Jews.
The arid soil of Colorado where irrigation at that time was
impossible, and where the spring torrents wrought devas-
tation upon everything in their paths, disheartened little
Jewish colonies which had been planted in that State, also.

These are some of the tragic incidents in the lives of
the pioneer Jewish farmers in the west. They were heroic
as were the non-Jewish farmers, and even a trifle more so
since most of them were pitifully poor and were strangers
in a strange land. All through the eighties and nineties
in numberless out-of-the-way places groups of these courageous and industrious Jews made efforts to get a
foothold in agriculture and away from the cities. They
may be traced to the forest lands of Oregon where one
sturdy group set out to hew its way to a homestead by
chopping down trees and cutting them into railroad ties
while clearing the land for a future planting. For eight
years they stood the hardships and labor and deprivations
of that backwoods' life, and then, the railroad completed
which had sustained them, they gave up the struggle, as
did many non-Jewish pioneers whose courage was no
better.

This and similar Jewish endeavor to enter into agriculture may be traced in every State in the Union. In
every State individuals have succeeded where large colonization was not always successful. The numerical strength
of the Jewish farmers, however, is difficult to ascertain,
owing to the fact that races are not indicated in the Gov-

ernment statistics but only the country of nativity. So late as 1922, there were upward of seventy thousand Russian and Roumanian and Hungarian farmers listed, the immigrants from which countries are very largely Jewish. What is far more important than numbers in viewing the Jew in agriculture, is the intelligent effort the race is making in the education of its youth for agricultural careers. This is the first fruits of the de Hirsch Fund planting, and also of the incomparable service to his race of Rabbi Joseph Krauskopf, of Philadelphia. The de Hirsch Fund Trustees with millions at their command, founded the new Jersey farming colonies that have become a source of pride and satisfaction to the State, first at Woodbine and then at Vineland, and established there agricultural schools from which intelligently trained farmers have gone out into many States in the Union. Dr. Krauskopf, having no money, gave himself to the founding of the National Farm School at Doylestown, Pennsylvania, the fame of which, and many of the graduates of which, have reached the farthermost parts of the world. Two of its graduates but recently have been called to Argentina to give agricultural instruction to the special schools that have been opened in that country.

The Woodbine School and colony was started in 1893, the pupils receiving instruction in planting, in plant surgery, and in the care of fruit trees and growing plants. The colonists almost without exception were made up of that despised class, the Russian Jew. One such, a brilliant plant chemist, was made supervisor and organizer of the school. The meaning to the community of the work of this school may best be shown by a glance at the careers of some of the earlier pupils there.

Among the colonists was a family of Russian Jews, by name, Lipman. They would at once come into the category of un-worthwhile Russian Jews which the *"World's*

Work" has seen fit to denominate as detrimental to our American thought and life.

One of the sons of this family, Jacob G. Lipman, entered the de Hirsch Agricultural School at Woodbine and was graduated therefrom, and later from the New Jersey State Agricultural College and from Cornell University. Since the family were scarcely in "easy" circumstances, his path could hardly have been one of ease. Today he is Professor of Soil Chemistry in the New Jersey Agricultural College and Director of the State Agricultural Experiment station; the authority to whom the agriculturists of the State look for counsel on all points in connection with their problems. Charles Bernard Lipman, a younger brother of the same family began as a student at the Woodbine Agricultural School going later to Rutgers, and is now Soil bacteriologist and chemist at the University of California.

Another Russian-born agriculturist, a graduate of the School of Forestry at Yale, J. G. Levison, was for a long time Chief Agriculturist of the Brooklyn Department of Parks. Under Gifford Pinchot he was in charge of Prospect Park for ten years, making it, as has been said, "the famously beautiful Park it now is." A lecturer at Yale, specializing on shade trees, he has also developed some of the most beautiful estates on Long Island.

Many practical farmers, horticulturists, dairymen, stock-raisers have come from the de Hirsch School and the National Farm School of Doyleston, and from both have issued a brilliant succession of professorial scientists to fill chairs of Agriculture in various parts of the world. Jacob G. Taubenhaus, a Doylestown and Cornell graduate, fills the office of Assistant Professor of plant Pathology at the Delaware Agricultural College and Experiment Station; Maurice Mitzmain, from the same school, and, later from the University of California, was Chief Entomologist for the United States in the Department of Agriculture in the Philippine Islands. Professor H. L. Sabsovich, first superintendent of the Woodbine School was afterward Chemist at the California Agricultural Experiment Station. Jacob Kotinsky, a graduate of the Woodbine School was for several years Chief Entomologist and Assistant Director of the United States Experiment Station at Honolulu. M. E. Jaffa, graduate of the de Hirsch School is Nutrition Expert at the California Agricultural Experiment Station.

Nor do these, by any means, cover the activities of the American Jew in avenues agricultural; and the technical training which the youths of the Jewish people are receiving in this field, gives promise of a growing importance to the country of this people. But surely enough testimony is here presented to indicate that if there is a shortage of farmers in the country, the fault does not lie with the Jews who contribute a just quota, but rather with that class of non-Jew who neither knows nor cares where his food comes from so long as it is at hand when he is hungry. The Jew today is probably a little more alive to the possibilities and interests of agriculture than any other class of citizen.

It was a Jew, Bernard Marks, who not only founded a number of Jewish farming colonies in the west, but led in the irrigation activities of that land. It was Mr. Marks, too, who was so closely identified with the introduction of alfalfa grass into the country. It is the Jewish farmers who are the quickest to see the advantages of new labor-saving devices for farm work, for the dairy, for the creamery. The Jewish agriculturist, not only has his Farmers' Exchanges, his Farmers' Reviews, but keeps closely in touch with the Department of Agriculture at Washington, and avails himself alertly of every scientific discovery as to soil treatment, soil enrichment, and plant development.

Mr. David Lloyd George, in his work, "Where are we going"? says of the farmers of Palestine: "Everywhere the Jew cultivator produces heavier and richer crops than his Arab neighbor. He has introduced into Palestine more scientific methods of cultivation, and his example is producing a beneficent effect on the crude tillage of the Arab peasant." Something very like this may also be said of the Jewish farmer in the world, generally. He is no longer "a brother of the ox;" The Jewish "man with the Plow" has risen erect and to his true place beside the chemist and scientist.

CHAPTER XIV

The Jew in Jurisprudence; in Statesmanship; in Diplomacy

"The same passionate intensity which makes the grandeur of the Hebrew literature . . . gives them the peculiar effectiveness that comes from turning all the powers of the mind, imaginative as well as reasoning, into a single channel, be that channel what it may. They produce, in proportion to their numbers, an unusually large number of able and successful men as any one may prove by recounting the eminent Jews of the last seventy years."

JAMES BRYCE.

(In "Biographical Studies")

IF we may judge by the existence of the Noachic, as often spoken of as the pre-Sinaitic laws, even from before the time of Moses, law-giver, leader and liberator of his people, law was a study, and it and its related activities in statecraft and diplomacy a natural calling of the Jews. The development of their law systems from those of tradition to those contained in the Book, and the tracing of the Rabbinical interpreters and framers of the later laws to the entrance of the Jew into the practice of the Roman and English secular law systems, is far too vast an enterprise to be undertaken in a work of this scope; but it may be said that law schools and academies were known among the Jews in the beginning of the present era in their centres of learning in the East and in Spain, and that laws covering all the points of friction between members of a community, were plainly in operation among them. Maimonides, whom Grotius quotes frequently, in his law writings specifically defines, for example, the powers of attorney, and methods of suing and defending clients in their courts.

Equally, from century to century are to be found "wise" Jews who have served potentates and peoples as legal and diplomatic advisers, and as ambassadors between negotiating countries; and while the Justinian Code in Christian countries deprived them of civil rights and as often of common human rights, yet it is certain that individuals of the Jewish race were, every now and then, to be found even in public offices; for in the late thirteenth century canonical prohibitions were renewed against "trusting the Jews with public offices." They were for centuries the necessary intermediaries between the Christian and the Mohammedan world; the confidential advisers of the Spanish and Portuguese monarchs. It will have been seen elsewhere the height of power to which Joseph Nasi, as Turkish statesman, rose in the early sixteenth century. Great "feats of diplomacy" were performed in those days which were at least shared in by Jews; but we must deal here with those which are especially linked with the last and the present centuries in which the Jew has taken a truly great part, the time being the first in the ages in which he has been free to do so as other men have been. His appearance as an active factor in law is not, in view of the past tendencies of his race, surprising, nor is his success in this field, though it has been little short of unparalleled; but as statesman and diplomat in the modern world systems, so various, and so much more difficult than the simpler systems of an earlier period, his stride to the front commands both wonder and admiration from the student of foreign and home relationships.

Mr. Marriott says in his work, *"The European Commonwealth,"* that the public is not half interested as yet in this new thing, diplomacy, which, he says, is a word that only came into being through Edmund Burke toward the end of the eighteenth century, though what it stands for may be traced to the fifteenth; and Mr. Marriott outlines, in a concise summary, the new era of nations as we know them today, the process of forming which, he says, was not completed until nearly the end of the nineteenth century. We may most easily be conducted into a position in which to judge the Jew in this field, and in that of statecraft, by reviewing this brief and informing summary.

"Not until the decade of 1870 and 1880 was continental Europe exhaustively parceled out among the independent States, based, for the most part, upon the recognition of the national idea. France, Spain, and the United Provinces," Marriott says, "emerged as Nation States in the course of the sixteenth century; modern Austria came to the birth with the virtual death of the medieval Empire of the Treaty of Westphalia (1648); a unified and self-conscious Russia was brought into being by the genius of Peter the Great early in the eighteenth century; the birth of Prussia, due to the industry and persistence of the Hohenzollern Electors of Brandenburg was almost co-incident with that of Russia. But the rapid multiplication of Nation-States came only with the nineteenth century. Belgium as a Nation-State dates from 1830; Greece from the same time; while the Balkan States, Roumania, Serbia, Bulgaria and Montenegro gradually re-emerged from the superimposed dominion of the Ottoman Empire between 1859 and 1878. From the same period must be dated the birth," the author continues, "of still greater Nation-States. The Italian *Risorgimento,* originating, as Mazzini admitted, in the Napoleonic occupation, stimulated by the sporadic revolutions of 1848, helped on—a further stage—by the calculating intervention of Napoleon III in 1859, brought near to fruition by the wise statesmanship and adroit diplomacy of Cavour and Victor Emmanuel, finally attained its zenith in 1870-1. In the same year, Bismarck, with the help of Roon and Moltke, completed the fabric of a united Germany."

It happens that in all this reforming of States, the Jewish element has played a significant part.

It may be said that in the last century revolution has produced evolution, and evolution has brought the Jew into the possession of his long withheld political rights. It has freed his forces in new fields, in which, even in that short period, he has risen to the most dignified heights, and this not in any one special territory, but in all in which he has made his home and to which he has given his patriotic devotion. There is not a government in modern Europe nor, for that matter on the Western hemisphere, which has not been benefited during all this evolutionary period by Jews, trained in the law; none wherein, given the opportunity, or allowed to seek it, the Jews have not become ornaments to the bar, distinguished in Statesmanship, and invaluable diplomatic representatives or assistants in international relationships.

Friedrich J. Stahl, whom the Prussian King appointed as a life-member of the first Chamber—afterward designated as the Herrenhaus—was the first Jew to attain fame in German diplomacy. Lord Acton, who, however, is not wholly safe from the suggestion of a bit of personal feeling—he was too great an admirer of Gladstone to do full justice to that statesman's great rival—wrote of Stahl: "He has had a more predominant influence and showed more political ability than Lord Beaconsfield." However, Stahl is but one of many statesmen of the race who have had conspicuous parts in the political re-forming of the European States.

The late Mr. Andrew D. White, who wrote of another Jew, from the standpoint of close observation and personal knowledge, said in his "Seven Great Statesmen": "Edward Lasker was one of the most eminent parliamentarians during the formation period of Germany. He was an accepted leader of the National Liberal Party, and in his ability to sway thinking men, and in his influence over liberal-minded men throughout the Empire, he was one of the foremost statesmen of his time." Nor can we do better, in view of one of the last flings at the Jew to be made by an editor of the *"World's Work"*—he denies them ability to rank high in the field we are now entering— than to follow Mr. White somewhat farther in his estimate of Herr Lasker. He continues:

"At the first elections to the Imperial Parliament Lasker had been chosen by a half dozen districts, and he represented in the Prussian Parliament the important constituency of Frankfort-on-Main. As a jurist, publicist and debater, he stood among the foremost; his integrity was unimpeachable. He had won a victory over financial misdoing on a large scale by which he had driven a finance minister out of office, and he had dared to attack the business enterprises of one of the proudest princes in the Empire. In various exigencies he had been one of Bismarck's most important supporters, and, notably, one of his main aids in reforming German Jurisprudence: but"— and here is another instance of the many thousands that might be cited of the Jew's non-mercenary spirit, of his willingness to sacrifice his personal ambitions for a principle—"in sundry other measures dear to the Chancellor's heart, Lasker opposed him. He could not be reckoned on for thick and thin support and Bismarck's antipathy toward him became passionate."

Lasker was on a visit to America, in connection with the opening of a great western railroad (the Northern Pacific), when death struck him. Shocked, and profoundly moved, the House of Representatives at once sent its sympathies to Germany through the proper official channels. But, to the astonishment of everyone, continues Mr. White, "Bismarck cynically withheld it from the Diet and by the speediest channel returned it to America with a verbal message more curt than polite— its significance being: 'Mind your own business!'" Nor did the matter end there, Mr. White informs us, "for the Iron Chancellor showed his displeasure—even showered it upon the American plenipotentiary, driving him, at last, to resign."

In Austria, at about the same mid-century period, Freiherr von Winterstein took his seat in the House of Lords; and Adolf Fischer, as counsellor to the liberal Government, and Kuranda (one of the most progressive spirits of that exciting period which marked the emergence of the Jews from their political obscurity of centuries) began to take part in the re-forming of their State. In that changing period every country in Europe had its own distinguished Jewish light. They burst forth in jurisprudence, statecraft, and in every avenue of diplomacy. In Italy, Samuel Alatri, a native Roman, sat in Parliament for the Second District of Rome, where for sixty years he worked for the uplifting of his people. For years Alatri headed the delegations from the State which waited upon the Pope. Such was his persuasive eloquence, that Pope Gregory XVI nicknamed him "our Cicero." The re-organization of the financial department of Rome was entrusted to him by Victor Emmanuel, who later put into his hands the adjustment of the Italian budget. When Alatri died (having survived his son, a most revered philanthropist of Rome) it was said by the Syndic of Rome that his city "mourned for Alatri as for a father."

Italy has been especially free from bias in her dealing with her several classes of citizens, and, in consequence, has bred many notable Jewish statesmen and jurists of whom the world has heard much in the last half century. Luigi Luzzatti, whose family for several hundred years have been notable among Italy's scholars and philosophers, has not only filled the Chair of Law in several of her great Universities, but sat in her Parliament for upward of three decades. A Minister in Giolitti's cabinet, he became Premier, in time, and continuously has served his native country in the most delicate negotiations. His name will go down in history with that of Baron Sydney Sonnino, who, with him, represented Italy during the Versailles conferences. Baron Sonnino, an internationally recognized statesman and diplomat, came into world notice when, in 1906, he was called upon to form a ministry. He made this ministry one of the most successful in modern years. The Baron, however, had already represented his country in diplomacy; serving it at Madrid, Vienna and at Berlin; and last, at Versailles, with Luzzatti, his confrère. He was one of the three speakers at a highly important session of that famous gathering, the others being ex-President Wilson and Mr. David Lloyd George.

In view of the wonderful use the Jews have made of their short political freedom, it is increasingly amazing that any should be found among the professedly intellectual, who could continue to indulge in comparisons which are especially odious in this racial discussion. "In statesmanship," admits the writer in the *"World's Work,"* whose pen has been especially active in the work of belittling the Jew, "they have a Disraeli, but no Cromwell or Pitt, or Washington, or Lincoln." To which one might reply: But they had a Moses. "What Jewish orator is there," asks this writer, "to put in the same class with Burke, or Fox, or Sheridan?" To which one may respond truthfully: Non-Jews, at least as capable of estimating their fellowmen accurately as this critic, have ranked Judah P. Benjamin with these famous men. The Jews have not produced a Blackstone or a Grotius, he says, forgetting that both spoke from the inborn consciousness of a people living free for thousands of years; and that they drew upon the Hebrews for precedents. But they have produced the author of the Ten Commandments in which lies the seed of all modern concepts of Law. They have been for a hundred years identified with the administration and even the codification of law in every modern land and have helped to shape and to steady international relations throughout what is called the civilized world. They have strengthened and enlarged empires, even while still handicapped by political disabilities and by the need for meeting the constant foe of racial prejudice, and injustices arising from it.

Nothing could reveal more plainly the deep roots of this prejudice, which even superior minds, it may be unconsciously, continue to cherish and to pass on to posterity, than the various literary attempts that have been made to paint a portrait of Benjamin Disraeli, afterward Lord Beaconsfield. The late Mr. James Bryce has written of him, one of England's foremost premiers, that he is "one of the six or seven—Pitt, Fox, Wellington, Peel, Disraeli; possibly Canning, or O'Connell, or Melbourne—whose names are on our lips today". But Mr. Bryce's biography itself contains much that is disappointing; he devotes sixty-eight pages to an analysis of Beaconsfield as statesman, as man, as novelist, and allows him some rare gifts; but in the end, and especially in his differentiations between Beaconsfield and that other great statesman, Gladstone, he demonstrates the truth of Taine's saying: "Change a virtue in its circumstance and it becomes a vice; change a vice in its circumstance and it becomes a virtue."

In his *"European Commonwealth,"* Mr. J. A. R. Marriott credits Beaconsfield with "England's purchase of the Khedive's shares in the Suez Canal in 1875," which diplomatic activity gave England a quick path to her pos-

sessions in the East; with the bringing about of the proclamation of Victoria as Empress of India in 1876; with the
acquisition of the Transvaal in 1877; and with that of
Cyprus in 1878 (three years before Beaconsfield's death,
at a ripe age), all of which mark, says Marriott, "the
realization of a definite and conscious policy." These
great diplomatic accomplishments escape Mr. Bryce's
attention save by an observation that suggests that
Beaconsfield's eastern policies and acquisitions were negligible. Though always politely, he diminishes all the benefits which Beaconsfield conferred upon England, accentuates his personal shortcomings, and with the same
politeness accentuates Gladstone's virtues while entirely
overlooking his known weak points. A lack of candor
exists in these omissions in connection with both statesmen. Beaconsfield's service was great. He never failed
in an emergency, nor blundered as did Gladstone in selling Heligoland to a rival nation. Both were great men, and
both eminently human. What is striking in Mr. Bryce's
appraisals of both, is that he is at pains to describe as
Semitic in Beaconsfield the traits which reappear in his
descriptions of Gladstone; which traits appear, upon
examination, to be very plainly human ones.

These human characteristics in the case of Mr.
Gladstone are never "Scottish" or "Presbyterian"; never
"English" or "Episcopalian"; but they are in Beaconsfield's case always "Hebraic," "Semitic"; the result of
"his Jewish origin," of his "Hebrew intensity," or his
"Hebrew detachment"; and again and again does he
speak of him as "an alien," as one under "the disadvan-
tages of not being really an Englishman," though, as elsewhere stated, Beaconsfield was the second of his race to
be born in England and the third to reside there for a
lifetime. Surely our language requires a new defining

when "alien" can be applied to a case like that of Beaconsfield's, by a scholar of Mr. Bryce's standing.

This diplomat-author carries his reiteration of race
even to his closing paragraph. History, he thinks, will
not leave Beaconsfield "without a meed of admiration."
When all possible explanations of his success have been
given, he goes on, "what a wonderful career! An adventurer, foreign in race, in ideas, in temper, without money
or family connections, climbs, by patient and unaided
efforts, to lead a great party, master a powerful aristoc-
racy, sway a vast empire and make himself one of the four
or five greatest personal forces in the world. His head
is not turned by his elevation. He never becomes a dema-
gogue; never stoops to beguile the multitude by appealing
to sordid instincts. He retains through life a certain
amplitude of view, a due sense of the dignity of his position, a due regard for the traditions of the ancient assem-
bly which he leads, and when, at last, the destinies of
England fall into his hands, he feels the grandeur of the
charge and seeks to secure what he believes to be her imperial place in the world." Well might Mr. Bryce add,
that whatever judgment history may ultimately pass upon
Beaconsfield, she will find in "the long annals of the English Parliament no more striking figure."

Marriott, writing fourteen years later, has no dis-
qualifying word to say in his brief appraisal of the great
part this statesman played in the establishment of England's prosperity during his connection with the Government. He says that Disraeli had the imagination to perceive—even Mr. Bryce allows him "an occasional flash
of insight"—and this long before the truth was revealed
to the mass of his countrymen, that a new era was dawn-
ing, and Marriott quotes this from Disraeli, himself:
"You have," he said, "a new world, new influences at
work, new and unknown objects and dangers with

which to cope. . . . The relations of England to Europe are not the same as they were in the days of Lord Chatham, or of Frederick the Great. The Queen of England has become the sovereign of the most powerful of Oriental States. On the other side of the globe there are now establishments belonging to her, teeming with wealth and population . . . there are vast and novel elements in the distribution of power . . . what our duty is at this critical moment is to maintain the Empire of England." Mr. Marriott adds, with sincere and just feeling, it would seem:

"Lord Beaconsfield was denounced by opponents as a political charlatan, an Oriental adventurer. . . . Posterity will decide whether the denunciation was just or whether the accusations will recoil upon the heads of the accusers; but this is certain: Lord Beaconsfield perceived that a vast change was taking place under the eyes of his contemporaries, though by the majority of them unperceived, in the centre of political gravity. 'A new world, new influences at work.' Lord Beaconsfield was at least enough of an Englishman to entertain an ardent hope that the new world might be predominatingly English; that the new influences might be directed into channels which would subserve the interests of England, and therefore (as an Englishman may be forgiven for believing) the interests of mankind."

Disraeli, who combined so many potentialities; so many qualities which lesser man could not perceive, who hid his every smart under a smiling face, making himself such a mystery of self-control that his followers fancied that he must have "some hidden resources of wisdom as well as of courage; who never had familiars, was admitted by Mr. Byrce to have attained the heights to which he rose "without patronage or support" and even against opposition "more often concealed than in the open."

Nevertheless he regards his subject as "a favorite of fortune rather than as one who in himself is entitled to credit for any part in his rise. First, Mr. Bryce says, Disraeli had the "fortune" of belonging to the "right political party," though, contradictorily, he points out that it was the opposite of "right" if we may take popularity as an evidence. Such "rightness" as it came presently to have was through the efforts of Disraeli himself. Moreover, the weakness of that party was really responsible for the admission of Disraeli to it. They needed votes. They needed support. They even came to need the Jew. The question of a changed faith may have and did have, unquestionably, a small part in relieving his position, for Jews, as a race, were still many decades from political enfranchisement. Disraeli has left records in his letters to his sister, that his race was never forgotten. "What did you talk about?" he was once asked after an interview held with another great man. "Race, as usual," was his laconic reply.

Mr. Bryce says that the conspiracies hatched against Disraeli to keep him out of an active leadership of his party —and he ran five times before he succeeded in winning a seat in the House—might well have prospered had there been at hand another candidate capable of crossing swords with the leaders in possession. The story of the obstacles Disraeli encountered, of the strenuous rivalries, often with worthy competitors, furnish some of the most engrossing pages in the political history of England. Even Mr. Bryce perceived this. He writes: "Nothing so fascinates mankind as to see a man equal to every fortune, unshaken by reverses, indifferent to personal abuse against apparently hopeless odds with the sharpest weapons and a smiling face. . . . Beaconsfield laid his spell upon the imagination of observers in continental Europe," he adds, "and received at his death a sort of canonization from a large

section of the English people." Mr. Bryce includes Mr.
Gladstone's reply made to a lady who asked him what he
thought of Beaconsfield. "Two things have struck me as
very admirable," Gladstone is said to have responded; "his
perfect loyalty to his wife and his perfect loyalty to his
race." There was also his perfect loyalty to England,
but this was omitted.

Brilliant biographer as he is, Mr. Bryce displays this
tendency to the politely invidious in another biographical
paper on Sir George Jessel, who, Mr. Bryce has written, "had confessedly, the strongest judicial intellect on
the English Bench. . . . He never had an equal and
in our own days a rival in dealing with facts."

Probably none of the factors that go to the support
and upkeep of the law and order of civilization today, is
so little heard of, reaps so little acclaim as those who have
to do with the administration of the law in what is known
as the Courts of Equity. There is nothing in such practice, as Mr. Bryce points out, of the sensational, that may
attract the public. The cases handled are of such nature
as to call for the most absolute knowledge of facts and of
legal precedents, and subtle definitions. Reputations and
legal values in this field are only made by and known to
"the legal fraternity". This was the case, says Mr. Bryce,
with Sir George Jessel, whose fame among his fellows as
Master of the Rolls was extraordinary, even though his
name was seldom heard (until toward the end of his short
career) by his fellow-Britishers.

Sir George Jessel rose through sheer ability, the first
Jew to attain a high judicial position without disavowing
his ancestral faith. He was a Queen's Counsel at forty-
one, and at forty-four Mr. Gladstone called him to his cabinet as Solicitor-General. Next we find him in the House
of Commons, and in 1873, the office of Master of the Rolls
becoming vacant, he was appointed to that office which he

held until his death in 1883. Six judges presided in the Chancery Court, (afterwards to be termed the Court of Appeals), but Jessel took and held the highest rank among them. He decided some of the most important commercial cases of last century. With the exception of Lord Cairns, whose high capacities were known wherever law was practised, he had no equal. His decisions, though delivered on the spur of the moment, "had the merit of carefully considered utterances", so clear and direct was their style, so concisely and so cogently are the authorities discussed and his grounds of decision stated. "The judgments of the Master of the Rolls", Mr. Bryce continues, which fill so many pages of the English Law Reports are among the best that have ever gone to build up the fabric of the English law,." We find historians describing Sir George as impatient with older practitioners who came to court unprepared, but notably gentle with inexperienced and young lawyers; Mr. Bryce finds him an "illustration not only of the advantage of throwing open all places to all comers . . . but also of having a judge at least equal in ability to the best of those who practice before them. . . . His premature death was felt to be a national misfortune."

And yet—the pity of it that it should stain his pages—Mr. Bryce finds that certain mannerisms of this great judge—again those which we see constantly and commonly exhibited in non-Jewish mankind—are racial; that Jessel was "not a cultured man though he knew a great deal besides law—for instance, mathematics, Hebrew literature, botany; and had an intelligence of extraordinary power and flexibility eminently practical . . . and scientific". This tendency of the teachers of the world, of literary leaders, to drag in at every turn the race of the Jew, and always by way of pointing a moral of depreciation, is far more efficient in the transmission of racial prejudices than the broadsides of a Ford, a Chamberlain, a Belloc could possibly be and is deplorable from whatsoever side it is viewed.

Since practice of the law and participation in its political life have been opened to the Jews of Great Britain, innumerable men of this race have performed valuable services for that government. Sir David Salomons, the first English Jew to take an important political post, served first as sheriff, then as magistrate, and rising rapidly to be alderman, he later entered Parliament and became, in the course of time, Lord Mayor of London, in 1855. Sir Salomons was the first Jew to hold this office. His career was a long and dignified battle for the removal of the political difficulties from which his race in England suffered until the last decade of the nineteenth century. During his occupancy the Mansion House became a centre of great brilliancy. As Mayor, Salomons showed a particularly broad spirit in securing the removal of a tablet from a London monument, which, attributing the famous fire of London, of 1666 to the Roman Catholics, was a continual source of indignation among many London citizens. Another Judge Salomons became notable, as a Queen's Counsel in New South Wales, for his successful defense of O'Farrel, a Fenian who had shot the Duke of Edinburgh in 1868. Sir Julian E. Salomons (for that was his name) was Chief-Justice in New South Wales, and served previously in the Ministries of Cowper and Robertson. Notable Jewish jurists and statesmen have had great parts in the organizing of Britain's most important colonies, and, generally are linked with the efforts that have eventuated in a development of the Empire. It has been characteristic of them, and frequently is remarked upon, that Jewish statesmen have never complicated their political operations with their private hatreds, which offers a marked contrast to many who have sought to win political sainthood by the persecution and even attempted annihilation of those who opposed them.

Since the office of Lord Mayor of London was filled by Sir David Salomon, he has had several distinguished successors of his own race; Sir Marcus Samuel, and Sir Benjamin Phillips among others, and the second son of the latter, Sir George Faudel-Phillips, who made his term of office famous for his philanthropic activities. He was responsible for the raising of one million pounds sterling for the famine sufferers of India.

No greater proof of a nation's confidence in the honor and integrity of a Jew has been offered to the modern world than the sending of Lord Reading of Earley, in vice-regal capacity, to India, to have and to hold the interests of the Empire intact, and comprehendingly to administer its laws. The inner reasons for this extraordinary choice and honor to the race will doubtless be elucidated by historians of the future; the stating of them is not the function of a contemporary. But known facts already establish the worth of this diplomat in this great trust, in that peace has been restored to India, which, at the time of Lord Reading's appointment, was torn by conflicting influences and elements. A false diplomatic move, a tactless or autocratic vice-ruler, the presence of the wrong representative among a highly wrought and religiously excited people might have proven a match to highly inflammable material. Only a great man, in whose greatness was comprised both wise statesmanship and delicate understanding of his fellow-beings, would have been equal to the task Lord Reading undertook, and in which he has succeeded.

An acumen as wise has led to the appointment of Sir Herbert Samuel as Governor of Palestine, a country politically unorganized, and where no Jewish experience that might co-operate was available. Sir Herbert already had served England as Post Master General and in other offices. His work in Palestine is not that of bringing harmony among a restless nation but actually of organizing that nation; of developing it; of establishing between it and its neighbors a mutual understanding that will ultimately bring back to that ancient land the glory of its earlier history. He has already succeeded, quietly, in putting it on the map of the world as it has not been for centuries. A large part of the success that has attended the re-establishment of Palestine is also said to be due to our American Ambassador, Morgenthau, who had the oversight of the American philanthropy which has contributed largely to the rebuilding of Palestine to the present.

The name of Adolphe Cremieux brings up in the minds of the legally learned what has come down as the "Damascus Affair," of 1840; but his fame does not rest upon nor was it first attained in his conduct of that famous case. He was practising law at the age of twenty-one, at Nîmes, where, before he had reached his thirtieth year he was recognized as a brilliant orator, learned in legal lore, and skilful in its practice. Paris became aware of him when he secured the conviction of a daring bandit, one Trestaillon, who had been a figure in Royalist activities and was supported by powerful friends. The talk of Paris, we find Cremieux there shortly, defending the case of a group of young men who had been imprisoned for singing the *"Marseillaise"*. The story that tells of his handling of the case states that he concluded his presentation of the case to the jury by an eloquent and dramatic recital of a paraphrase of the famous marching song, which so moved those who heard him that his clients were promptly acquitted. His fame rose steadily after he took up his residence in Paris. Here, in the late '30s he secured the abolition of the *More Judaica,* a very humilitating oath which to that time had been imposed upon the Jews who sought justice in the Courts.

The "Damascus affair" was one of the most notable in the legal annals of the first half of the 19th century. It arose from the disappearance of one, Father Thomas and his servant, under circumstances which seem never to have been cleared up. The priest had practiced medicine among all classes, including the Jews and the Mohammedans. He had a hot dispute with one of the latter who ended by accusing him of blaspheming Mahómet, and threatened the priest with vengeance. A few days later he disappeared, and a fanatical official who was in conflict with the Jews of Damascus, found a way of making political capital out of the case. He circulated the suspicion that Jews had killed the Priest and his man for ritual purposes, and, the calumny gathering force, it was not long before thirteen eminent Jews of the community were arrested and thrown into prison on the accusation of ritual murder. Here they were kept, being tempted by gold to betray each other, and, when this failed, put to excruciating tortures. Among others, these tortures took the form of pulling out the beards of the helpless ones; drawing their teeth, searing their flesh with hot irons. One feeble member of the group died under these tortues and one other is known to have turned Mohammedan rather than suffer longer. One even signed a confession of participation in the crime of which he was accused.

Nor were these prisoners the only Jews who suffered in Damascus. The local synogogue was destroyed together with the sacred scrolls of the law, the heirlooms of centuries. Pamphlets were disseminated over Europe accusing the Jews of the practice of ritual murder, and passions lashed to such a height that the most disastrous consequences were feared. Such Jews as had the power sent to the English and French of their race a heartrending appeal for help. Diplomatic means were tried, but, unsuccessfully, to obtain the release of the prisoners. Finally, with credentials from their respective governments to fortify and protect them, the notable journey was begun, (of which so much has been written) of Sir Moses Montefiore, Adolphe Cremieux and Solomon Munk, famous as an Orientalist. These met and reasoned with the Khedive and later, with the Sultan Majid at Constantinople. Many delays occurred and much tedious international correspondence passed between these rulers and those of the European countries; but the mission eventually succeeded and a firman was issued which freed the prisoners and declared the charges on which they had been held to be absolutely groundless. No amends were made for the horrible sufferings of body and mind which had been endured; but a great public sentiment was stirred up by the case, which, together with another most vicious outbreak of violence against the Jews in the same city some twenty years later culminated in the establishment of the protective *Alliance Israélite Universelle.*

Under the Republic which eventuated from the Revolution of 1848, M. Cremieux served as Minister of Justice and was instrumental in abolishing capital punishment for political offenders; in doing away with the barbarous custom then practiced of exposing condemned prisoners to the gaze of the public. He experienced an imprisonment from the perfidy of Louis Napoleon whose cause he had espoused, but his patriotism was in no way affected, and when "the inglorious peace" was declared which was to rankle in the very heart of France quite to the present day, Cremieux offered a large part of his means to help meet the payments which Germany exacted so uncompromisingly. Gambetta served M. Cremieux as secretary and later became his colleague in the Government of Self-defense.

A man of scrupulous integrity, of unblemished nobility, M. Cremieux who had the reputation of always being ready to aid his race, was inexorable in his attitude towards those who were guilty of unworthy acts. It is said that the scalawag who brought accusations against the Duchess de Berry appealed to M. Cremieux, on the ground of race, to defend him; but that he was met with a scornful reprimand for his audacity. But what is still more remarkable in his career was his quick sympathy with human distress irrespective of race or creed. When, in their turn, the Christians in the East became the object of religious persecution, he sent this strong appeal to his fellow-Jews:

"The Christians of the East are being subjected to the most horrible persecutions. Tortures, rape, assassination, pillage, burning; the murder of women, children and old people—even the mutilation of corpses—such is the picture presented by the entire region of Lebanon . . . Mohammedan fanaticism, even against the wish and forces of the Turkish Government, is destroying a dense population whose sole crime is that they worship the Christ. French Jews! let us not await diplomacy; let us be the first to come to the aid of our Christian brothers" . . .

Even Russia has had its famous Jewish jurists and statesmen within a century, among them, Emanuel Bank whose powers as a debater were the wonder of the legal fraternity. Koni, himself called the "Russian Cicero", having listened to a famous debate in which Bank took part spoke of it as "the most brilliant oratorical tournament he had ever listened to." Bank's memory, especially its accuracy, has passed into a saying in Russia.

The Asser family of jurists and statesmen, in Holland, have been identified with its legal and political life for more than a century. Moses S. Asser, in 1798 was a member of a legislative commission appointed for the readjustment of the Holland laws to meet the requirements that arose when the United Provinces were changed into a Republic under a French protectorate. When the Napoleonic code was imposed upon the new Republic, Asser again became a member of the commission formed by Louis Bonaparte to draft a commercial code as "part of the uniform system of laws which was projected for use throughout the government."

Carel Asser, a member of the same family was one of the three delegates to the Sanhedrin, called by Napoleon in 1807, and for twenty-one years held the post of referendery of the first class in the department of Justice at The Hague. The high pinnacle of legal attainment in this family however, was reached by Tobias M. C. Asser, who died in Holland in 1913, two years after the Nobel Peace Prize had been awarded to him. From the beginning of his career, so early as his twenty-third year, Asser was a man of mark in Dutch jurisprudence. At that time the Dutch Government made him a member of an international commission to negotiate a settlement in connection with the abolition of tolls on the Rhine. Before and after it became a University he held the Chair of Jurisprudence at the Athenaeum. He took part in many important conferences on International Law with distinguished foreign authorities before he had attained his thirtieth year. At thirty-seven he became Assistant Secretary of State holding the office for eighteen years, when he rose to membership in the highest body in the Dutch Government, the Council of State.

Nothing could better tell the story of his standing, his rating in Holland than to glance at the record of the offices he has filled. In 1905 he was made permanent Chairman of the Diplomatic Congress on International law, which Congress was brought into existence mainly through his efforts. He was delegate to the Peace Congress that was convened at the Hague in 1899 and presided over one of its divisions. Asser wrote works on International Law which before the opening of the present century had been translated into all the European languages. Fragments of his most potent speeches are to be found in the biographies of noted statesmen, which other statesmen have published during the last two decades.

The records of the Ambassadors to foreign lands from the United States—to come to a glance at the history of Jewish diplomats of the present who have performed distinguished public services for the United States—every page of these records of the Honorables Abram I. Elkus, Oscar S. Straus and Henry Morgenthau, Ambassadors to Turkey, and of Ira Nelson Morris to Sweden, bears testimony to the consciousness in each of the full weight of responsibility in his office, and offers proof that each diplomat kept continually before him the axiom that one false step in diplomacy may disarrange the peace of the world. As caretakers of the interests of the nation abroad, they have been perfect stewards of the government, and benefactors as well to their fellow-citizens.

A conscientiousness as marked attaches to the services of other Jews in the foreign relations of the United States; in those of Louis Marshall, an acknowledged great authority upon international law, who took part in the Versailles negotiations. Our American Jewish jurists have their representatives upon the Supreme Court Bench; they have issued from the leading law schools of the land, and are active factors in the growth of our legal and legislative systems, trusted alike by clear-seeing non-Jews and their own religious group.

But previous to the present century the United States has had her own truly distinguished Jewish jurists and statesmen. One of the most brilliant names associated with the practice of law, with the Congress, with the period of the Civil War, is that of Judah P. Benjamin, remembered chiefly in these days for his connection with the attempt to found a confederacy of the Southern States. But Mr. Benjamin, long before his activities in that connection, had a nation-wide reputation. A native of St. Croix, he was brought up in North Carolina, and afterwards studied at Yale. He was admitted to the bar of the Territory of Louisiana when he was twenty-one, and already was recognized as having a philosophical mind and great reasoning powers. In some respects his early career resembles that of Beaconsfield, whose junior he was by seven years. While he made the earliest known "Digest of the Reported Decisions of the Territory of New Orleans", he began life as an agriculturist experimenting in the extraction of saccharine from sugar-cane.

Quite like certain later adventuring agriculturists upon the Mississippi border of whose trials we have spoken, his plantations were ruined by floods, and to reimburse himself for his losses, Benjamin took up the practice of law. He became famous for his handling of the land-title cases to property in California which was long in litigation. Very shortly he was practising before the Supreme Court and President Taylor considering him for a cabinet position. It has been said that President Pierce offered him an Associate Justice-ship of the United States Supreme Court. He was then United States Senator from Louisiana.

Messrs. Nicolay and Hay, in their life of Lincoln describe Benjamin as one of the ablest and most persistent of those who were passionately occupied with the establishment of a Southern Government. Famous as an orator in his day, he has been included in volumes that treat of great orators. Charles Sumner considered him "the most brilliant orator in the United States," and many times the story has been told of the impression made by his farewell speech in the Senate on the dramatic occasion of the withdrawal of the Southern Senators in 1861. There were present in the Senate on that occasion the families of the withdrawing Senators and representatives from many of the foreign Governments housed in the Capitol. It is said that Sir George Cromwell Lewis asked Lord Sherbrooke shortly afterward: "Have you read Benjamin's speech? It is better than our own Benjamin [Disraeli] could have done."

That serenity of bearing which so often was remarked upon in Disraeli was characteristic of Judah P. Benjamin. To him fell the responsibility of the foreign correspondence of the young Confederacy, but when arms failed, diplomacy was weakened, and when at last the southern group met failure, Benjamin was obliged to flee the country. His American property was confiscated and he was proscribed. From the accounts of Messrs. Nicolay and Hay, Mr. Benjamin, long after his own conviction had been formed that the cause was lost, clung to the responsibilities he had assumed. But the wonderful part of his career, the most remarkable element in his character was still to be revealed. At the age of fifty-five he made his way to England, and there, beginning life anew, took up the practice of law. A few years later, in 1872, he was made Queen's counsel; and, becoming recognized as one of the leaders of the English bar, was able to retire, eleven years later, his fortunes amply repaired and his reputation the highest.

Schmoller's saying that "the greatest efficiency of great men begins after their death" is particularly applicable to the case of jurists, statesmen, diplomats. Theirs is the work, the danger, the accomplishment that the average man enjoying the benefits of, is yet scarcely aware of. They are the safeguards of national, international and individual liberty. A mighty charge, and one in which the Jew has played a great part and rendered important services to mankind.

CHAPTER XV

The Jew as Moral Force

"For the whole civilized world the Jewish race has been the source of all the highest conceptions of God, man and nature. Through this race was developed not only the Hebrew religion, but also the Christian religion. . . . I say that the highest conceptions of God, man, and nature are all Jewish. . . . The Jews originated and still preserve the loftiest descriptions of the attributes of God. For them, thousands of years ago, He was the one only God, a pure spirit, infinite in knowledge, power and good will."

CHARLES W. ELIOT.

(In address delivered at Boston. November, 1905)

IT would be unnecessary, today, to measure the Jew as a moral force, but for the overgrowth of erroneous belief which from time to time is permitted to obscure what should be left free to the common knowledge. In this field, he has been assailed, is being assailed with the most unscrupulous disregard for common consideration, for truth, forgetful, as some one has said, "of the dangerous homing tendency of facts".

All races in the course of their development have arrived at moral codes, at standards of conduct; but of all races of which anything is definitely known, only the Jews merged their moral codes with their religion, adhered to them, preached and practised them for thousands of years, from the beginning associating them with their frequent oblations to God in whom they continually acknowledge themselves "to live and move and have their being".

Though to adhere to these standards has carried them literally through stonings and insults, through slavery, and massacres, pogroms, and revilings and contumely from men even to this third decade of the twentieth century, yet to them the ways of the Law of their God have continued to be accepted as "ways of pleasantness" and their paths those of "peace." Their never-flagging message to the world has been: "If thou hadst walked in these ways, thou shouldst have dwelt in peace forever."

The Law and peace: these are the great recurring words of the Jewish prophets from the beginning. The keeping of the one produced the other. The thought of their teachers, their patriarchs and prophets from Abraham to Moses; from Moses to Malachi; from Malachi to Hillel; from the Galilean, Meir, Maimonides, and on down through the great list of their inspirational leaders to those as devoted and heroic today, their continual word to humanity is the attainment of peace through just and righteous conduct. One voice dies out but another reiterates the admonition to their people to learn to distinguish and choose between right and wrong; to deal and to live righteously. "Righteousness tendeth to life": "the way of the transgressors is hard"; only by the living of a just and righteous life may the road to peace be found. Every prophet voice proclaims the same truth. The keeping of the Law is the starting-point; the goal the attainment of peace for troubled humanity.

The teachers of the race have always been punctilious as to the minutiae of conduct. They rebuke the slothful and the sluggard: the sleeper, the glutton, the tippler, the vain, the back-biter, him who cheats, who thinks evil in his heart, as well as those who commit the major sins of the decalogue. Always the reward of righteousness is to be able to lie down in green pastures, beside still waters, the attainment of peace. This was never to be won by the Jews through warrings and bloodspillings—"whoso sheddeth man's blood by man shall his blood be shed" is one of their early great commandments—but by the right conduct of the individual. Of all the ancient peoples, the Jews alone visioned a time when swords might be beaten into ploughshares. Of all modern races it was a Jew whose plea for world peace touched the Russian Czar in the last years of the nineteenth century and led to the calling of the first Peace Conference at The Hague.

Peace and the perfecting of human conduct, of human character has been the great quest of the race from the earliest records we may come at. The path to their goal was alone through their Law which was to be kept in mind forever. They were exhorted, they are today still exhorted to teach this law of conduct, this law of blended worship of God with just dealing with man, to their children; to "talk of it when thou sittest in thy house; when thou walkest by the way; when thou liest down, and when thou risest up." "Impractical idealism" say those who move uneasily under the consciousness that they would not have the moral stamina to meet such rigorous laws; yet the Jews go on undeterred. They are "essentially idealists," Bishop Lawrence has said; and he credits them with possessing "insight which through the wars, social revolutions and political overthrows, saw always God's hand"; with having wrought always "for higher spiritual truth," and for having "brought the righteousness of heaven into the affairs of this earth." For sixteen hundred years non-Jewish idealists have drunk at these Jewish springs, and have been applying the pure religious ethics of the race, and often its ritual forms, to the building up of their later religions or faiths.

But how are these facts to be squared with the utterances of the bigots of today, who reach, unfortunately, the many, where wiser men are heard by but few? A Bishop may preach to a thoughtful if self-concerned city congregation, but an irresponsible editor or publisher may send his manifolded libels into every news-hungry village of the land; inject his poisonous propaganda into impressionable minds, and so "mould public opinion" as to lash the innocent mind which is fundamentally just, into a fury against a people who have never offended them; whose only fault is that they have been stung into a state of sensitive self-defense by incomparable and unprovoked attacks from amazing sources? The editor and publisher, it would seem, even more than the minister with his limited congregation, should hold in mind the critical importance of the preservation of respectful tolerance between the varying groups that form a nation. Two examples of the acrimonious spirit which such "authorities" are displaying, suffice to show both the state of mind of modern Jew-baiters, and the shamelessness with which they make anything serve their purpose.

An editor of the *"World's Work"* complains of the Jew's "continual communings" with his God. He finds that it leads the Jew of today to such lengths of devotion that he would rather go hungry than accept employment in which he would be obliged to labor on the Sabbath. Devotion so quixotic in these practical days is incomprehensible to this editor. It frets him, and evidently sets his reasoning powers awry, for he is able to construct out of these super-religious tendencies of the Jew, qualities unbefitting to citizenship in the United States. This devotion of the Jew to his law and to the customs of his forefathers, far from appearing to this editorial gentleman as a praiseworthy moral example, represents the opposite to him. We live in an age when other religious groups have pooled their day of devotion; organized it in such way as to have it all over and done with, with as little inconvenience as possible. It rankles him that the Jews do not act similarly. This complaint is, of course, mere fretful faultfinding, which, moreover, was once quite commonly made against the Seventh Day Baptists. When we come to the conscienceless attacks upon the Jews which Mr. Ford of Detroit, Michigan, has launched, we find a horse of quite another color. He says:

"The Jews are a race that is the moving spirit of the corruptive, subversive and destructive influences abroad in the world today"; and, quoting from an alleged foreign source, he adds: "they have stirred up the people in all countries, have incited them to war, revolution and to communism. . . . Youths, mostly circumcized, [no data is supplied as to how this fact was obtained] are often drunk or half drunk," etc. It is surely unnecessary to quote farther from a case so obviously the over-elaborated labor of prejudice, but it should be quite clear as to which is the force that at present is making for subversion, corruption and destruction among the people.

The pity of it is that so many supposably responsible beings are still willing to act in violation of the laws and precepts of humanity while with their lips they confess the justice and propriety of these laws; that so many are willing to take as true the dogmatic utterances, which, but a slight examination would usually prove to be unwarrantable and even entirely baseless. We should make sure before accepting them, as Walter Bagehot has outlined it, that such deductions are the truth and nothing but the truth, for who is not almost sure beforehand, he asks, by their very fierce dogmatism, that they do not contain such a mixture of error and truth as to render it not worth while to spend time in reasoning over them? "In a word," he ends, "they are the superfluous energy of mankind flowing over into fields which might better be passed by."

Matthew Arnold wrote that most of the theological systems that had come up to rasp the world, most of their extravagances have arisen "out of the talents of able men for reasoning, and their want—not through lack of talent, for the thing needs none; it needs only time, trouble, good fortune and a fair mind . . . their want of literary experience." He has traced at length in his "Literature and Dogma," the steady quest of the Jews for perfect living; for perfect morality; for closer union with the *Eternal:* and this by following behind the prophets, as each urges his people to seek for righteousness and peace. He finds the Jews to be the one people who have not been led away by the distractions which merely moral propositions offer to the brilliant reasoners along theological lines.

Arnold quotes Ovid as excusing himself for the immorality of his verses on the ground that the mention of the gods has incited them; and, the English poet adds (a bit mischievously, it must be admitted) "Even at this time of day, the grave authorities of the University of Cambridge are so struck by one of them [the god] of pleasure, life, fecundity . . . that they set it publicly up as an object for their scholars to fix their minds upon, and to compose verses in honor of; which is all very well at present:" Arnold says, "but with this inclination in the University of Cambridge, and in the Indo-European race to which they belong, where would they be now if it had not been for Israel, and the stern check which Israel put upon the glorification and divinization of this natural bent of mankind? Going, perhaps, Vice-Chancellor, bedels, masters, scholars and all, in spite of their Professor of Moral Philosophy, to the Temple of Aphrodite. It is Israel and his seriousness that have saved the authorities of the University of Cambridge from carrying their divinization of pleasure to these lengths." It may be said with equal truth that it is this restraining influence of Israel that lies at the root of the rancor Mr. Chamberlain so indefatigably displays in his voluminous effort to decry the Jewish race.

Examine into the ethics of the Jew as seen in the

Scriptures and in the later Rabbinical writings—and
notable European University scholars today are urging
an acquaintance with, at least, the literature of Ibn Ezra,
Ibn Gabirol, and Maimonides, Levi ben Gerson, and
Hasdai Crescas, as enlightenment that is necessary to a
comprehension of the New Testament—and it will be
found that the most rigorous moral codes ever devised
for human conduct are there imbedded; that they are
devised for the elevation of human character.

The Old Testament ethics are universally applicable
and have been universally applied. They deal with practically every phase of human thought; they point continually to the fact that the wages of sin is death; that
the hope of the world lies in the uplift of the individual.
Most of the Jewish kings, like Josiah, "began while
yet young, to seek after the Law". Most of them,
and all of their prophets, have been reformers. Every
time the race has fallen into the error of departing
from their way of worshipping their God, the rebuking
prophet has risen to point them back to God. Hosea,
Isaiah, Jeremiah, Ezra were the great moral forces
of their times. They roused their people to their
better selves when temptation had overwhelmed them;
when evils had crept in among them that worked
for their undoing, even as many later representatives of
their race have worked, with an energy which is racial,
and affected great moral changes in the modern world.
Ezra and his co-worker, Nehemiah, worked a great moral
reform in Israel, by their call upon their people to return
and pledge themselves anew to their God. Today the
race still feels and the non-Jewish world no less, the
force of those two personalities. Ezra was the Blue
Law man of Jewry, who emphasized the Sabbath laws
which the Jewish people, faithful to the pledges their
forefathers made to him, still adhere to. Many historians

perceive these prophets as agents who have set in motion
currents of religious thought which are still most forceful
in the modern world.   It is unnecessary to dwell here
upon the moral force which Jesus, the Teacher, of Jewish
birth, and thought and training, and Paul his follower,
have exercised in the world.   They are the foundation
stones on which great Church organizations have risen.

But Jewish teachers did not cease to teach, they did
not cease to be great moral forces in the world with the
destruction of Jerusalem; rather, they, too, entered upon
a new era in their moral life.   Name after name arises
in the early and Middle Ages, of great Rabbis who have
left their imprint on their times.   They were forces for
enlightenment when the world at large was still battling
with what to our modern eyes seem like the most childish
superstitions.   They were teaching forgiveness and forbearance even in the face of martyrdom; teaching, too,
human justice, and, above all, just conduct.   Justice
Stafford has said of them: "Israel's ideal of justice has
taken permanent possession of the human mind," and he
added to the Jews: "Give up every other claim to the
world's gratitude before you surrender this: The world
owes its conception of Justice to the Jew."

Maimonides, Rabbi, philosopher, scientist, physician,
from his home in Egypt in the twelfth century, was one
of the first to strike a blow at the superstitions of his time
when he denounced astrology as "not a science, but a
disease."   His *"Guide to the Perplexed,"* an edition of
which, prepared by Rabbi Stephen S. Wise, was brought
out early in the present century, has influenced every
Jewish thinker and many non-Jewish theologians and
students to the present day.   Maimonides, like all innova-
tors, was criticized and opposed even by the orthodox of
his own race, who in later generations went back to his
teachings.   He is generally regarded as the steadying

force of his time that safeguarded the Scriptures which the conflicting and confusing philosophies of his time threatened to overturn. Aristotelian physics possessed the scientific minds of the period and threatened the security of the theory of God on which both Church and Synagogue rested. It is claimed and evidence exists in the writings of eminent Church authorities of that day, that the writings of Moses ben Maimon remained a force and bulwark of the Church writers for centuries. Certainly his philosophies formed the mental food of later thinkers who have enlightened the world.

The Kabbala cult which engaged alike the non-Jewish and Jewish scholastics of Europe for a century, arose from Jewish speculative theories. Faulty, mystical, it was, nevertheless, a progressive step in its day of confused thinking, and of conflicting efforts for the finding of truth. It has been said that but for the contributions of the Jewish scholars of the Middle and later ages, indefatigably translating the philosophical deductions of Greek and Arabian authors and uttering their own, as well, Europe might still be in the state of conservative inaction which for so many centuries has bound present day China in the chains of the past.

A perfect treasurehouse of wisdom in imperishable sayings have been accrued from the Jewish teachers of those times, many of which have passed into general literature: from Ibn Gabirol, Rashi, Ibn Ezra, Halevi and many others. "He who soweth hatred, soweth regret"; "Who questions is halfway to wisdom," are typical of the progressive and broad-minded spirit of the Jewish leaders of those days. Abraham Judaeus, another great moral force of his time (the twelfth century) wrote, it is said, with a wonderful fervor, always exhorting his readers to lead holy lives, and devote them to purity and to well doing. Rabbi Meir of Rothenberg,

Chief Rabbi of Germany, and called the Father of Rabbis, was a great spiritual leader of his people through times very troublous for them. He was a jealous guardian of everything that touched the Jewish honor, and constantly warned them against descending in their business transactions from the lofty precepts of their prophets.

The list of remarkable theologians among the Jews in the Middle Ages is large, and their contributions to the philosophical literature was voluminous, especially in the commentaries of the Scriptures, and in the Aristotelian debate which occupied so much of the general thought. It was the time of the discovery of printing; of the multiplying of books and the spread of learning. Philosophies of the ancients were available now for many, and modifications were taking place in the thought of the world in many directions. Science, the new element in life, was making great strides, and opening up intellectual vistas that previous ages had never dreamed of. A great influx of Jewish scholars from Spain and Portugal had taken up their residence in Holland, where speculative thinkers were especially active. It was from among this group of Jews of Europe that there was to arise one of the greatest moral forces of modern times.

Baruch Spinoza has been called "the God-intoxicated Jew." His life was short, but his influence is already three centuries long and will last in some degree while literature lives and men think. His forty-four years of life were spent in poverty, and even in obscurity. "Like every Jew," as one biographer puts it, "Spinoza learned a trade"; and while pondering on the mighty thoughts that were to carry his name down the ages, which were to be fused thereafter with the life thought of modern civilization, he polished lenses, and was otherwise interested in optical instruments. He was physically delicate, like those hollow-chested Jews whom an editor elsewhere quoted, finds so unpleasant a sight for the eyes of prosperous Americans to look upon. He lived and died apart, as another has written, "in the great spiritual isolation which enabled him to regard human affairs with complete detachment." He lived also in continual communion with the Almighty, which would again bring scoffing from the editor referred to, though from a million pulpits each week, of all known faiths, the world weary are urged to seek their strength in such devotion. Spinoza had so little in him of that commercial spirit which is so insistently declared to be characteristic of all Jews that, while living on six sous a day, he had the moral courage to refuse a gift of two thousand florins on the ground that the possession of so much money would deflect him from his studies and occupations. He was wont to say: Nature is satisfied with little, and when she is content, I am so.

It was in lowly surroundings that the great philosopher evolved his doctrine of God as the Imminent Cause of all things, a doctrine so lucidly put forth that it has acted magically upon many groping minds since it was formed, though it brought much woe upon Spinoza himself. The gentlest accusations brought against him in life was that he was a Pantheist.

Much capital has been made of the action of the Jews of Amsterdam, who, themselves refugees from the persecutions of Spain and Portugal, in turn persecuted Spinoza, excommunicating him, as the story goes, "with the anathema wherewith Joshua cursed Jericho, with the curse which Elisha laid upon the children, and with all the curses which are written in the Law"; but when this is reached it leads to recrimination. Religious history is one long paradox when matters of this sort are looked into. It is unnecessary to cite the case of Galileo or the very late cases of harsh dealing with clergymen whose ripened reason repudiated items of dogma to which their unripe reason had earlier subscribed. The history of mankind, of Jews and of non-Jews proves that every progressive thought has endangered its utterer. To paraphrase Bergson, our perceptions of truth widen slowly. The victim of yesterday's outraged beliefs, today is perceived to have erred only in seeing a little farther than his fellows. Faraday pleaded in vain for "the meanest place in which he might test his scientific theories." He was rejected and put aside on every hand. Happily, in his case, he lived to decline the highest honors which the scientific world which had refused him, afterward desired to confer upon him.

Spinoza knew no such triumph. He met with oppression in life and contumely after death. Hume spoke of him as a "famous atheist," and it is recorded that Lessing said of him: "People speak of him as if he were a dead dog"; and yet, fifty years later, we find Goethe acknowledging with joy "how much the views of that great thinker answered the wants of his youth. In Spinoza," he said, "he found himself, and in him, therefore, could he fortify himself to the best advantage." Spinoza's writings, through their interweaving and transfusion into the writings of later philosophers, Hegel, Schelling and others, were to have a large part in coloring the philosophic thought of the last and present centuries.

Like Maimonides, Descartes, and Bacon, his predecessors, looking upon the religious disputes which for centuries had been destroying the peace of the world, Spinoza shared in the labor of giving to humanity such freedom as it today possesses from the bondage of superstition. His philosophy went far toward uprooting the hedges which half-seeing theologies had been setting about the human mind, and toward leaving the individual free to seek his God. That there are yet barriers to be overcome we have conclusive proof in the sectarian and national walls, overgrown with hideous prejudices, hatreds and rivalries, that still postpone the coming together in friendliness of the human family.

Spinoza, followed closely after Descartes, who "led Europe in the attempt to found a new philosophy based on reason and not upon past customs," but he rose higher spiritually. A great moral force, he taught that "minds are not conquered by armies, but by love and magnanimity"; that "intellectual love of God" is more permanent than that born of a transitory emotion. His teachings were caught up in the course of time by the Dutch theologians, among whom a Spinoza school of thought was founded. Leibniz, first his friend, "veered round" after Spinoza's death, and joined the groups which proclaimed the Jewish philosopher an atheist; nevertheless, historians say, he was the direct beneficiary of Spinoza's moral force. In an article on *The Philosophy of Leibniz,* written in 1900 by B. Russell, that author finds passages, he says, with but slightly changed phraseology, but without acknowledgment, in Leibniz's works, which "contain the views of the derided Spinoza." "There is but one philosophy," said Lessing, one hundred years after the death of Spinoza, "the philosophy of Spinoza." Hegel declared that to be a philosopher, you must first be a Spinozist.

The name of this Jewish thinker, execrated by ecclesiastics of all classes, ecclesiastics who now generally are forgotten, shines out against the skies of his century like a clear planet. Schleirmacher's fine apostrophe to Spinoza has often been repeated, but will bear still another telling. He bids the world "to offer a lock of hair to the manes of the holy and excommunicated Spinoza." The basis, the inner kernal, the sum total of this Jewish philosopher's teaching was that God was in all and all in God, a thought which permeates all religious thought of today; which is being preached from every pulpit and which none disputes.

What is interesting above all else in this "new" philosophy is that it lies imbedded in the first writings of the Jews and may be found in Genesis, in the names the early Hebrews employed to characterize the all-supplying, all-nourishing Providence, the All-in-All. Spinoza's was a gospel of love, as well, which gospel has been similarly incorporated with Jewish teachings from the beginning. The power of love for one's fellow-men, even for the beasts of the field, to whom, the patriarchs taught, man should show pity and give succor, again and again is emphasized throughout the Old Testament. It has been, for that matter, theoretically recognized among all groups of men, by all races and civilizations. Like other fundamental truths, it is only on rare occasions applied. Emerson has been quoted as saying: "Were Christendom to accept the sentiment of love even for a season, it would bring the felon and the outcast to our side in tears with the devotion of his faculties to our service. Love would put a new face on this weary old world in which we dwell as pagans and enemies too long; and it would warm the heart to see how fast the vain diplomacy of statesmen, the impotence of armies and lines of defense would be superseded by this unarmed Love."

The function and force of the "third Moses," Mendelssohn, was to dissolve prejudices and to operate for the political freeing of his people. No man of his time affected human thought more, or set so many moral forces in operation, which, threatening and eventually overturning many of the social inequalities and injustices that had prevailed in his time, has brought about universal suffrage, and a democratic freedom which has no precedent in world history. The decades of the nineteenth century, examined one by one, will each, in turn, show some special Jewish force at work upon the solving of some moral problem which kept "the people" bound, or suffering. To the unthinking, the unobservant, many of these Jewish forces have been passed by as "revolutionary"; as troubling the peace of the world. But every great reforming personality that has come into the world at some point in his career has been similarly characterized, whether non-Jewish or Jewish. What principally matters is: What did this one or that accomplish to better the condition, spiritually, physically, for mankind?

It was a "terrible Jew," Ferdinand Lassalle, a disciple of Hegel, who proved a moral force in combating the "iron law of wages," and set in motion the battle between Capital and Labor, the end of which is not yet in sight, but the object of which was humane; for it sought to raise the standard of living for the greater part of the human family. Today we are so far removed from the conditions which gave rise to "Social Democracy," founded by Lassalle, that it is difficult to measure them. Lassalle believed, and labored for his belief, that labor as the creator of value in any given product, should itself receive the value of that product; that wages should keep pace with that product's increasing value and not remain confined to fixed terms that furnished but the barest subsistence for the laborer and his family.

In his day, all but the smallest possible sum returned to the wage-earner, while the mass of profit went back to capital in return for its investment. Lassalle's problem was "how to dispense with the interposition of capital so that labor might secure the profit of its industry" and not be perpetually limited to a pittance. His work was humane but necessarily revolutionary, since Capital clings to its prerogatives and custom had established its privileges. So dangerous did Lassalle's ideas appear to Germany, herself a leader in many later struggles, that when he not only espoused the cause of the working-classes as a great "Fourth Estate," but foresaw as well the coming of universal suffrage, all political forces attacked him. Nevertheless, he succeeded in establishing the "German Labor Organization" mother of all future labor organizations. After his death, it weakened for lack of a leader, but his idea had been projected, to thrive, to live and to spread over the earth, and this by the moral force of another, born of the same race.

The histories of Jewish moral leaders hold a singular resemblance to the old Greek torch-races, in which the mounted participants rushed over their course holding aloft a flaming torch; and as each reached the end of his allotted race he flung his torch to him who came after, who in turn dashed forward with it. Karl Marx caught up the torch from Lassalle's hand and scarcely a year after Lassalle had passed away the International Workingmen's Association was founded. Established in 1864, its progress is known. Today the Labor interests are active the world over and prophets are not lacking who declare that the religions of the future will involve tenets defensive for the workingman's protection.

As the author of *Kapital*, the moral force of Karl Marx has tremendously affected modern life. In a comparatively recent voting contest for the greatest men of their day, ten to be selected from a thousand, Marx was given place among the chosen ones as the greatest humanitarian of his time. He came in for serious criticism, none the less, for having encouraged the workmen to take part in the Paris Commune, in 1871. By the peace-loving of the Jewish race, from whose tenets Marx was quite divorced, he has never been held as a Jew, but his race, none the less, spoke through his great visions of freedom for the worker and for a more even distribution of the comforts of life as between the industrial producer and the moneyed employer.

Few will dispute the moral force which has effectively helped the world in the present day through the active Jewish mind of Felix Adler. The time has not arrived for making even an approximate appraisal of all he has meant and all he means to his generation. Reverent and serious, the offspring of a rabbinical house, which in itself was a powerful moral force—through his father, Rabbi Samuel Adler of the Temple Emanu-El of New York City—Felix Adler, with charity toward all and malice toward none, founded the Ethical Culture movement many years ago, which today has its branch organizations in many American and European cities. Beginning with the proposition that moral ends are supreme above all human ends and interests, the aim of the Ethical Culture Society has been to teach "that the moral law has an immediate authority not contingent upon the truth of religious beliefs, or upon philosophical theories; and to advance the science and art of right living." It does not seek to detach men from their preferred religious forms, or sects, but only to draw their attention to the moral problems which each day of life erects.

Dr. Adler's Society has founded free kindergartens, a workingman's school. It has undertaken movements for the improvement of the dwellings of the poor; and had its important part in securing the adoption in public schools of courses in science and art; also in manual training. Unique in its hope and in its organization for the attaining of it, the Ethical Culture Society is the single body today that exists for the purpose of uniting men to their fellowmen in a bond of human understanding, of mutual comprehension and for the purpose of "linking up the world's activities in science, art, politics, business to the supreme ethical end."

Someone has said of Dr. Adler: "He works among the intellectuals"; but his true work has been to raise the intellectual standards, even of workingmen. This is characteristic of the peculiar democracy of the Jewish teachers throughout the ages and the world over. It has been the mission of Jewish Rabbis in America, in every locality in which they are found domiciled; to raise the intellectual standard, especially of those new-arrivals in America from lands where for centuries they have been denied the opportunity of an education at all comparable with that open to non-Jews.

No man has left a greater impression upon the communities that knew him than the late Rabbi Isaac M. Wise, long identified with the State of Ohio and to whom the Rabbinical School at Cincinnati stands as a memorial. It was not enough that the people of his race should be educated, but he foresaw the need of widening the education of their teachers. His people were scattered, each group a law unto itself in matters relating to Synagogue services, and Judaism, the oldest of all religions, lacked the organization which was necessary to build it up. Dr. Wise, to put an end to conditions which were chaotic and lacking in order, travelled and wrote constantly until he had roused his people to the point of warmly co-operating with him. The outcome of his zeal was not only the establishment of the Hebrew Union College in Cincinnati, but a fusing and bringing together of differing groups of Jews which, as one has said, "had an incalculable effect upon the Jewish citizens of the United States."

Looking over only the past fifty years of the story of the Jew as a moral force in America, a record of the

most unparalleled zeal and unflagging self-sacrifice may
be traced—not in the instance of one, but of innumerable
rabbis and teachers of the race. During that period, the
"race-consciousness" and "Jewish organization" which the
vicious have been so industriously misrepresenting, has
spoken steadily through the erection of schools for their
less fortunate members. A great publication society has
been founded, not for the dissemination of "red" literature
as the careless reader of Mr. Ford's recently uttered fiction
about the Jew might infer, but for the spread among the
Jewish people of knowledge of their own wonderful secular
as well as religious literature, of which the non-Jewish
world is at present equally in need. "For most readers"
says R. T. Herford, in the Hibbert Journal, "Rabbinical
or post-Biblical literature is entirely unknown"; but he
speaks also of "the increased attention which is being
given to Jewish literature other than Biblical," and adds
elsewhere that the man who has missed a close study of
the Old Testament is not yet completely educated.

In the great educational campaign which for the past
half century has been conducted by the more fortunate and
highly educated Jews of the world for the enlightenment
of the less fortunate members of their race, many who have
passed on and many of their successors have taken zealous
part. Dr. Jastrow, a member of a violently assailed
group, the Polish Jews, gave a quarter of a century of life
in America to a translation of the Old Testament; participated in the preparation of the Jewish encyclopedia which
appeared some twenty years ago; and at the same time
taught and preached the moral life to his people. Dr.
Morais, founder of the Jewish Theological Seminary
which stands on University Heights, in New York City,
and President of it until his death; Rabbi David Phillip-
son, Professor Solomon Schechter, Dr. Joseph Krauskopf,
who lectured the length and breadth of the land to raise

funds for his National Farm School, and who was one of the most beloved and honored Jewish teachers of his time; Dr. E. G. Hirsch, of Chicago; Rabbis Samuel Schulman, Joseph Silverman and Stephen S. Wise of New York and Dr. Henry Berkowitz, Dr. Cyrus Adler of Philadelphia—these and unnumbered Jews of America have been and are moral forces of incalculable value today. Nor should Dr. Henry Leipsiger be forgotten, who established "the People's University" Course of Public Lectures under the auspices of the Board of Education of New York City, the first course of the kind to be established in any city in the world. He deservedly must be reckoned a moral force of as yet incalculable benefit to his community.

But these by no means compass the meaning to the world today of the Jew as a moral force. A host of European Jewish thinkers are carrying on the "Humanist" spirit that has distinguished this race through all time. In everything that has to do with the welfare of mankind they take and have taken active part.

The Jews again and again are accused of desiring war, though their efforts, their creed is for peace. "Peace" is their greeting; the Galilean pressing home this racial tenet was the "Prince of Peace". Blioch of Russia, wrote his plea to the nations to take counsel together to devise some means of preserving perpetual peace among the nations, which plea bore fruit in the first Hague Conference.

Among today's philosophers, it is again a Jew, Henri Bergson, who opposes the agnostic tendencies of the times. Professor Bergson, at Oxford, told his listeners that "but for the narrow range or weakness of our perceptive powers" there would be no reason for "philosophy". That, in itself is a message of hope to humanity. It may look forward to a time when our perception, now so limited, will recognize the folly (and worse) of hugging to our breasts the asp of racial prejudice, and cause us, for our own protection, to eliminate this horrid and venomous thing as thoroughly as we would and do other poisons, once we have identified them.

John Burroughs named Bergson the "Prophet of the Soul", His *"Creative Evolution"*, which may be called a text-book of Bergson's philosophy, has been printed and reprinted many times. Balfour has mildly objected to the proposition advanced by this philosopher concerning the "vital impulse," that it has no goal more definite than that of acquiring an ever fuller volume of creative activity"; but to Burroughs, the American philosopher, Bergson has opened a new world, "and to open a new world to a man is within the power of unique and original genius only. Bergson's is a philosophy that goes well with living things," Burroughs wrote. "It is a living philosophy . . . an interpretation of biology and natural history [presented] in terms of the ideal. In reading him I am in a concrete world of life, bathed in the light of the highest heaven of thought. It exhilarates me like a bath in the stream or a walk on the hills. Those who go to Bergson for scientific conclusions only, will find bread where they were unconsciously looking for a stone; but those who go to him in the spirit of life, will see him work a change in scientific facts like that which life works in inorganic matter."

Nothing could better demonstrate the honor in which M. Bergson is held by his contemporaries than the dignities that have been conferred upon him in the last fifteen years. Named President of the French Academy of Moral and Political Science in 1914, he became, in 1917 a member of the Clemenceau Cabinet, and, among many degrees awarded him by the universities of the world was that by Cambridge, of the doctor's degree *honoris causa*. In 1922 he was elected President of the Commission of the League of Nations for Intellectual Intercourse among the Nations. He is thus appraised by the world as a great teacher, an inspired philosopher. He is no less valued as a literary artist. "His method" writes Burroughs, so well able to sum up the work of a fellow-craftsman, "is always such that, looking at the processes of organic evolution through his eyes is like looking into the mental and spiritual processes of a great creative artist. He is *sui generis*. . . . One cannot read far without being carried into the poetic and romantic . . . the world of organic nature is seen for the first time through the creative imagination of a great literary artist and philosopher combined. For his competent reader" Burroughs adds, "Bergson recreates the world by showing it as issuing like a living stream from the primal, cosmic energy".

Certainly to the student of philosophic literature the newness, the vigor and grace of Bergson's literary manner, and his fresh imagery have proven powerfully attractive, and have made him, in two decades, a moral force throughout the world. He is the latest flowering of the Jewish mind. May not the race's contributions on the moral side, to the civilization we know today, safely be placed in the balance?

CHAPTER XVI

Summary

"Here is a great body of our Jewish citizens from whom have sprung men of genius in every walk of our varied life; men who have become part of the very stuff of America; who have conceived its ideals with singular clearness, and led its enterprises with spirit and sagacity. They are playing a particularly conspicuous part in building up the very prosperity of which our Government has so great a stake in its dealings with the Russian Government with regard to the rights of men. They are not Jews in America; they are American citizens. In this great matter with which we deal tonight, we speak for them as for representatives and champions of principles which underlie the very structure of our Government. They have suddenly become representatives for us all. By our action for them shall be tested our sincerity, our genuineness, the reality of principle among us."

WOODROW WILSON.

(In an address before the Committee on Foreign Affairs, House of Representatives, December, 1911)

IN approaching the closing paragraphs of this book there comes a keen awareness of how inadequate, after all, has been the effort here made to the task undertaken, in view of the power of the ignoble to sway the more impressionable minds. To excuse the violence of their own rancor, to what ends have the enemies of the Jews not gone in misrepresentation, in vilification? In the fifteenth century the same class offered such excuses as these for the pillage and massacre of their fellow-men: "This accursed race were unwilling to bring their children to be baptized. . . . They dressed their stews and other dishes with oil instead of lard; abstained from pork; kept the Passover; ate meat in Lent; sent oil to replenish the lamps in their synagogues; with many other abominable ceremonies of their religion, etc., etc."

Looking back at the printed spleen of today will future humanity have reason to feel that this age really had progressed beyond that earlier one? What will it think of the Beilis case, in Russia, so late as 1911-13, when race hatred and superstition spoke again so cruelly, with such a vicious disregard for human life as to draw a protest from the just-minded of the world against the persecution of a race, the near-martyrdom of a Jew, most obviously innocent, upon a flimsily concocted charge of having murdered a boy for ritual purposes? It was the old Apion charge of two thousand years ago. Well did Great Britain, under the signatures of hundreds of her greatest men protest: "This blood accusation is a relic of the days of witchcraft, a cruel and utterly baseless libel on Judaism and an insult to Western culture." Again: "We deem it our duty" ran the German protest, this, too, fortified with the names of her most thoughtful men," to protest against that unscrupulous fiction spread among the people, and which has, from the Middle Ages until recent times led the ignorant masses to outrage and massacre, and has driven misguided crowds to stain themselves with the innocent blood of their Jewish fellow-men. We deem it the duty" continued this memorable paper, "of everyone to whom the moral progress of mankind is dear, to raise his voice against such deplorable occurrences."

Similarly France and the United States denounced this sowing of ancient superstitions, the first declaring that "so far from requiring blood for its rites, the religion of Israel prohibits its use both for ceremonial purposes and for food, and this absolute prohibition is rigorously respected by all Jewish sects." The second added a lengthened testimony as to the lack of foundation for this especially spiteful accusation. "It has been subjected," said the American protest, "to the most careful investigation for centuries, and no evidence warranting the slightest credence has ever been discovered. As history shows, the same accusation was frequently directed against the early Christians." "Invented by hate" runs another protest, as ably signed, "adopted by blind ignorance, the absurd invention has become an instrument of enmity and dissension even between Christians themselves. The pogroms caused by it have drawn a trail of blood through the history of this era."

Grotius, whose aim was to substitute reason for unbridled rancour, light for darkness, said that no man's life was of such importance as to violate the general rule of forbearance by which the peace and safety of the individual is secured; and he referred frequently to his predecessors in the search for peace, to the Jewish writers; notably to Moses Maimonides' *"Guide for Doubtful Cases,"* as he interprets the great work written by Maimonides in the twelfth century. Today, ignoring the recognition of the wise, which clearly proves the Jews to have been, from the beginning of time—and the violent anti-Semites insist again and again that the Jews have not changed character in thousands of years—the advocates of peace, and of reason. "Come, let us reason together," were the Israelite Prophet's words, which Grotius returned to when he, as David J. Hill has said, "sought to create a system of illuminating principles to light the way to the paths of peace and general concord; to make intelligence triumph over irrational impulses and barbarous propensities."

Today, unfortunately, and universally, social facts have become so disordered, that the reasoning of the world itself would seem to have ceased to function. How will the unthinking, with only their prejudices to guide them, react to the confidant and bold assertions which have been made of the existence of a world-wide plot among the Jews to pollute the morals of the human family? These insidious statements, made upon the authority of the

"Protocols," since proved to have been instruments not of the Jew, but of the enemies of the Jews, have been sent into every hamlet of the United States. The first knowledge which the present writer had of this "Jewish Peril," was received from a little town in Alabama which, since, has heard nothing of the fraudulent character of the documents on which most heinous charges have been made, though such information should have been forthcoming to stop the growth of the evil those charges gave rise to.

Nothing could be more illogical, when you come to examine into it, than that a race, religion-bound for thousands of years, which has suffered martyrdom for the preservation of that religion, which has, as the tap-root of its racial strength the most devoted love and preservation of the family—which, as its enemies insist, cultivates and holds to its ancestral habits and faith even at loss to itself—should now, in the twentieth century be occupied with a diabolical scheme which could only culminate in its own destruction, and this for the following reasons: The accusation on which so many other cruel charges have been founded declares that the proposed pollution of the world will be through literature; through degrading art; through the theatre; through evil-arousing music by which the *morale* of non-Jewish humanity will be undone to such an extent that the subjection of the great mass will be easy, and the rise of the Jew to imperial power even more so. But, look at the facts, which may be obtained from any statistical librarian today. It will be found that the great mass of eager readers are the Jewish young. Can they read pernicious matter without their own race being "poisoned at the very spring"?

There is no class or group in the world today which spends so liberally, according to its numbers, at the theatre; at the moving pictures; in the support of music.

As the Jews in America, among the hundred million and more citizens of the United States alone, are an exceedingly small group, were a large percentage of that small group to give themselves up to the re-enacting of the lessons of salacious and immoral plays, to those of unworthy pictures, to evil literature and so forth, who but the race itself, is injured? Some degraded Jews may, for profit, engage in the purveying of the venal, but against them there is a great army of Jews who protest them. This was the conspicuous case awhile ago in New York City, when a devout Rabbi took the lead in applying to the courts for the closing of a play written and produced by members of his own race.

The facts in connection with the Jewish family life should be sufficient to refute these abominable charges. The foundations of such solidarity as has existed among Jews for ages has lain in their safeguarding of their home from just such pollutions. "God dwells in a pure and loving home" is a basic saying in the sacred writings of this people. Down to their great Dispersion, when families were ruthlessly torn apart, and children bunched and flung indiscriminately together, were carried in one direction while their parents were scattered in others, the one idea of the Jewish people was the close co-operation of the family. It was the old patriarchal idea which led Abraham, in coming out from Chaldea, to take with him every member of his family. With the Jewish people family-building, race-building was a natural instinct. "In their family relationships," said ex-President Eliot, some years ago, "the Jews are singularly pure, tender and devoted. This, in part, may be a consequence of the cruel persecutions to which almost all Jewish communities have been, first or last, subjected. Each family was bound together by the pressure of external wrongs, and only in the family home could consolation and hope be

found; but, clearly, their religion fostered filial piety."
Bishop Lawrence, commenting on this statement, concurred with it, saying: "Allow me to emphasize what President Eliot has already mentioned and what was in my mind to say, that the integrity of the family for which the Jew has always stood is a tradition of the greatest value to this day and nation."

Someone has said that the observances of the Jewish faith are so entwined with everyday customs in the home as to make the Jewish religion and the family life a unity, bound together in sanctity. Nor can it be overlooked that the history of the Jews reveals on its every page exacting fundamental principles of righteous conduct, which must be held to if Judaism is not to die from the earth. They find their punishment for deflexion from these rules marked clearly in their own histories. Every time great numbers of the race have fallen away from the practice of virtue the hand of God has smitten them. A notable Jewish scholar has been heard to express the thought that the luxury which obtained in Spain, being far removed from the simple precepts of the Jewish religion, had caused a pride in his race which brought its antidote in expulsion. This is the noblest of humility; it is the signature of greatness on this people, that in each crisis of its history it has held true and sincere men who have gathered the fragments of the race together again, and in humility and renewing faith they have gone back to their first and eternal principles.

Where the Jew has fallen away from a faithful adherence of his religion, even when he has wandered into the avenues of "free thought" which, during some periods, allure both Jew and non-Jew, even those who have foresworn their membership with the Jewish religion, maintain, nevertheless, their ideal of family love, and it is rare indeed that they do not extend a quick sympathy to their own kind in trouble. Heine measured what are called the happinesses of life through his own childhood and youthful experiences in "the charm of true Jewish family life" which his memory dwells upon. "If pride of descent were not a foolish contradiction," he wrote, "I might feel proud that my progenitors were members of the noble house of Israel, and I a descen- dant of those martyrs who have given the world a God and a morality."

A volume might be written on the Jewish woman as exemplar in the home; as indefatigable social and wel- fare worker; as an educational force and contributor to modern art and letters. A friendly examination into their women's part in the race's life and history will reveal a procession of remarkable heroines though we begin no further back than with the classic "mother in Israel," Deborah, the warrior matron whose fame by thousands of years preceded and exceeded that of Jeanne d' Arc, and whose war song has placed her among the immortals. Judah has its companion, too, to the Mother of the Gracchi, in the wife of Rabbi Meir, who lived in the second century. It has not been esteemed beneath the dignity of the assailers of the modern Jew to go back to the Middle Ages to attack a very delightful human character, one Glückel, whose life was full of vicissitudes, and whose devotion and courage and wit as wife and mother make her a classic example of which any race might be proud. Judith Montefiore and the Baroness de Hirsch were both heroic women, and women, too, who left great impress on their times for their practical work for mankind. New York has its monument to Julia Rich- man, long identified with the Public School system of that city, in the Julia Richman High School. Someone has called attention to the fact that of the three great nations of antiquity, neither Greece nor Rome has in its history, or associated with its glory a feminine figure which humanity has exalted as it has exalted the Jewess, Mary.

This, however, is but another instance of the inconsistency of a world hating its victim, while possessing itself of that victim's most valued treasures. The world has appropriated to its use the Jew's scriptures; his prophets; his teaching, his services in a hundred fields; a supreme example, it would seem, of men's inhumanity and ingratitude to man. It furnishes, indeed, the paradox of the ages. "The whole Christian Church," Bishop Lawrence once said, "is under obligation to the faith, history and traditions of the Hebrews. I cannot forget that every time we offer our prayers and praises in our Christian Churches, we are expressing our faith in the language of the ancient and chosen people. From the beginning to the end of the service, the Psalter, lessons, prayers and hymns are either in the very words of the Jewish lawgivers, singers and prophets, or else saturated with their thought and character." The same might be said and amplified by other Christian sects; yet how many who follow the religions of our era, appear, as Goethe said, to feel "that the descent of the Holy Spirit was in the form of a vulture and not in that of a dove!" And this interpretation of that descent has gone on the world over, especially in Christendom.

Bayard Taylor, visiting Jerusalem in the middle forties of last century, wrote of what he saw there, as follows: "Here, although the Jews freely permit Christians to enter their synagogue, a Jew who should enter the Holy Sepulchre would be lucky if he escaped with his life. Not long since, an Englishman who was mistaken for a Jew was so severely beaten that he was confined to his bed for two months. What worse than scandal," exclaims Mr. Taylor. "What abomination that the spot looked upon by many Christians as the most awfully sacred on earth, should be the scene of such brutish intolerance!" This was told of conditions that existed less than a hundred years ago; and recent travellers, less horrified, but more cynical, report a not greatly altered attitude on the part of those who watch over the hallowed (!) spot.

Moses Mendelssohn has left a pathetic picture of the experiences of his family in a letter to his friend Winkopp. "Papa," asked his children, returning from a walk, "why do those boys throw stones at us? Why do they run after us and call us 'Jew-boy! Jew-boy'? Is it a disgrace to be a Jew-boy, Papa?"

This was happening in Berlin nearly two hundred years ago; and notwithstanding the world has progressed so mightily in material things, its non-Jewish children are still being taught that which leads them to pursue Jewish children with the cry: "Dirty Jew!" and "Christ-killer." This is happening in orderly countries in conservative towns the modern world over. It is happening daily in the streets of our great cities, and adults smile at it when they do no more. The first thing that Jewish and non-Jewish children become aware of as they get to the school age is the right of the one to attack, to deride and to mistreat, and the need for the other sometimes to weep and chafe under sneers and taunts; to withdraw from, mistrust and resent. If here and there an embittered Jew "kicks over the traces," where is the wonder? You cannot gather figs of thistles.

The more the question is studied, the more it will be recognized that evil passions and prejudices continue among the peoples of the earth because from their first apprehending days they are imposed upon the child mind —let us hope not with a deliberate intention to hoodwink or mislead, but certainly with a thoughtless indifference as to the wrong twist it may give to the individual's mind in the future. " 'Tis education forms the common mind; just as the twig is bent, the tree's inclined," was a truth recognized long before Pope so phrased it; yet the warring ideals of Rome, and those of Greece where the killing of a fellow-man was an heroic art and lust a godly attribute—though they led Rome to ruin and Greece to decay, are still held high before the child's and youth's mind, while the moral ideals of Israel, whether through the prophets or the Nazarene, never more commonly and theoretically acknowledged than today (if we may measure it by the Church edifices that stand as monuments to them the world over) are left as bones for theologians to quarrel over, and only come to light from time to time as they issue from such debates in the form of isms, schisms, sophisms and fanaticisms. Is this a too radical stand to take? But in false education lie the evils of race hatreds which today trouble mankind. It begins about the roots of life, entering the minds of children, and there thriving and multiplying for a lifetime. This evil can only be eliminated, if at all, by probing to those roots, and cutting the evil out; tares sown, cannot yield wheat. That is common knowledge.

"Thou shalt love thy neighbor as thyself"—all of the ten "Thou shalt nots," preach the "natural laws of equity which are common to all races". Confucius taught the overcoming of evil by good; Buddha said: "Let a man overcome anger by love, let him overcome evil with good. For hatred does not cease by hatred at any time; hatred ceases only by love." Hillel preached the refraining from harming others. Every prophet and priest who has labored for humanity has taught the same lesson in almost identical words, even before the teachings of Jesus, which incorporated the wisdom of his race. He re-affirmed its truths, and simplified them for the people.

Always he stressed the all-important necessity that will always exist for forbearance, for forgiveness; for the need of personal purity before casting the stone of reproach; for removing the mote from our own eye before concerning ourselves with the beam in that of our neighbor's. Forgiveness was his theme, as it had been that of the Prophets of Israel. Not theirs to punish those who injured, but God's. "Vengeance is mine. I will repay, saith the Lord of Hosts," was the ancient equivalent for a truth which is everywhere preached today: Do unto others as you would have them do unto you, and leave the working out of Justice to the Divine.

One of the most impressive of all the Galilean's teachings was that offenses would continue to come in the world, "but woe to him through whom they come! It were better for him," he said, "that a millstone were hung about his neck and he cast into the sea than that he should offend one of these little ones." Yet what greater offense can be put upon the innocents than that they should be saddled, from their first lispings, with racial and religious prejudices against any group of their fellowmen? What greater offense to young minds than that the Pauline doctrine of "Christ Crucified" should be substituted in their first lessons for that of Jesus who taught of forgiving love—that love and forgiveness should be applied even unto seventy times seven? Those lessons he continued to teach—unless we are to discount the truth of the Gospels through which his teachings and story have come—when, even on the cross, he said: "Father, forgive them, for they know not what they do." That prayer was not for sinning Jews, as so many prefer to believe, but for a sinning world. Its mixed representatives stood around on Calvary, Romans and others, jeering and sharing in the thing done. It is a prayer which many victims of the savagery of zealots, Jews and non-Jews, have since uttered. Prescott alludes to the shedding of Christian blood by Christians, as well as to the racial crimes that stain the present era's past, saying: "In every country the most fiendish passions are kindled in the name of religion."

That prayer upon the cross is one that should be prayed with especial fervor today, on behalf of those who are responsible for the vicious appeals to racial antipathies which have been flooding our bookshelves. These new prophets of hatred and persecution, are the real menaces to the peace of the world. Enmity, not amity, is their creed, as Spencer has said, who saw clearly that men "merely believe that they believe in the religion of amity."

There is not a statesman today who does not realize the need for freeing the world from its age-long fetters of racial, religious and class strife. But how go about it? Wise men on every side see the weakness of a civilization divided against itself. They recognize that world peace will never be attained until such time as shall see these artificial barriers down, and each man able to look into his brother-man's eyes in confidence and trust; but how is that happy state to be reached when, individuals may project the most distorted ideas, broadcasting them into this and that even remote corner of the world, for the unblushing purpose of increasing the circulation of a weekly, or creating a demand for a book? Nations are not secure that are made up of groups warring with one another. To make a country strong there is need for its citizens to be brought together, to be bound together by a common understanding and by such common service as will insure a mutual respect. It is declared by the hopeless, that racial strife is ineradicable; that to try to stop it is as futile as was Canute's command to the inrolling waves. But we know that given the will all things are possible. Duelling has been put out of fashion ever since the reason of the world cleared, and the folly of it was perceived. Those who still persist in fighting duels are no longer heroes of romance, but weaklings in reasoning upon whom the world will scarce waste a shrug of the shoulder. The Italian vendetta is heard of no more. Even the peasantry, their education widening, perceive the utter uselessness of life-wasting and the still worse undermining of national life by the carrying on of hatreds. Feuds among American mountain groups, which were once transmitted from generation to generation, have ceased to be the fashion even in the back counties of Kentucky and Tennessee.

Coming back to charges against the Jews which should be touched upon here: In a screed published by Mr. Ford and quoted elsewhere, a group of Jews in Russia are described as being "drunk or half drunk" and, by implication, the race is accused of a propensity to excessive drinking. But the facts are: From the beginning of history, in matters appertaining to the appetite, the Jews have been and are models of sobriety. Samuelson, writing on the *History of Drink,* says that the Jews are notoriously a sober race, which is due to two causes; first, their partial isolation from other religious groups has had a tendency to make them more careful of their morals, and, second, and the more important reason has been that they do not follow occupations that require great physical exertion. "On the whole," he says, "they are a sober and exemplary race whose habits in this respect are worthy of universal imitation." Dr. Norman Kerr, another observer of the race, has said: "I have never seen a case against this distinctive people of a strong impulse to alcoholism or other narcotism." Professor Commons, in summing up the tendencies of immigrant races, and naming them in the order to which they

are addicted to this or that weakness, names nine in his
list of drinking groups, and names the Jews ninth. It is
unnecessary to adduce further testimony in a case which
is readily open to examination through hospital and
prison statistics.

Let us, too, in hastening to our close, glance at the
charge of duplicity and evasiveness uttered in various
tones by the *"World's Work"* author, and Messrs. Belloc,
Chamberlain and Ford, and which stresses, in particular,
the fact that Jews enter a country as "natives" of this or
that other country, when, in fact, they should enter as
"Jews." "Why do they not sign themselves Jews?" cry the
frenzied, and elaborate their complaint until the incom-
ing stranger has begun to look like a menace and
criminal. What are the facts? These: that the United
States Immigration Laws neither require nor record the
religious faith of intending settlers in this country. They
do require and record the country of birth and of citizen-
allegiance of such entrants; but, in addition, the Jews have
no alternative in the matter of not naming themselves
"Jews" in the majority of European countries, where, so
late as 1919, they were prohibited from filling out the cen-
sorship blanks as "Jews," which, by preceding practice they
were forbidden equally to omit doing. They were, for
instance, compelled to fill out such documents as "Germans," or "Czechs." Acting in conformity with the law
in emigrating from those countries, they had no choice
but to register in the same manner, as citizens of the
countries in which they had been born or long domiciled.
As such, and in good faith, they have arrived at their
destination only to be met with accusations of intentional
deception.

Like other immigrants, the Jew, with few exceptions,
comes here to gain health, home, education for himself and his children; willing to attain them by fru-

gality and industry, but unable to turn aside the harmful suggestions of the unfriendly, by his unacquaintance with English. Looking into forbidding and doubting eyes, the only defense of these immigrants is to shrink back among themselves, so beginning that "exclusiveness" which gives ground for new complaint. The Jews from the Levant have come in for especially malevolent suspicions because they linger in the sea-board towns, while the German Jews are praised or blamed, according to the mood of the critic, because they have gone in larger numbers inland. None enquires into the reason for the choice in either case. It is so much easier to insinuate into the public consciousness the idea that they are gathering in special places as part of a plot to undo modern civilization. The fact is that German Jews go inland in greater numbers because as a people, the Germans are inland dwellers. Their coast line is not large; whereas the Levantines for centuries have lived and traded in the coast cities of the Mediterranean. Each merely follows, in his new home his earlier habits until a confidence comes that he will not be molested.

It is this confidence that the representative Jews of America have trusted and are seeking to instil in the newcomers. Their zeal is seen on every side to raise the standard of living and of character in the late arrivals here. They are quite as aware as impatient critics could be of the newcomers' shortcomings; of their often uncouth and fear-stamped manners. Sir C. G. Montefiore has made a passionate appeal for just this class of the poor of his people, in a recent number of the Hibbert Journal:

"Give the Jew, even for a short time," he writes, "a respite from hatred and prejudice . . . and there is no reason to suppose that these various products of disability and persecution will not entirely disappear. . . .

Where every man's hand is against you, you may be tempted to hit back. It does no good but you may yield to the temptation. Is it too much to ask of Christendom after centuries of persecution, a few years of patience? Certain ugly characteristics of the hunted animal—fear, cunning, untruthfulness—may have shown themselves in a few Jews . . . but the Jew learns very quickly. Indicate to him what you *want* him to learn and that you will *welcome* his learning. Even as things are the learning is going on apace. Give them a little encouragement; a little surcease from suspicion and hatred; a little breathing space.

"Anti-Semitism tends to make the people it hates worthy, at last, of hatred; for hatred will breed hatred, and suspicion will breed suspicion. Equality, fairness, love—these are curative. To make the Jews as like you as possible, treat them as fellow-citizens. They will soon resemble you—in your failings as well as in your virtues."

Apropos of the effect upon both the body and the soul of the Jew, of long continued oppression and its offspring, a manner of fear and suspicion, as well as resentment and general coarsening, Bayard Taylor has left a peculiarly valuable testimony in his work earlier referred to. "The native Jewish families in Jerusalem, as well as those in other parts of Palestine," he writes, "present a marked difference to the Jews of Europe and America. They possess the same physical characteristics—the dark, oblong eye and prominent nose, the strongly-marked cheek and jaw—but in the latter these traits have become harsh and coarse. Centuries devoted to the most debasing forms of traffic, with the endurance of persecution and contumely, have greatly changed and vulgarized the appearance of the race. But the Jews of the Holy City still retain a noble beauty, which proved to my mind their descent from the ancient princely houses of Israel. The forehead is loftier, the eye larger and more frank in its expression, the nose more delicate in its prominence, and the face a purer oval. I have remarked the same distinction in the countenances of those Jewish families of Europe, whose members have devoted themselves to Art or Literature. Mendelssohn's was a face that might have belonged to the House of David."

And Mr. Taylor adds a description of a Jerusalem experience which is even more memorable. He writes:

"On the evening of my arrival in the city, as I set out to walk through the bazaars, I encountered a native Jew, whose face will haunt me for the rest of my life. I was sauntering along, asking myself 'Is this Jerusalem?', when, raising my eyes, they met those of Christ! It was the very face which Raphael has painted—the traditional features of the Savior, as they are recognized and accepted by all Christendom. The waving brown hair, partly hidden by a Jewish cap, fell clustering about the ears; the face was the most perfect oval, and almost feminine in the purity of its outline; the serene, childlike mouth was shaded with a light moustache, and a silky brown beard clothed the chin; but the eyes—shall I ever look into such orbs again? Large, dark, unfathomable, they beamed with an expression of divine love, and divine sorrow, such as I never before saw in a human face. The man had just emerged from a dark archway, and the golden glow of sunset, reflected from a white wall above, fell upon his face. Perhaps it was this transfiguration which made his beauty so unearthly; but during the moment that I saw him, he was to me a revelation of the Savior. There was still miracles in the land of Judah. As the dusk gathered in the deep streets, I could see nothing but the ineffable sweetness and benignity of that countenance, and my friend was not a

little astonished, when I said to him with the earnestness
of belief, on my return: 'I have just seen Christ!' "

Not all, perhaps, can rise to the rhapsody of the
poet and so see God in their fellow-man; but all seekers
of truth can find good in him, if they truly seek it. Not
in diplomacy, but in good faith between man and man,
will world peace be found. Good faith, said Grotius, is
"the keystone by which the larger society of nations is
united." It does not exist when the better element in a
nation or community by silence gives a tacit consent to
the persecution by one group of another.

This volume goes out into the world with a great wish
that it may incite the conservative good who have been
negative to the thought of a better understanding of their
neighbor, the Jew, to take part in the suppression of those
forces for evil which would set the nation, and the nations, once more upon a course of Middle Ages persecution. We have our special days of celebration and prayer;
our Hospital Sunday; our Mother's Day; our Flag Day;
our Independence Day. Fancy what might happen if but
one nation were to inaugurate the setting apart of a single
Better Understanding Day, seeing to it that on that day all
teachers, preachers and spiritual pastors and masters, yes,
and the editorial teachers as well, shall concentrate their
thought upon the bringing about of peace on earth
and good will among men! The outcome of even
a single hour so set apart in a year, of a single honest
thought sent forth with the concentrated force of the
world—each human being led to consider the need for
mutual kindness, the existence of mutual rights and the
duty of protecting them—ah, there is no way of measuring
it! Then, indeed, might we hope to see swords beaten into
plowshares, and that universal peace established for which
men and nations pray.

THE END

BIBLIOGRAPHY

Aspects of Judaism. ISRAEL ABRAHAMS.

The Voice of America on Kishineff. CYRUS ADLER. *Philadelphia* 1904.

An Ethical Philosophy of Life. FELIX ADLER. *New York* 1920.

Physics and Politics. WALTER BAGEHOT. *London and New York* 1900.

Our Modern Debt to Israel. EDWARD C. BALDWIN. *Boston* 1913.

The Religion of Israel. GEORGE BARTON. *New York* 1918.

The Jews. HILAIRE BELLOC. *Boston* 1922.

The Development of Palestine Exploration. FREDERICK BLISS. *New York* 1906.

Poland, Study of the Land, People and Literature. GEORGE BRANDES. 1903.

Studies in Contemporary Biography. JAMES BRYCE. *London* 1904.

The Scapegoat. HALL CAINE. *New York*.

Foundations of the Nineteenth Century. Translated from the German by John Lees, M. A. HOUSTON STEWART CHAMBERLAIN. 1910.

At the Foot of Sinai. GEORGES CLEMENCEAU. *New York*.

Races and Immigrants. JOHN R. COMMONS. *New York* 1915.

The Dreyfus Case. F. C. CONYBEARE. *London* 1898.

Philo-Judaeus on the Contemplative Life. CONYBEARE. *London*.

The Impeachment of President Israels. FRANK B. COPLEY. *New York*. 1913.

The Culture of Ancient Israel. C. H. CORNHILL. *Philadelphia* 1914.

The Settlement of Jews in North America. CHARLES P. DALY. *New York* 1893.

Jewish Artisan Life in the Time of Jesus. FRANZ DELITZSH.

Spirit of the Laws. DE MONTESQUIEU. *London* 1900.

Philo-Judaeus; of the Jewish Alexandrian Philosophy. JAMES DRUMMOND. *London* 1888.

Daniel Deronda. GEORGE ELIOT. *New York*.

The Chief Works of Spinoza. Translated by ELWES. 1884.

The Holy Land and the Bible. J. H. FINLEY.

History of the Philosophy of History. ROBERT FLINT.

The International Jew. HENRY FORD. *Detroit* 1921-2.

Where Are We Going? DAVID LLOYD GEORGE. *New York* 1923.

The Principles of Political Economy and Taxation. E. C. K. GONNER.

History of the Jews, translated by Bella Lowy and various others. H. GRAETZ. *Philadelphia* 1891.

The Rights of War and Peace, with Introduction by David T. Hill. HUGO GROTIUS. *London and New York* 1904.

Post-Biblical Hebrew Literature. BENZION HALPER. *Philadelphia* 1921.

The Spirit of the Ghetto. HUTCHINS HAPGOOD. *New York* 1902.

The Yoke of the Torah. HENRY HARLAND. *New York* 1885.

Music and Morals. H. R. HAWEIS. *New York* 1899.

The Jews and the English Law. H. S. Q. HENRIQUES. *London* 1908.

The Mendelssohn Family. SEBASTION HENSEL. *New York* 1882.

Christianity in Talmud and Midrash. R. T. HERFORD. *London* 1903.

Pharisaism. R. T. HERFORD. *London and New York* 1912.

Antiquities of the Jews. Whiston's Translation. FLAVIUS JOSEPHUS. *London* 1900.

The Works of Philo. PHILO-JUDAEUS 1896.

Critique of Pure Reason. IMMANUEL KANT.

Dynastic America. HENRY H. KLEIN. *New York* 1921.

Prejudice; its Genesis and Exodus. JOSEPH KRAUSKOPF. *Philadelphia* 1909.

History of European Morals. W. E. H. LECKY. *London, N. Y. Reprint* 1921.

MacMillan's Guide to Palestine and Syria. MACMILLAN. *London* 1911.

Guide to the Perplexed. Translated by M. Friedlander. MOSES MAIMONIDES. *New York* 1919.

The European Commonwealth. J. A. R. MARRIOTT. *London* 1918.

A Study of Spinoza. JAMES MARTINEAU. *London* 1883.

Liberal Judaism and Hellenism. CLAUD GOLDSMID MONTEFIORE. *London* 1903.

Aspects of Judaism. C. G. MONTEFIORE.

Life of Disraeli. WILLIAM FLAVELLE MONYPENNY. *London* 1910.

History of Religions. GEORGE F. MOORE. *New York* 1920.

Interpretation of History. MAX NORDAU. *London* 1910.

Stories and Pictures. ISAAC LOEB PEREZ. *Philadelphia* 1906.

The Jews in America. MADISON C. PETERS. *Philadelphia* 1905.

Researches in Sinai. WILLIAM M. F. PETRIE. *London* 1906.

History of the People of Israel. ERNEST RENAN. *London* 1891.

Fresh Light from Ancient Monuments. A. H. SAYCE. *New York* 1895.

Races of the Old Testament. A. H. SAYCE. 1891.

Studies in Judaism. SOLOMON SCHECTER. *Philadelphia* 1908.

History of Jewish People in the Time of Jesus. E. SCHURER. Edinburgh 1892.

The Prophets in Israel and Their Place in History. W. ROBERTSON SMITH. *London,* 1895.

The Jew and American Ideals. JOHN SPARGO. *New York* 1921.

The Nature and Elements of Poetry, Lectures delivered before Johns Hopkins University. EDMUND CLARENCE STEDMAN. *Boston* 1895.

The Tragedy of Dreyfus. G. W. STEEVENS. *New York* 1899.

The Renaissance of Hebrew Literature. NAHUM SLOUSCH. *Philadelphia* 1909.

Education of Ancient Israel. FLETCHER H. SWIFT. *London.*

The Land of the Saracens. BAYARD TAYLOR. *New York* 1855.

Prolegomena to the History of Israel. J. WELLHAUSEN. *London* 1885.

Sketch of the History of Israel and Judah. J. WELLHAUSEN.

Outline of History. H. G. WELLS 1921.

Zangwill's Jewish Works complete. ISRAEL ZANGWILL. *Philadelphia.*

INDEX

DATE DUE

GAYLORD			PRINTED IN U S A.